# RESPONSE TO DECLINING ENROLLMENT

## School-Closing in Suburbia

## Jean Stinchcombe

UNIVERSITY
PRESS OF
AMERICA

LANHAM • NEW YORK • LONDON

TO BILL

# CONTENTS

# CONTENTS

# ILLUSTRATIONS

## Maps and Graphs

## Photographs

# Acknowledgments

This study results from experiences and reflections dating back to 1977. As a resident of the Jamesville-DeWitt Central School District, I participated in the events described and during a five-year period had countless conversations with school administrators, board members, teachers, parents, and residents. Without attempting to name them, I offer thanks to all.

After completing a draft of the manuscript I benefited from the suggestions and comments of the following readers: Robert I. Rotberg; Stephen Saunders Webb; James C. Carroll; Annette Muir; Lynda Rill; John H. Fennessey; Mary Jane Fennessey; Betty G. Hayes; my father Eldridge Lovelace; and my husband William Stinchcombe. For their continuing interest throughout the project I especially thank Barbara Nosanchuk, Nancy Sharp, Anita Iannotta, and Richard Lovelace.

George McVey of the New York State Department of Health, Office of Biostatistics, was extremely helpful in providing records of live births. James Brady, New York State Department of Education, Office of Education Statistics, and Deborah Williams, Syracuse-Onondaga County Planning Agency, answered numerous questions. The Jamesville-DeWitt District Office placed district newsletters, budgets, and board minutes at my disposal. Eldridge Lovelace is responsible for the maps and graphs. Photographs are reprinted with permission of Syracuse Newspapers.

For my longstanding interest in community decision-making I thank M. Kent Jennings, who directed my doctoral dissertation at the University of Michigan and encouraged me to return to research and writing in political science. At Swarthmore College Charles E. Gilbert first sparked my imagination as he set forth the challenging questions to be unraveled in the study of local politics.

My family and friends all shared in the experiences and writing of this work. I thank my mother and father for their unflagging interest and help. My aunt who had a career as a writer offered an example. Not to be overlooked is the sufferance that Tom, Marjorie, and John sometimes gave as they distributed newsletters or found their mother at the typewriter. No one had a greater part in this undertaking than my husband. As a partner in school politics and in writing he offered both the inspiration and the criticism essential to this book.

# PREFACE

Almost twenty-five years ago Thomas H. Eliot called upon political scientists to consider the public schools as part of government--an appropriate and important subject for political analysis. During the 1960s and 1970s a number of studies discounted education's apolitical ideology, but analysis of the public schools progressed slowly. Local school districts truly remained the "lost world" of political science.[1]

The study of public schools fell largely in the province of education schools devoted to training administrators and teachers. Social scientists, meanwhile, turned their attention to the distribution of power in local communities. This vital interest produced now-classic studies, including Arthur J. Vidich and Joseph Bensman's **Small Town In Mass Society**, Robert A. Dahl's analysis of New Haven in **Who Governs?**, and Edward C. Banfield and James Q. Wilson's several works on political influence in Chicago, among others.[2] These scholars addressed such questions as who rules? In what sense is the system democratic? How are conflicts resolved and goals established? Although these themes are by no means novel in political science, they receive negligible attention in the literature on public education. The few available studies of school decision-making are thus repeatedly cited and reused.[3]

This study is a detailed analysis of school decision-making at the local level. The work entertains the community power study's central questions: who wields power, how, and for what ends? In **Governing American Schools** L. Harmon Zeigler and M. Kent Jennings used democratic theory to assess school board recruitment, relations between school board members and their constituencies, and the role of professional educators in decision-making.[4] Instead of drawing upon statistical data from many districts as they did, I explore these subjects as seen in one suburban school district's experience of school-closing. In a once-tranquil upstate New York district, a four-year battle over closing dramatically revealed patterns of school decision-making and underlying community conflicts. I first participated in these events by resisting the closing of my children's elementary school and later studied the unexpected sequence of decisions for what it said about school politics and suburban communities.

i

During the decade of the 1970s total public school enrollment declined by 11 per cent and thousands of schools were closed, often in the face of bitter opposition. In urban areas school-closings are politically and legally challenged as hurting the disadvantaged or destroying a precarious racial balance. In suburban areas the genteel agreement not to disagree is destroyed when a school is closed. As the process of closing accelerates through the 1980s, future community conflict is a certainty. The issue clearly provokes the rancorous controversy considered in previous community studies, covering issues as diverse as public housing, urban redevelopment, water fluoridation, sex education, and racial desegregation and control.[5] In recent years, however, the vigorous interest in local communities has faded, and social scientists have not looked at school-closings as a way of examining both demographic trends and decision-making at the local level.

Declining enrollment itself has received scant attention in even recent surveys of public education. Many studies make only passing mention of a phenomenon affecting every area except for a few southern and western states. Publications on declining enrollment are frequently written to guide superintendents in controlling the public's response to painful but necessary decisions.[6] This study places the subject squarely in the context of community politics and choices.

During decades of expansion, administrative decisions usually prevailed, particularly in relatively homogeneous suburban areas. School districts offered programs and facilities to meet every need and satisfy each new demand. Presiding over a growing enterprise, school superintendents consolidated resources and communities remained respectful of technical authority. Only in the process of giving up rather than adding did residents of complacent suburbs finally challenge education's mythology of non-political decision-making. In school-closing the administrative habit of improvised solutions and crisis-to-crisis management revealed its inadequacy.

As the percentage of the population with children drops and financial constraints loom large, the need for careful planning and public understanding are now more important than ever. In a new era of "private-regardingness," the willingness to provide public services has waned, and many communities no longer have a sense of shared purpose in supporting their schools. The "one best system" should not be disassembled in a piecemeal fashion to accommodate to each year's changing pressures or in accordance with how-to-do-it handbooks that emphasize the preservation of administrative interests.[7] Long neglected democratic standards should be reinvoked to guide local communities in a process of discussion and planning preceding the decision to close schools, reduce staff, or eliminate programs. Moving from decision-making by the "polite priesthood" of professional educators to public participation will be difficult. But the effort is essential to renew public commitment to the schools. Writing in a period of high birth-rates and school expansion, Eliot insisted that local school districts be considered as political entities, because the future of public education "is not only a political issue but an increasingly crucial one." Words written in 1959 are even more compelling today.

## NOTES

1. Thomas H. Eliot, "Toward an Understanding of Public School Politics," **American Political Science Review,** Vol. 53 (Dec. 1959), 1032-1051.

2. For example, Edward C. Banfield, **Political Influence** (New York, 1961); Edward C. Banfield and James Q. Wilson, **City Politics** (Cambridge, 1963); Robert A. Dahl, **Who Governs?** (New Haven, 1961); and Arthur J. Vidich and Joseph Bensman, **Small Town in Mass Society** (Princeton, 1968).

3. The Jefferson School District is often used as a case study, for example. Daniel E. Griffiths, et al., **Organizing Schools for Effective Education** (Danville, 1962), 225-293.

4. L. Harmon Zeigler and M. Kent Jennings, **Governing American Schools** (North Scituate, Mass., 1974).

5. Among many see William A. Gamson, "Rancorous Conflict in Community Politics," **American Sociological Review,** Vol. 31 (Feb. 1961), 71-81.

6. Katherine E. Eisenberger and William F. Keough, **Declining Enrollment: What to Do?--A Guide for School Administrators to Meet the Challenge of Declining Enrollment and School Closings.** (Arlington, 1974). David Tyack and Elisabeth Hansot's excellent new work examines decision-making in a period of contraction in the conclusion but does not explore enrollment trends or the magnitude of decline. **Managers of Virtue: Public School Leadership in America, 1820-1980** (New York, 1982).

7. The "one best system" from David B. Tyack's title, **The One Best**

System: **A History of American Urban Education**(Cambridge, 1974);
James Q. Wilson and Edward C. Banfield, "Public-Regardingness as a
Value Premise in Voting Behavior," **American Political Science
Review**, Vol 58 (Dec. 1964), 876-888.

# I. The Suburban School District as the One Best System

"It was bitter and theatrical," said **Time Magazine** in describing school-closing in Evanston, Illinois. Meetings drew audiences of 400 to 500 people, as residents demanded to be heard and the school board struggled in vain to find a satisfactory policy to deal with declining enrollment. "It was neighborhood against neighborhood, teachers against administration, north Evanston vs. South Evanston."[1] Candles were burned and a coffin symbolically displayed; residents lamented not only the closings but the loss of quality education. In the end the school district had "more losers than winners," an experience repeated in cities and suburbs across the nation. "TAPS" ran a three-inch headline describing school-closings in suburban Philadelphia. As in Evanston, these closings produced "catcalls and boos" from more than 700 parents and an immediate decision to file suit against the school board. The schools remained closed.[2]

Despite tears and placards, administrative appeals and lawsuits, nearly 10,000 public elementary and secondary schools closed between 1968 and 1977. Publications as diverse as **McCall's Magazine** and the **New York Times** alerted readers to the damaging effects of closing controversies. Rarely does a school district accomplish reorganization without divisive but usually futile resistance from parents or community residents. In the words of Evanston's superintendent, "You don't make friends closing schools."[3]

Only two decades earlier headlines had called for the construction of new schools. Edward R. Murrow deplored the use of army barracks and prefabricated buildings to overcome classroom shortages, and **Life Magazine** referred to a "tidal wave of students" inundating "already inadequate schools."[4] Between 1940 and 1961 the number of live births in the United States rose dramatically. Starting in the war years and continuing through the period of postwar prosperity, each year brought record numbers of babies, soon to swell the ranks of school children. The birth total of two million in 1941 doubled to reach 4 million babies born in 1955. In 1957 fertility in the United States reached a peak of 3.8 lifetime births per woman, and a **Kiplinger Report** declared that "the population of the United States grows so fast you lose track of it."[5] The year 1961 established an all-time high of 4.3 million births.[6]

The rising birth rate fueled an unprecedented expansion in American education. Between 1950 and 1970 elementary enrollment in the United States increased from 22 million to 37 million, while secondary enrollment more than doubled, going from 6.5 million to almost 15 million.[7] Each year a greater percentage of children and youth not only attended school but completed high school, and record numbers now went on for higher education.

The teaching staff in American public schools increased from only 960,000 in 1949-1950 to over 2,200,000 in 1969-1970.[8] Programs in colleges and universities expanded to meet the apparently endless demand for teachers, and ambitious teachers turned to degree programs and positions in the growing field of school administration.

To meet the challenge of growing enrollment, educational leaders urged a consolidation of the nation's many school districts. The familiar schoolhouse of the past could not efficiently serve a burgeoning population of children. Educational authorities such as James B. Conant also found the course offerings of small schools to be lacking.[9] American students needed specialized training if the United States was to compete successfully with the Soviet Union--an added spur to educational expansion during the 1950s and 1960s.[10] The federal government fortified the schools for competition with Soviet expertise by the National Defense Education Act of 1958 and increased funding of the National Science Foundation. State governments, meanwhile, encouraged consolidation by offering additional state aid to centralized districts. In 1960 the nation had less than half as many school districts as in 1950.[11]

The newly-consolidated districts floated bond issues, rapidly constructed modern one-story buildings, recruited new teachers, and expanded their course offerings. Local residents willingly supported property tax measures to build entire new school systems, and state and federal aid increased as never before. Between 1950 and 1970 expenditures by elementary and secondary schools increased from $6 billion to $40 billion, far outpacing the growth in enrollment.[12] The public schools had entered the era of big business. The need and the possibilities for growth seemed limitless.

2

Nowhere was education's period of "boom" more pronounced than in the suburbs, the growing edge of America's postwar population.[13] Between 1940 and 1950, the suburbs grew at two times the annual rate of central cities, a ratio that doubled in the next decade.[14] The federal government's mortgage-guarantees encouraged the purchase of new houses in the suburbs, and the construction of freeways made suburban locations convenient for business and industry as well as residential developments. In the 1950s younger and middle-income Americans poured into the suburbs, leaving central cities with a disproportionate share of the old, the poor, and the black.[15]

As the suburban migration transformed sleepy villages and created new neighborhoods from onetime farmlands, communities "grappled with the growing tide of children who invade their borders." Writing in 1958, Robert C. Wood observed, "Following the Pied Piper lure of better schools, family after family lists consideration of their young as a primary cause for the suburban trek."[16] In the Chicago suburb of Skokie, for example, the number of children under age 10 rose from 2,500 to 10,500 during the 1950s, and education became the "chief target of Skokie's ambitions."[17] Throughout the country suburban school districts vied for the distinction of being their metropolitan area's "best system." School systems defined communities. In **Crestwood Heights,** a classic study of suburban culture published in 1956, a member of the board of education is quoted as saying that "Crestwood Heights and the school are one and the same; that the Crestwood Heights social and municipal organization virtually exists to make to make the school possible; that the school is the center of the community, and that everything revolves around and within it."[18]

In the upstate city of Syracuse, New York, the same population trends were at work. Syracuse, too, experienced the cycle of rise and decline common to central cities. The city is now ringed by scores of suburban communities and eighteen school districts in Onondaga County alone. Located at the intersection of ancient Indian trails, Syracuse first developed as a transportation center early in the nineteenth century. The completion of the Erie Canal in 1826 accelerated the city's growth and stimulated its first industry, the manufacture of salt from local deposits at the foot of Lake Onondaga. The advent of the railroad in 1839 brought both goods and people to Syracuse, and the city's brought both goods and people to Syracuse, and the city's population grew steadily during the nineteenth century.[19] Irish, German, Polish, Italian, and Jewish immigrants established distinct neighborhoods, giving the city a variety of newspapers, religious institutions, and social organizations.[20] By the turn of the century manufacturing companies such as Crouse-Hinds, Syracuse China Corporation, Crucible Metals, Edward Joy Plumbing and Lighting Company, and Oberdorfer Foundries were doing a flourishing business in Syracuse. The nineteenth century's ornate public buildings, banks, and stores gave the city a distinctive appearance that survived even the extensive bulldozing and highway construction of the 1950s and 1960s.

In the twentieth century Syracuse has continued to have a diversified, albeit diminished, economy. No one industrial employer dominates a local economy known for the manufacture of electrical equipment, air conditioners, candles, china, shoes, and drugs. Major national companies are located in Syracuse, and in recent years some local firms, most notably Carrier Corporation, have been absorbed into national and international corporations. In addition to varied industry and the service trades that have grown rapidly since 1950, the city serves as a retail and wholesale center for its region.[21]

Syracuse is also an educational, cultural, and medical center for the surrounding area. Founded by the Methodists in 1870, Syracuse University developed from a local sectarian institution to a national university. During the 1950s and 1960s the university's professional schools and graduate programs grew, attracting students and faculty from many parts of the United States and abroad. By the early 1980s Syracuse University had an enrollment of about 16,000 on its main campus alone and was the city's single largest employer. Adjacent to the Syracuse University campus are those of the highly-regarded State University College of Environmental Science and Forestry and the State University College of Medicine. Originally part of Syracuse University, the medical school became a state institution in 1950. In the last three decades the medical school and associated hospitals have expanded rapidly, creating a medical complex that serves the entire region. Other educational institutions in the area include LeMoyne College, a coeducational institution founded by the Jesuits in 1947, and Onondaga Community College, opened in 1962 and now located on a suburban campus.[22]

4

Despite a diversity of economic interests and educational enterprises, Syracuse has lost population. First, an extensive urban renewal program and, more recently, local boosterism extolling a renaissance in arts, sports, and government have failed to revitalize the city or stem out-migration. In the postwar years city dwellers began an exodus to the suburbs of Onondaga County. In 1950 the city of Syracuse accounted for 65 per cent of the county's total population, a figure that had dropped to 41 per cent by 1970, and 37 per cent by 1980.[23] During the 1950s business and industry also shifted to the suburbs, as the city lost several major employers. The percentage of taxable property and jobs outside of Syracuse grew even more rapidly than did the population.[24] By 1980 Syracuse had a population of 170,105, a decline of about 50,000 from the peak reached in 1950.

During the period of suburban expansion, the Town of DeWitt became a prime location for residential development. In the twentieth century's early years, the city's middle-income and professional classes had moved eastward into the neighborhoods surrounding Syracuse University.[25] When the postwar housing boom began, easterly migration continued and DeWitt was transformed into a first-ring suburb on the city's east side. As a community, however, DeWitt had its origins in the late eighteenth century. The first settlers had appeared in 1790, building their homesteads in the Butternut Creek valley. By 1815 a small settlement on the Genesee Turnpike had its own hotel--which survived until a fire in 1979--stores, and church, as well as a post office under the name Orville. In 1835 the community's name was changed to DeWitt in honor of Moses DeWitt, who had surveyed the entire upstate region in the post-Revolutionary era and laid out the Genesee Turnpike as well as other public roads. Before his death in 1794 at the age of 28, Moses DeWitt also had an instrumental part in creating Onondaga County, served as a judge on the county's early courts, and earned renown as "one of the first, most active and useful settlers of the county," according to his epitaph.[26]

The opening of the Erie Canal and a feeder canal to the Butternut Creek stimulated the development of mills and boat landings, giving DeWitt a period of early prosperity. Several other settlements in the area flourished in the early nineteenth century. Two miles east of the hamlet of DeWitt, Revolutionary war veteran Captain Samuel Wilcox purchased land south of the Genesee

Turnpike, including property that his son later developed as a profitable quarry--a land use that would long be important in the area.[27] Later, Joseph Edwards purchased nearby land extending northward beyond the Erie Canal, and the Wilcox and Edwards families became the nucleus of a settlement that thrived on east-west traffic. Men transporting grain from Buffalo to Albany stopped to huddle at taverns during their journey, thus giving the community its first name. In 1875 residents discarded "The Huddle" in favor of a more dignified name, Lyndon, a community whose identity is still upheld by descendants of the original settlers.[28]

Seven miles south of DeWitt was another hamlet, originally known as Sinai. Renamed Jamesville, this settlement depended on the Butternut Creek for its prosperity. By the early 1800s several woolen, grist, and saw mills operated along the creek, and a factory, post office, and church were soon established.[29]

The Town of DeWitt, a political jurisdiction created in 1835, encompassed Jamesville, DeWitt, The Huddle, and other hamlets to their north and northeast. Early signs of industry and commerce to the contrary, the township remained primarily agricultural throughout the nineteenth century. With the coming of the railroad, the canal's importance faded and the "hustle and bustle of life dimmed to a sleepy, quiet tempo," according to one fragment of local history. East Syracuse developed as a railroad switching center and became an incorporated village in 1881, but other communities in the township remained unaffected by Syracuse's growing industry. Near the turn of the century the little hamlet of DeWitt had a business core consisting of its hotel, two stores, and a cider mill, surrounded by a scattering of residences.[30] In 1898, however, the railroad brought DeWitt's still-isolated settlements closer to Syracuse. The Syracuse and Suburban Railroad provided trolley service down the Genesee Turnpike to the city, and in 1903 a spur line connected DeWitt and Jamesville.[31]

Only with the coming of the automobile did the Town of DeWitt begin to see significant change. New roads made DeWitt and Lyndon easily accessible. The suburban railway ceased operation, and a major section of the Erie Canal was paved to make a thoroughfare into DeWitt. The availability of city water and electricity also spurred development in the 1920s, first in the area known as DeWittshire. Located directly behind the hamlet's original business section on the Genesee Turnpike,

DeWittshire became a neighborhood of spacious three and four-bedroom houses along wide streets. Lawns and shade trees were planted to provide the amenities of suburban living. In 1931 residents formed the DeWittshire "C" Community Club to foster neighborliness. Mingling at social occasions sponsored by their Community Club, DeWittshire residents sent their children to school nearby, first in an 1811 building that had once served as a church and after 1931 in the new four-room brick school named for Moses DeWitt.[32]

During the 1920s and 1930s development also created another residential tract across Jamesville Road from Moses DeWitt, a neighborhood that regarded the new school as a sign of community progress.[33] To the north of the Genesee Turnpike the decade of the thirties saw the development of the Orvilton section. Here, too, large houses along tree-lined streets made a suburban neighborhood in the heart of DeWitt, still referred to as Orville by some residents.[34] In Lyndon the 1920s and 1930s brought the beginnings of construction. Once known for its taverns and little red schoolhouse dating to 1875, Lyndon was to become an area of country club grounds and imposing houses behind stone gates.

Nearby, Jamesville remained a village, still removed from the path of suburban expansion. The village was primarily a center for the surrounding agricultural region, but in the twentieth century quarrying and stone-processing again became a significant local industry. Operations in the Rock Cut Quarry began before World War I, and another major employer, the Alpha Portland Cement Company, opened its first plant in 1917. In 1950 Alpha Portland began construction of a new and enlarged plant. The Allied Chemical Company had substantial property in Jamesville, using close to 2,000 acres for quarrying and processing stone. Unlike other communities in DeWitt, Jamesville had its own high school, built in 1894, and operated a K-12 school system for the village.[35]

In the years following World War II residential development in DeWitt became intense. The period of the early 1950s produced a variety of new neighborhoods. Among the early developments was DeWitt Acres, a subdivision of small houses close to the core of the original hamlet. Then came the larger ranch-style houses in the former orchards along Jamesville Road, parallel to the old Butternut Creek feeder canal. In Lyndon were enormous houses, separated by vast lawns.

7

Excluding East Syracuse, the population of DeWitt was to rise from 6,300 in 1940 to 17,000 in 1960. Existing school buildings and contract arrangements with other communities could no longer serve the newly-suburban population.

In the postwar period school centralization proceeded apace in New York State. Since 1925 state law had provided for central school districts, formed by a combination of common and union free districts. The common school districts, once numbering close to 10,000 in New York State, were designed to serve small areas and authorized to offer only elementary education.[36] As common school districts, DeWitt and Lyndon contracted for students to attend high school in Syracuse or the nearby village of Fayetteville. The union free district usually followed the lines of a village or community and offered a high school program, as in Jamesville or Fayetteville. Like the common school district and the union free district, the central district was empowered to levy taxes subject to annual approval of the voters. Officials in New York as in other parts of the country recommended central districts, because they offered more "economical financing of better school programs and buildings" in addition to "equalizing educational opportunities for all children."[37] In the postwar years local leaders eagerly embraced this view. By 1980 New York State had 300 central school districts--independent taxing jurisdictions--and 62 city school districts, in which the school budget is part of the municipal budget and not voted upon by the electorate. Only 20 common school districts and 92 union free districts remained in operation in 1980 as relics of a previous era in school organization.[38]

In 1950 educational and civic leaders from DeWitt, Lyndon, and Jamesville came together to propose a centralization plan for their area. Joining these districts were three others: Kimber-Genesee Hills, a residential section to the north and west of Orvilton in DeWitt; a rural district in the Town of Pompey that already contracted to send children to Jamesville for all grades; and Southwood, a small hamlet of semi-rural poverty, located just outside Jamesville in the Town of Onondaga. The proposed central school district fell largely within the Town of DeWitt, although the peripheries around Jamesville extended into four other townships. Leaders in nearby school areas were simultaneously pursuing their own centralization plans, and these boundaries would also cross political lines.

8

In the late nineteenth and early twentieth centuries political reformers and professional educators had agreed that public schools must be sheltered from the baneful effects of local politics.[39] The new school districts would not be coterminous with political jurisdictions and, hence, intentionally safeguarded from capture by local political interests, according to conventional wisdom of the day.

The proposal to centralize schools in the DeWitt, Lyndon, and Jamesville area was presented to the voters in June 1950, following many years' consideration. After consultation with the New York State Education Department, local leaders decided that the proposed union "would best serve the interest of the area."[40] (See Figure 1.) The centralization plan joined three suburban districts with three essentially rural districts. Boundaries were defined on a north-south basis, although the course of suburban development was eastward. Directly to the east of DeWitt, the Fayetteville Union Free School had long educated children from nearby Lyndon and DeWitt. Although Fayetteville was rapidly becoming a suburban community like DeWitt, school leaders there were committed to a separate centralization plan.

Members of the centralization committee for DeWitt, Lyndon, and Jamesville did not attempt to chart the course of future residential development or define a homogeneous school district. The committee proposed meeting an immediate need. Children in the component districts attended school in the nineteenth-century buildings or in old houses, and had classes in basements and hallways. Furthermore, increasing numbers of children were expected to enter kindergarten: a projected 111 children in 1952 and 134 in 1954. The centralization committee proposed construction of a new elementary school in Jamesville; additions to Moses DeWitt School; provision of an adequate school in Lyndon; and improvement of Southwood's elementary school.

The centralization proposal further provided that the new school board be composed of nine members: the key areas of DeWitt, Lyndon, and Jamesville were to have two members from within their original districts, while each of the three remaining districts would have one member. Geographical representation on the board of education played an essential part in drawing the different districts together as one unit, and the

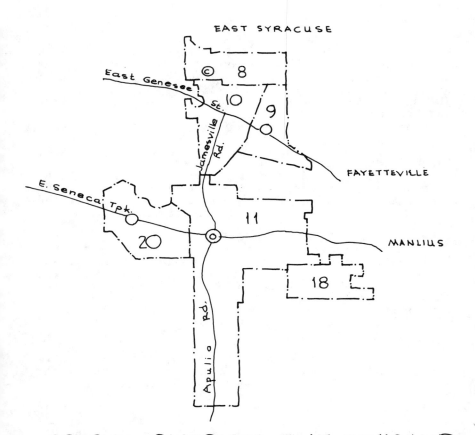

# SCHOOL DISTRICTS THAT COMBINED
# TO FORM JAMESVILLE-DEWITT

DEWITT 8 KIMBER-GENESEE HILLS   DEWITT 11  JAMESVILLE
DEWITT 9 LYNDON             POMPEY  18
DEWITT 10 DEWITT          ONONDAGA 20 SOUTHWOOD

Ⓒ SCHOOL CLOSED
◯ ELEMENTARY SCHOOL OPEN
◉ HIGH SCHOOL OPEN

**FIGURE 1**

10

importance of the distinctive areas was recognized in the composition of the school board, a representational system periodically modified but never discarded.

Residents considering centralization received assurances that "our area lends itself to simple bus routing schedules....No child should spend more than fifteen minutes riding the bus at either end of the day."41 Furthermore, according to state law of the time and the original proposal, "neither the voters of the central district, nor the Board of Education" could close an individual school unless residents of a particular area voted to do so. State law on this subject was amended in 1964, however, to eliminate the requirement of local approval.

Centralization received approval in the component districts, opposition coming mainly from Jamesville residents apprehensive about losing their high school and their local autonomy. In 1951 the president of the board of education, Richard Wiles, wrote, "Our new central school district is a wonderful organization. It was not easily achieved, nor is the job of making a perfect union yet complete."42 An early district newsletter referred to the problem of locating elementary schools as "difficult."43 The site for the high school presented an even more trying political question.

Nevertheless, the emphasis of early newsletters and reports was on growth and progress. One account noted that the area within the new school district is "now one of the more rapidly growing suburbs of Syracuse."44 (See Figure 2.) Each year's census and registration were higher than the last's, and these figures were set forth in reports to the voters. Because of the influx of new families, school district officials used a 5 per cent factor to account for in-migration in projecting the next year's enrollment. A 1954 headline carried the announcement: "Our Enrollment to Increase to 2500 by the Year 1960."45

Accommodating the increasing numbers of children seemed an unending problem. As the district grew, the voters supported plans for new and better elementary schools. Additions to Moses DeWitt School were approved in 1951 and 1953, and in 1953 the electorate also approved the construction of the Jamesville Elementary School which opened in February, 1955, with 350 students. In 1956 voters approved the construction of the Genesee

11

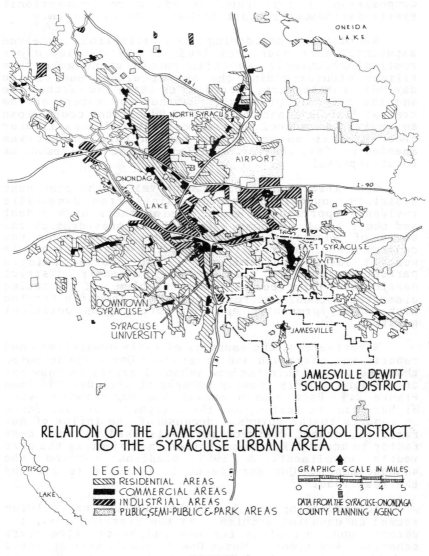

RELATION OF THE JAMESVILLE-DEWITT SCHOOL DISTRICT
TO THE SYRACUSE URBAN AREA

LEGEND

▨ RESIDENTIAL AREAS
■ COMMERCIAL AREAS
▨ INDUSTRIAL AREAS
▨ PUBLIC, SEMI-PUBLIC & PARK AREAS

GRAPHIC SCALE IN MILES
0 1 2 3 4 5

DATA FROM THE SYRACUSE-ONONDAGA
COUNTY PLANNING AGENCY

**FIGURE 2**

Hills opened in 1958. Following several years of discussion between the two school boards, Jamesville-DeWitt residents voted to annex the common school district in the Tecumseh area of residential DeWitt. Located near the Syracuse border, this district had previously contracted to send children to city schools. In 1960 voters approved the purchase of property for the construction of an elementary school at Tecumseh and Waring Roads, to open in the fall of 1962.

Local officials anticipated a continuing demand for facilities. Town of DeWitt planner Arthur Reed observed in 1961 that school enrollment in Jamesville-DeWitt had increased 214 per cent since 1950. The populaton ages five to eleven had increased the most rapidly, and Reed's **Plan for the Development of DeWitt** [1961] forecast that "this group is expected to grow at an increasingly high rate during the next 20 years and to be continually reinforced by high birth rates and the in-migration of families that will supply substantial reserves in the under 4 years group."[47]

While providing for growing numbers of elementary-school children, the district was also building and enlarging other facilities. (See Figure 3.) In 1952 voters approved the purchase of property and construction of a junior-senior high school in DeWitt, which held its first classes in September 1954; in 1957 they approved a junior-high addition to the building. In 1965 voters approved the purchase of property and construction in DeWitt of a middle school. Opening in 1966, the new middle school grades 6-8 was located off Randall Road, the connecting link between the Tecumseh area and other DeWitt neighborhoods.

Within a fifteen-year period a small but reliable constituency provided unfailing support for the construction and improvement of Jamesville-DeWitt's six school buildings. Additions to the buildings all received public approval, as in the construction of a swimming pool at the middle school in 1967. Still-cramped conditions brought additions to Genesee Hills (1959), Jamesville (1966), and Tecumseh Elementary Schools (1966), as well as the high school (1970). In 1968 the district acquired property for the possible construction of another elementary school near the middle school. "From studies made there appears to be future growth in the area, and the land would be cheaper and more available now than after the area is developed," a district report observed.[48]

13

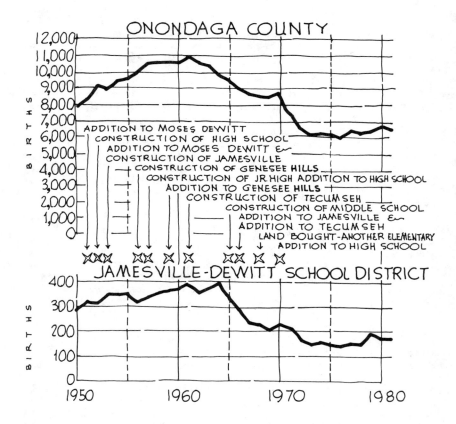

ONONDAGA COUNTY

BIRTHS

12,000
11,000
10,000
9,000
8,000
7,000
6,000
5,000
4,000
3,000
2,000
1,000
0

ADDITION TO MOSES DEWITT
CONSTRUCTION OF HIGH SCHOOL
ADDITION TO MOSES DEWITT &
CONSTRUCTION OF JAMESVILLE
CONSTRUCTION OF GENESEE HILLS
CONSTRUCTION OF JR. HIGH ADDITION TO HIGH SCHOOL
ADDITION TO GENESEE HILLS
CONSTRUCTION OF TECUMSEH
CONSTRUCTION OF MIDDLE SCHOOL
ADDITION TO JAMESVILLE &
ADDITION TO TECUMSEH
LAND BOUGHT-ANOTHER ELEMENTARY
ADDITION TO HIGH SCHOOL

JAMESVILLE-DEWITT SCHOOL DISTRICT

BIRTHS

400
300
200
100
0

1950        1960        1970        1980

DATA FROM NEW YORK STATE DEPT. OF
HEALTH-BUREAU OF HEALTH STATISTICS

# TREND IN RESIDENT LIVE BIRTHS

**FIGURE 3**

14

Only the small Southwood Elementary School closed, holding its last classes in June 1965. But district publications in the early 1960s saw the possibility of real estate development and a new school in the Southwood area.[49] Lyndon, too, seemed an area for future school construction.[50] Named in the centralization proposal as needing an elementary school, Lyndon and surroundings were the site of high-priced residential development in the 1960s. No demographic trend, political issue, or economic downturn broke the forward momentum of these years. During the period of almost-constant building, the electorate that invariably passed both bond issues and the annual budget was often only a handful, or at most, 415 residents who voted on the 1970 budget--a turnout of three per cent of eligible voters.

By the 1970s Jamesville-DeWitt was a comfortable suburban area, considered the most affluent school district in Onondaga County. (For county school districts, See Figure 4.) The district's population numbered slightly more than 18,000 in 1970, the year that school enrollment reached a peak of 4,490. A 1972 bond prospectus described the community as one of "upper middle-class home-owners and, primarily, professional people." According to the 1970 census, the median income in the district was $15,637, a figure that had jumped close to $30,000 by the end of the inflationary seventies.

Nevertheless, social-economic contrasts continued, along the lines of the communities that originally created the central school district. With a population of only several thousand, Jamesville had not merged with the suburbs growing to the east of Syracuse. The educational and economic characteristics of Jamesville residents indicated a population not as solidly middle or upper-middle class as that of DeWitt. According to 1970 census figures, the median income of Jamesville was $10,871, or only about 63 per cent of that in DeWitt. By 1980 the median income in Jamesville had reached $19,622 but remained unchanged as a percentage of DeWitt's median income; one major section of DeWitt reported a median income of twice that of Jamesville.

In most areas of DeWitt between 55 and 60 per cent of residents reported four years of college (or more) in the 1980 census; in Jamesville only 16 per cent fell in this category. Responses to a 1977 school district survey had earlier revealed differences between DeWitt and Jamesville.[51] Wage-earners in Jamesville were less than

15

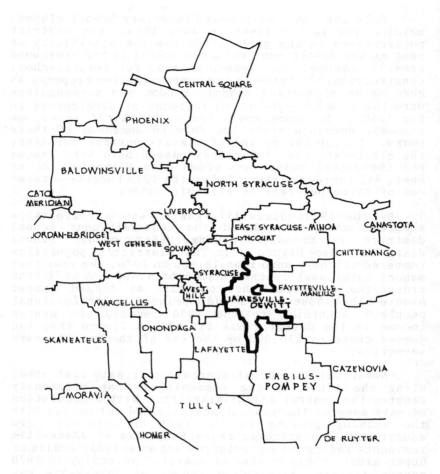

# SCHOOL DISTRICTS IN ONONDAGA COUNTY

**FIGURE 4**

16

half as likely to describe their occupations as
professional or executive and six times more likely to
rank themselves in the skilled labor force.

Lined with three-story frame houses, Jamesville
retained the feeling of a rural village. Community
activities revolved around long-established Catholic and
Protestant churches and the 1950s elementary school that
replaced the venerable 1890s K-12 building. Disrupting
this peaceful atmosphere, however, were the smokestacks
and truck traffic of the nearby cement plant and quarries
as well as a congested commercial section crossed by
railroad tracks. Outside the village remote country
roads with only occasional clusters of houses seemed far
removed from the 1950s and 1960s suburban subdivisions
seen in DeWitt. Despite some new neighborhoods,
Jamesville continued to have large undeveloped areas
throughout the 1970s.

DeWitt, too, contained some variation. Census
figures from 1970 showed the neighborhoods surrounding
Moses DeWitt and Tecumseh Elementary Schools to be the
district's upper-income areas. The residents in these
sections were clearly the upper-middle class
professional people depicted in the school district's
self-description. In 1970 the median income in these
two areas was about $19,000; by 1980 it was over $30,000.
Within the Moses DeWitt school area the tract including
Lyndon and the environs of the high school reported a
median income of over $40,000 in 1980. In the Tecumseh
and Moses DeWitt areas close to 60 per cent of residents
had completed four years of college, and wage-earners
overwhelmingly described their occupations as
professional or executive.

The Genesee Hills area included residential
sections not unlike those in other parts of DeWitt, and
wage-earners described their occupations similarly.
But the presence of several apartment complexes affected
the area's social and economic characteristics.
Students at nearby LeMoyne College added a younger, more
transient population, and rent-subsidized apartments
drew lower-income residents. Over the decade of the
seventies much of the district's non-white population
came to live in apartments in the Genesee Hills section,
as the number of non-whites grew from only 164 in 1970 to
873 in 1980, or five per cent of the total. According to
the 1980 census, a decided majority of the district's
non-white population lived in the vicinity of Genesee
Hills School.

17

In 1970 the median income in the Genesee Hills area was $13,231, or close to $6,000 below the median income in other parts of DeWitt. By 1980 the Genesee Hills median income of $18,532 was the lowest in the district, or under 60 per cent of that in the nearby Moses DeWitt and Tecumseh areas. Likewise, 25 per cent fewer residents had completed four years of college than in other sections of DeWitt.

Unlike Jamesville, DeWitt retained little if any trace of the onetime hamlet. Punctuated by shopping areas and neon-lighted commerical strips, DeWitt no longer had a community center. Crowded parking lots and a welter of signs occupied every corner of the hamlet's original intersection at Jamesville Road and Genesee Street, and close to this corner the former turnpike and the filled-in Erie Canal created what a local writer extolled as "one of the busiest intersections in the state."[52] By the 1970s extensive commercial and residential development left little acreage for future building. Housing varied from conventional cracker-box design, to the 1960s split-levels, and in DeWitt's upper reaches, large colonials and modern designs, separated by manicured lawns and gardens or shielded behind private woodlands. A survey of all houses sold in one section of DeWitt in 1977-1978 showed most prices in the $50,000-$70,000 range, reaching $200,000 at the most expensive.[53]

The DeWitt of the 1970s had a full array of volunteer organizations from scouting troops to senior citizens' groups, many of them meeting in the schools. An interfaith survey conducted in 1965 showed about one-fourth of DeWitt's residents to be Roman Catholics.[54] Syracuse's Irish and Polish neighborhoods had moved primarily to suburbs on the city's north and west side, but the eastern suburbs also had an active Catholic congregation. With a membership of 950 families the Holy Cross Church provided a network of formal and informal ties in DeWitt. Protestants, about thirty per cent of all residents according to the 1965 survey, were represented by churches of numerous denominations but most conspicuously by a large interdenominational community church dating to 1814.

Two Jewish congregations were established in DeWitt during the 1960s, and Jewish residents accounted for perhaps one-third of the population. The author of a history of the Syracuse Jewish community observed that temples and synagogues had followed the people in the postwar period. "The trend of the general population has been more toward the east, so that now DeWitt and Fayetteville....have a considerable number of Jewish residents."[55] First to locate in DeWitt was a new conservative congregation organized in 1962. On its hundreth anniversary in 1967 the Temple Adath Yeshurun announced plans to move to DeWitt. The oldest conservative congregation in central New York, Adath Yeshurun now has a membership of over one thousand families and serves several thousand on the High Holy Days.[56]

Politically, both Jamesville and DeWitt maintained a tradition of tranquility and conservativism. Overwhelmingly Republican, voters in these areas rarely sent a Democrat to the county legislature or the town board. The town board viewed development in the township complacently, and DeWitt showed all the signs of suburban sprawl. Instead of controlled growth as seen in some local suburbs, the town government long supported commercial interests and future development. In 1972 the town planner effectively protected the "gateway" to DeWitt along the interstate highway from a high-voltage line and instead recommended that it be located in residential DeWitt, because "visual encroachment into neighborhoods has become a tolerated fact of life."[57] Increasingly aware of commercial pressures on their neighborhood, residents in DeWittshire blocked the town's efforts to open a deadend street in their neighborhood, and in 1977 persuaded the town board to prevent a nearby supermarket from expanding close to Moses DeWitt school.

In Jamesville, too, residents sought to invoke community pride by recalling local history and establishing a historical museum. Community leaders worked to improve the village's appearance by eliminating abandoned structures and controlling traffic to an unsightly area of bars and grills. In both Jamesville and DeWitt local residents saw a need to strengthen their communities but these concerns remained, for the time being, separate and distinct from the school district.

During the years after centralization the Jamesville-DeWitt school district drew praise from satisfied residents and recognition elsewhere in the county and state. The district's 1977 survey indicated that fully one-third of residents chose to live in the area because of the schools, and over two-thirds

19

considered the schools to be doing an excellent or good job.[58] Real-estate advertisements listing "J-D Schools" confirmed the system's local reputation. School officials did not hesitate to refer to their district as a "leader" or "the best," a practice that drew withering comments from teachers and administrators elsewhere.

Jamesville-DeWitt's teaching philosophy emphasized the elusive concept of "individualized instruction" for each child. A statement of purpose written in the 1970s charged the staff with the responsibility "to diagnose each child's individual educational, emotional, and social needs vital to the child's full development." Since it was difficult to demonstrate that the district had offered every child "an opportunity for adequate academic preparation commensurate with his abilities, interests, and desires," school officials frequently turned to test scores as evidence of success. Elementary-school children consistently scored more than 20 percentile points above the national average on standardized reading and math tests. Virtually all eighth-graders passed the New York State competency tests in math, reading, and composition, and the high school's senior class often led the county in the number of students awarded Regents' Scholarships or named alternate winners. Eighty per cent of seniors pursued additional education, largely at four-year colleges and universities.

During the three decades following centralization Jamesville-DeWitt maintained unusual continuity in its leadership. Only four superintendents served the district in the years 1950-1981, in contrast to the frequent turnover often seen in school districts. The first superintendent, Ward Edinger, served from 1950-1961, the critical period in which the centralization plans were actually carried out. A local man, resident of Genesee Hills, Edinger had previous administrative experience as a supervising principal and a doctoral degree from Syracuse University. He successfully presided over the construction of new schools and located the central school district's new junior-senior high school in DeWitt despite resentment in Jamesville.

Following Edinger was Harold J. Rankin, who also had previous experience as a superintendent and a doctorate from Syracuse University. Rankin's career in Jamesville-DeWitt was highlighted by the opening of the middle school. Rankin helped develop the middle

20

school's philosophy, emphasizing the distinctive characteristics of children ages 10-13 and the need for a "more individualized program" for this age group.[59] With both the middle school and the high school now located in DeWitt, Rankin alluded to Jamesville in detecting both educational and "sociological advantages" in shifting sixth-graders from elementary to middle school. Because of different socio-economic levels within a district, "the sooner we can bring the youngsters together the better," wrote the superintendent.[60] The middle schools's teams of guidance counselors and specialist teachers drew the attention of visiting educators, and in 1972 Rankin retired to assume a position with Syracuse University's Utica College. He was followed by Dr. Rodney Welles, who had no strong local ties and left the district after a two-year period.

Succeeding Welles, first as acting superintendent in 1974 and then as superintendent, was Lansing G. Baker, who began his career in Jamesville-DeWitt as a math teacher in 1959. In 1966 he became the first principal of the middle school, serving until 1973, when he became an assistant superintendent. Baker completed a doctorate in education at Syracuse University in 1972. In his dissertation, a study of the change from a junior-high organization to a middle school, Baker focused on achievement by seventh-graders. Closely associated with Rankin, Baker's many local ties made for an easy transition to the superintendency. In the central office Baker had the assistance of three administrators--for finance, curriculum, and busing and cafeteria--all of whom had experience in the district dating to the 1950s. Jamesville-DeWitt had yet to experience a turnover of superintendents that indicated community dissatisfaction with policy.

The board of education, too, varied little in its character and composition over the years. In the period following centralization turnover on the board remained low. Most board members were business and professional men, joined in the 1970s by a few women recruited through the parent-teacher organizations. In 1965, for example, a district newsletter praised the caliber of the board, noting that it included one realtor, two engineers with General Electric, one engineer in private practice, one agent in a commercial insurance firm, one comptroller, one lawyer, one director of production in a manufacturing firm, and one executive with Syracuse University.

21

The school board's business-professional cast was not unusual, however. Starting with George P. Counts' study in 1927, many surveys have shown that school boards tend to be recruited from upper- and middle-income groups.[61]  In their 1974 survey L. Harmon Zeigler and M. Kent Jennings found that board members have qualities traditionally valued in American society. Compared with a member of the general public, the school board member is more often a white middle-aged male, Protestant and Republican, well educated and employed in a respected occupation, and a long resident of his community.[62] Zeigler and Jennings also found that civic-business activities provided much the leading avenue to the school board, followed distantly by political-governmental and, last, by educational activities. Of those previously involved in educational activities, most cited work or leadership in the hallowed but ineffectual PTAs. The Jamesville-DeWitt school board followed this pattern.

Few positions were actually contested in school board elections. Rarely did a candidate gain election without already having the advantage of incumbency gained by prior appointment, again a circumstance seen in many districts. In their sample Zeigler and Jennings found that elective board members often gained their seats by appointment.[63]  Only a handful of self-starting candidates ever reached the board of education in Jamesville-DeWitt's first twenty-five years. Instead of retiring, incumbents resigned to allow the perpetuation of a self-selected group. First screened and then appointed following a resignation, the board member had little experience in campaigning, debating issues, or answering public criticism. During the decade of the 1960s, for example, the same group of board members remained intact with only one change. Service of more than ten years was compiled by a number of Jamesville-DeWitt officeholders, and one board member retired in 1981 after twenty-two years.

The composition of the school board also reflected the original agreement by which the district was centralized. The voters preserved and respected the principle of geographical representation on the board of education. As explained in the **Jamesville-DeWitt Policy Handbook,** "Traditionally, representation on the Board has been one member from each of the following: Jamesville, DeWitt, Lyndon, Genesee Hills, Southwood, Tecumseh, At-Large North, At-Large South, and District-at-Large."[64] The north-at-large and south-at-large positions were added following the annexation of the

Tecumseh district in 1960. At that time a district newsletter explained that "since the district was first organized in 1950 the board of education has been based on the principle that each former school district be represented on the board." To allow representation for the Tecumseh district, the original "big-three" component districts--DeWitt, Lyndon, and Jamesville-- each sacrificed one of their representatives. According to the new apportionment, Southwood, Pompey, Genesee Hills, Tecumseh, Lyndon, DeWitt, and Jamesville were allotted one member. For the appearance of balance, a new south-at-large position was created to cover Jamesville, Southwood, and Pompey, while the north-at-large position included Tecumseh, DeWitt, Genesee Hills, and Lyndon. Later, in 1972, the Pompey position was eliminated, and the district-at-large seat established in its place.

All candidates are elected at-large rather than by local units, but residents agreed that the candidates for each given position live within the area. On a population basis the system was riddled with inequities. Using 1970 census figures Southwood's 628 residents received one representative, as did **eight** times that number of residents in Genesee Hills. On a nine-member board, 16 per cent of the district's population living in the Jamesville area was entitled to three seats. Securing Jamesville's acceptance of centralization continued as an important consideration in the board's composition. A populous part of DeWitt--the Lyndon and DeWitt area served by Moses DeWitt School--actually had a decrease in representation in 1960, and the residential areas of Genesee Hills and Tecumseh were never allotted representation on the basis of population. In 1981 voters overwhelmingly rejected a proposal to abandon this rotten-borough style of representation, traditional to Jamesville-DeWitt but far removed from the principle of one man, one vote.

The board of education holding office in the mid-1970s differed little from previous boards. The business and professional world received ample representation. Members from Jamesville and Southwood modified the corporate emphasis somewhat, and several women had emerged from PTA-good works to gain election to the board. The school board functioned much as it always had. The five-year term served to reenforce continuity and stability, because residents voted for just two positions each year and, every fifth year, for only one seat. Although public controversy had yet to touch

23

school affairs, voting turn-out had increased during the mid-1970s, rising from 554 in 1973, to 636 in 1974, and then to 1,462 in 1975. The 1975 budget proposal passed easily, but the number of "no" voters exceeded the total turn-out in most previous years. Neither administrators nor board members--much less residents--acknowledged any impending change in the district, however. Just as school officials and civic leaders had improvised to meet the problems of growth, they were soon to confront declining enrollment, a condition that placed a far greater strain on local decision-making.

## NOTES

1. **Time Magazine,** May 29, 1979.
2. **Main Line Chronicle**(Ardmore, Pennsylvania), March 29, 1978.
3. **New York Times,** June 29, 1979; **Time Magazine,** May 29, 1979.
4. Susan Abramowitz and Stuart Rosenfeld, "Setting the Stage," in Susan Abramowitz and Stuart Rosenfeld, eds., **Declining Enrollment: The Challenge of the Coming Decade**(Washington, D.C., 1978), 4.
5. **Ibid.,** 3.
6. **Digest of Education Statistics, 1980**(Washington, D.C., 1980), 1.
7. Russell G. Davis and Gary M. Lewis, "The Demographic Background to Changing Enrollments and School Needs," in Abramowitz and Rosenfeld, eds., **Declining Enrollment,** 19.
8. **Ibid.**
9. James B. Conant, **The American High School Today**(New York, 1959).
10. David B. Tyack, **The One Best System**(Cambridge, 1974).
11. Abramowitz and Rosenfeld, "Setting the Stage," in Abramowitz and Rosenfeld, eds., **Declining Enrollment,** 4.
12. Tyack, **One Best System,** 247.
13. Robert C. Wood, **Suburbia: Its People and Their Politics**(Boston, 1959).
14. Frederick M. Wirt, Benjamin Walter, Francine F. Rabinovitz, Deborah R. Hensler, **On the Ciy's Rim: Politics and Policy in Suburbia**(Lexington, 1972) 19.
15. Tyack, **The One Best System,** 276.
16. Wood, **Suburbia,** 187.
17. Civia Tamarkin, "Skokie Tries to Close a School," in Betsy Wachtel and Brian Powers, eds., **Rising Above Decline**(Boston, 1979), 77.
18. J.R. Seeley, R.A. Sim, E.W. Loosley, **Crestwood Heights: A Study of the Culture of Suburban Life**(New York, 1956), 4.
19. Roscoe C. Martin, Frank J. Munger, Jesse Burkhead, Guthrie Birkhead, et al., **Decisions in Syracuse** (Bloomington, 1961), 20-47.

20.  For example, see B.G. Rudolph, **From Minyan to a Community: A History of the Jews of Syracuse** (Syracuse, 1970).

21.  Martin, Munger, Burkhead, Birkhead, et al., **Decisions in Syracuse**, 26; also a pictorial history, Henry W. Schramm and William F. Rosenboom, **Syracuse: From Salt to Satellite**(Woodland Hills, California, 1979).

22.  On the city's educational and cultural institutions, Edward W. Muir, "Arts, Sports, and Politics:  Civic Humanism in Syracuse," in Stephen S. Webb, ed., **Essays on the Renaissance in Syracuse** (Syracuse, 1981), 8.

23.  Figures are from the U.S. Census of Population, Syracuse-Onondaga County Planning Agency.

24.  Martin, Munger, Burkhead, Birkhead, et. al., **Decisions in Syracuse**, 29.

25.  **Post-Standard**(Syracuse), Dec.  17,  1981(Neighbors East Section).

26.  For fragments of DeWitt history, see William M. Beauchamp, **Past and Present of Onondaga County, New York**(New York, 1908), 357-360.  Also a town publication, **Our Town:  DeWitt, New York**(DeWitt, 1976); on Moses DeWitt, William A. Comstock, Address to the Onondaga County Bar Association, undated.

27.  **Our Town: DeWitt, New York**, 5.

28.  Dick Case, "I Live in Lyndon, not Fayetteville, Ruth Wilcox Says," **Herald Journal**(Syracuse), Dec. 4, 1981.

29.  Jean Schutz Keough, ed., **Water, Wheels, and Stone:  Heritage of the Little Village by the Creek**(Syracuse, 1976).

30.  "A  History  of  the  DeWitt  Community,"  **DeWitt Directory**(DeWitt, 1974); also "DeWitt--Its History," mimeographed, no author.

31.  James D. Johnson, ed., **The Syracuse and Suburban Railroad** (Wheaton, Ill., 1967).

32.  Records of the DeWittshire "C" Community Club, DeWitt, New York; "A Church, Then a School," **Suburban Life**(DeWitt, East Syracuse), Dec. 16, 1981.

33.  Letter of Mrs. Margaret Levy to Jamesville-DeWitt Board of Education, **Post Standard**, Jan. 31, 1979.

34.  **Herald-Journal**, Dec. 4, 1981.

35.  Keough, ed., **Water, Wheels, and Stone.**

36.  Definition of types of school districts is from the **Handbook of Education Law**(Albany, 1980), Section 21:14, 224.

37.  **Handbook of Education Law,** Section 21:14, 224.

38.  **Ibid.**, 223.

39.  L. Harmon Zeigler and M. Kent Jennings, **Governing American Schools** (North Scituate, Massachusetts, 1974), 2; also Tyack, **The One Best System**, 126-187.

40.  **Proposed  Centralization  of  Schools  in  the  DeWitt-- Jamesville-Lyndon Area**(DeWitt, 1950), 5.

41.  **Proposed Centralization**, 13.

42.  Jamesville-DeWitt District Report, Feb. 1951.

43.  Jamesville-DeWitt District Report, Jan. 1953.

44. **Ibid.**

45. Jamesville-DeWitt District Report, Dec. 1954.

46. Jamesville-DeWitt District Report, Dec. 1955.

47. Arthur Reed, **A Plan for the Development of DeWitt**(DeWitt, 1956), 56.

48. Jamesville-DeWitt District Report, Mar. 1968; construction dates are from a four-page outline "History," Jamesville-DeWitt Central Schools, District Office.

49. Jamesville-DeWitt District Report, May 1960.

50. Jamesville-DeWitt District Report, Sept. 1961.

51. Jamesville-DeWitt Needs Assessment Task Force, Report (DeWitt, 1977), 5. All other data is from the U.S. Census, household income by tract for Onondaga County, 1970 and 1980.

52. Introduction, **DeWitt Directory,** 5.

53. Jamesville-DeWitt Demographic Committee, Report to the Board of Education (Jan. 1979).

54. The survey did not follow school district lines and is considered only suggestive for this description.

55. Rudolph, **From a Minyan to a Community,** 217.

56. **Ibid.,** 263.

57. Arthur Reed, "Statement on Behalf of the Town of DeWitt Regarding Niagara Mohawk Power, Inc. Proposed Oswego-DeWitt 345 KW Transmission Line," Testimony to the Public Service Commission (Albany, 1972), 1359.

58. Jamesville-DeWitt Needs Assessment Task Force, **Report,** 8, 10.

59. Harold J. Rankin, "Position Paper on Middle School," November 1966, 5, 6.

60. **Ibid.,** 11.

61. George P. Counts, **The Social Composition of Boards of Education**(Chicago, 1927); also Frank W. Lutz, "Local School Boards as Sociocultural Systems," in Peter J. Cistone, ed., **Understanding Local School Boards**(Lexington, 1975), 67-76.

62. Zeigler and Jennings, **Governing American Schools,** 27.

63. **Ibid.,** 31.

64. **Jamesville-DeWitt Policy Handbook,** p. 108; the system of traditional representation of areas was clearly violated for the first time in May 1983.

## II. Dealing with the "Baby Bust"

During the 1950s and 1960s the suburbs were ruled by children. "A term like **filiarchy** would not be entirely facetious," wrote William H. Whyte, Jr. in describing suburban life for **Fortune Magazine** in August 1953. "It is the children who set the basic design." If some social critics deplored the child-centered community, school administrators did not. Throughout the 1950s and 1960s they were accustomed to seeing increasing numbers of children enroll in school each year, and more growth seemed in sight. Using 1960 data, the Bureau of the Census published enrollment projections, including both high and low estimates--both of which forecast growth, accelerating after 1975.[1] In 1963 the National Committee for Support of Public Schools called for still more teachers and classrooms.[2] The standard of living was rising, the economy expanding, and the expectations of public education greater than ever.

Almost undetected the birth rate began to fall. Beginning in the early 1960s the number of births started to decline, at first gradually and then dramatically, bringing what became known as the "baby bust." By 1973 the birth total had fallen to a record low, 3.2 million-- or more than one million less than in 1960.[3] In the years after 1973 the annual number of births remained fairly constant at just under 3.2 million, a decline of more than twenty per cent from the peak established in the years 1957-1961. Demographers came to see the baby boom as an exception rather than the norm. "The decline is the long-term reality," explained Charles F. Westoff in the **Scientific American.**[4] In the Western countries decreasing death and birth rates had accompanied development. For two hundred years the birth rate in the United States has fallen, with the major exception of one period. The social and economic forces generating postwar America's "demographic excursion" remain unclear. "An unpredictable element of what might be called fashion seems to play a role in such changes," Westoff concluded.

Although fashion may again elevate the style which one Jamesville-DeWitt resident described as "the four-bedroom house and the four-child family," powerful trends militate against this. Reliable birth-control methods, postponement of marriage and childbearing, women's changing economic role are among the more important social changes affecting the birth rate.

27

Furthermore, the inflationary 1970s, followed by recession and unemployment, offered what one demographer describes as an unfavorable "economic milieu" for young families.[5] As a result of the baby boom, however, greater numbers of women are now entering the childbearing age, and recent years have seen higher birth totals. In 1980 there were slightly more than 3.5 million births--the highest total since 1970--followed by an additional modest increase in 1981.[6] But the number of births expected for each woman is now 1.8, in contrast to the 3.8 of the late 1950s.[7]

Within a few years the declining birth rate began to affect school enrollment. As early as the mid-1960s grade 1 enrollments began to drop, a precursor of the future trend.[8] In 1969 elementary enrollment reached a peak of 37 million. At first gradually and then more drastically enrollments in grades K-8 began a decline that has continued each year since 1970.[9] Current estimates expect elementary enrollment to increase by the mid-1980s, primarily because of the much larger numbers of women entering the prime childbearing ages.[10] High schools had an interval of grace before they, too, showed declining enrollment. In 1976 a record 15.6 million students enrolled in grades 9-12, a number that has decreased every year and is expected to reach a low point by 1990.[11]

The severity of declining enrollment has varied among states. Between 1970 and 1980, however, only Arizona, Nevada, Idaho, Alaska, Wyoming, Utah, and Florida did **not** experience declining enrollment. The Middle Atlantic and the North Central states experienced the decade's most pronounced decline.[12] Among school districts marked declines occurred in large city districts and in older suburbs without new residential building.[13]

In Jamesville-DeWitt a district newsletter in September 1971 reported the **first** decline in enrollment: a drop of 74 students, from a total enrollment of 4487 to 4413. The following year enrollment fell another 181 students, and by September 1973 the opening enrollment was 4232, a decline of 255 students or 6 per cent in a three-year period. In the next three years the trend continued, as an opening-day enrollment of 4145 in 1974 dropped to 3900 in 1976. Over only six years enrollment had declined 13 per cent. In the same period the total United States population between 5-17 declined by 5 per cent; in 1970-1976 the school-age population in the

Northeast dropped 7 per cent, as did that in New York State.[14] Thus enrollment in Jamesville-DeWitt fell at almost twice the regional and state rate of decline.

During the same period property taxes in Jamesville-DeWitt rose steadily. In the Town of DeWitt, a jurisdiction including 95 per cent of the district's population, houses were said to be assessed at about one-fifth of market value. A part-time political appointee assessed houses by neighborhood, generally at the time of sale. Assessments were not systematically updated, and no uniform standard was applied from one area to another.

In 1971 the tax rate per $1,000 assessed valuation was $84.46, rising a little over three dollars in 1972; by 1973 the figure had reached $94.51, followed by a modest increase of several dollars. In 1975 the tax rate per $1,000 assessed valuation was $103.90, and in 1976, $111.79. Over a five-year period that tax rate had increased 32 per cent, at the very time that enrollment had sharply declined. Through the years voters accepted every tax proposal and turn-out at budget elections remained low until 1975, when 1462 residents, or about 12 per cent of those eligible, voted. The following year a record turn-out of 1,725 residents came to the polls, and the budget passed by a bare 51 per cent vote. Between 1971 and 1976, the budget had grown from $6.6 million to $9.6 million.

The near-defeat of 1976 drew reactions from school officials proud of Jamesville-DeWitt's tradition of community support. President of the board of education at this time was William J. Hopkins, representing Jamesville, where he was postmaster. Hopkins was first elected in 1972 against nominal opposition. Representing Southwood was Anthony DeBottis, appointed to fill a vacancy in 1973, then elected without opposition in 1974. The proprietor of a service station centrally located in DeWitt, DeBottis was known as a booster of Jamesville-DeWitt athletic teams. Filling the south-at-large seat was Frederick P. Cargian of Jamesville, praised in an early 1970s newsletter as "an insurance man who has provided invaluable help to the school district." First elected to a two-year unexpired term in 1959, Cargian was elected to his first five-year term in 1961 and never received more than a handful of opposition votes in the successive elections that made him the board's most senior member.

In 1972 a resignation left the DeWitt seat vacant,

and Phyllis Perkins was appointed to represent the area served by Moses DeWitt Elementary School. A newsletter from the school district informed residents, "Mrs. Perkins has children in Moses DeWitt, Middle School, and High School and has been very active in Parent-Teacher and school affairs." In 1973 she was elected without opposition. Four years later her colleagues would elect Perkins president of the board of education.

The Tecumseh area was represented by Carolyn Coit, elected in 1975 in a four-way contest in which the winning candidate gained 30 per cent of the vote, running under the description "housewife." Also elected in 1975, the first year in which school board elections had generated such interest, was Frank Scibilia, a pharmacist who won the Lyndon seat by only four votes over his nearest competitor in a five-way contest. Scibilia's predecessor in the Lyndon position had served seventeen years on the school board.

Dr. John T. Mallan, a professor at Syracuse University's school of education specializing in teacher education, held the Genesee Hills seat, having won 885 votes to his opponent's 689 in the 1976 election, the highest voting turn-out then achieved in a school board election. Mallan's predecessor, Elaine Charles, had served ten years on the board, ending her career as president. Representing all of DeWitt as the north-at-large board member was Edward Beemer, a manager with Travelers Insurance Company. First elected in 1965, Beemer resigned in November 1976, creating a vacancy filled by the appointment of John F. Luchsinger, Jr., a young lawyer with a leading local firm. Luchsinger would gain election on his own in June 1977 by the narrow margin of 1490 to 1170. Thus board members Coit, Scibilia, Mallan, and Luchsinger were relatively new to a board characterized by long terms and low turn-over.

The district-at-large seat was held by Joyce Carmen, who was first appointed in 1972, when a longtime Pompey board member resigned and that position was redefined as district-at-large. At the time of her appointment a district report described Carmen as a person who "brings to the Board a concern for educational quality as demonstrated through her active and participatory involvement in parent-teacher organizations, service on community boards, and her own personal education." In 1973 Carmen was elected without opposition.

Jamesville-DeWitt board members had a record of community service. In a study of school board recruitment, Peter J. Cistone found that virtually every member had been active in some civic organization.[15] In Jamesville-DeWitt board members' community commitments included the Recreation Council, Heart Association, United Way, Rotary, Zoning Board, Scouting Troops, Community Library, and Little League--to name a few. A board member was often active in a local church or, in the rare instance, a temple. As characterized in Robert Salisbury's description of suburban school activists, board members were "family-oriented locals" who "like their town and their schools and work to maintain their quality."[16] Although they often took interest in party politics in town, county, or state government, board members considered any hint of partisanship or political ambition in school affairs suspect. The intrusion of political interest or competition could only degrade the public schools, according to a well-established orthodoxy.[17] In return for unpaid hours spent in meetings, board members gained the satisfaction of playing a strong civic role. As decision-makers they acknowledged themselves to be amateurs and expected to follow the superintendent's professional recommendation. Administrators, not board members, had that specialized training which gave them a "monopoly of....(an) esoteric and difficult body of knowledge" necessary to reach objective decisions about education.[18]

Even before the 1976 budget vote, Jamesville-DeWitt administrators had anticipated problems. Inflationary pressures had become more and more significant, as enrollment continued to decline. A newsletter in September 1975, for example, reported that the district was preparing enrollment projections for a five-year period. "Included in the projections will be building use, staffing patterns, and potential housing development in the community," the newsletter noted. In April 1976 a district report noted that consideration was being given to replacing the school nurse-teacher positions with registered nurses--an action later taken--and "to increasing the class size at Tecumseh, Jamesville, and Genesee Hills to 22-24," a modest adjustment never consistently applied. The near-defeat of the budget prompted a more comprehensive examination of the district's future, and in July 1976 the board of education appointed a committee "to initiate formation of a Task Force to study district organization." Citizen committees often appear as adjuncts to

31

governmental bodies in the United States, and the task force was an approach specifically recommended to school superintendents.

In 1974 the American Association of School Administrators had commissioned a study to offer administrators guidance in dealing with the "unique situation" of declining enrollment.[19] The resulting handbook by Katherine E. Eisenberger and William F. Keough, Jr. addressed declining enrollment strictly as a question of school-closing and making this prescribed remedy palatable to community residents, teachers, and parents, particularly mothers. "For decades, thousands of American housewives in communities across the country have looked toward the local school and school-related activity as an avenue for meaningful involvement," the authors explained. A mother participating in a neighborhood school has "provided an investment of time and effort while simultaneously reaping a harvest of fulfillment in terms of her psychological-emotional needs."[20] Her anxieties were to be assuaged by coffee hours, meetings, and visitations to ease the transition to another school.

In contrast to **Declining Enrollment: What to Do,** other publications of the 1970s observed that simply emptying a school building "will not go very far in reducing costs" and may require expenditures that offset cost-savings.[21] Many authors had emphasized the importance of schools in suburban communities. A particular school acts as a population magnet for a residential area and provides a focus of community interest and activity.[22] Close examination of school-closings across the nation in the early 1970s indicated a variety of effects, including accelerated outmigration of young families, neighborhood deterioration, transition from residential to commercial land-usage, and loss of school support--all complexities much beyond a mother's "personal investment" in a school or her "sphere of influence and general acceptance of herself and her school-age children," as emphasized by Keough and Eisenberger.[23]

Nor did the handbook **Declining Enrollment: What to Do** entertain the possibility of redefining the schools' mission. During the decades of rising enrollment, programs and course offerings had multiplied, supported by specialists including guidance counselors, social workers, psychologists, remedial instructors, speech therapists, and media and instructional-aides personnel.

32

"To reading, writing, arithmetic, and vocational training, modern educational doctrine adds instruction in social skills and group behavior, to ensure the development of the well-rounded personality," wrote Robert C. Wood, or as expressed in Jamesville-DeWitt's statement of philosophy, the school district is committed to each child's "development of an understanding and enjoyment of life and its environment to the fullest."[24] The school administrators' handbook did not propose a scrutiny of open-ended goals in the face of diminished resources. Instead it offered tactical advice: "The establishment of a Task Force of lay citizens is an essential ingredient of any school closing effort." Such groups serve to make the board's decisions acceptable to the public, because "task forces provide a direct line into the community" and "people tend to support what they had a hand in creating."[25]

The Jamesville-DeWitt Needs Assessment Task Force consisted of twenty members, nine of whom were appointed by the board of education to represent the school board, school administration, task force chairman, senior citizens, and non-parents. The faculty association appointed two members, and each of the district's six parent-teacher groups appointed a representative. The high school's student council sent two members, and the Town of DeWitt one, for a total of eleven. The Task Force did not represent neighborhood or civic improvement associations, or religious or charitable organizations, as recommended by the administrators' handbook, however. Nor did the group draw significantly from major companies, business and commercial interests, or real estate firms in the district. Despite the appearance of diversity, the total membership included few persons without a previous involvement in the school district, whether by past or present activity in parent-teacher organizations, a record of solid support on budget votes or bond issues, or personal association with school administrators. Only the representative from the Town of DeWitt came from **outside** the school system's own world.

Teachers themselves took only a minor role in the Task Force. In contrast to faculty members elsewhere who actively influenced policy on declining enrollment, aligned themselves with community or parents' groups, or attempted to thwart school-closings to save jobs, Jamesville-DeWitt teachers were decidedly non-political.[26] Organized as an association, not a union, these teachers had secured the highest pay scale in the county. In the year 1979-1980 a published list showed that almost half of Jamesville-DeWitt faculy members earned $20,000 or more, and each year 50 per cent received merit increases. Even with the onset of severe job-cutting--known as "excessing" or "reduction-in-force"--in the mid- and late-1970s, teachers continued on the path of cooperation and deferred to administrative leadership.

The Task Force was charged with investigating the "future educational needs" of the school district, but its implicit assignment was to save money and thus stave off the crisis of an impending budget defeat. Ways of improving curriculum and enlarging services, for pre-schoolers and adults, for example, received discussion at the same time that attention focused on possible cut-backs, as in music or foreign-language instruction. Without ever resolving this internal contradiction the Task Force organized itself into four separate subcommittees: 1.) needs; 2.) organization and facilities; 3.) demographic; and 4.) finance.

The subcommittees operated independently, under the general chairmanship of David Sher, then president of a real estate development consulting company and a part-time instructor in the school of hotel management at Cornell University. The chairman attended meetings of the individual subcommittees but otherwise they worked independently, drawing on the school administration for advice and direction. It was at this juncture that school administrators played a critical and to them familiar role. As described by one author:

> Official school department influence over the work of a supposedly autonomous advisory committee develops as pro-fessionals provide committees with help on technical aspects of policy making like budget analysis, program evaluation, facilities surveys and personnel poli-cies; they also, indirectly or otherwise, shape the committee's philosophy and approach to its task.[27]

Not surprisingly, committee members absorbed admini-strators' values about what the schools can and should do.

The needs subcommittee conducted detailed interviews with administrators, teachers, and parents to identify strengths and weaknesses in the district's offerings. Problems in discipline, in conferences, in dealing with the atypical child, in coordinating the school program between different levels were all identified. But this committee did not attempt to link these concerns to the overriding question of costs and reorganization. As a result, the subcommittee's efforts illustrate the opinion offered by the school administrators' handbook, "The Task Force should be given a specific charge clearly defined, rather than be asked to study nebulous areas not necessarily associated with the final decision."[28]

The organization and facilities subcommittee dealt directly with the major question, examining the school district's organization "with the initial focus on the four elementary facilities since the effect of declining enrollment will be felt at that level first."[29] Thus this subcommittee studied enrollment figures and projections through 1981 for the elementary schools; examined the number of staff members and personnel costs at each school; studied floor plans and utilization of classrooms; assessed the costs of operating and maintaining each school; and, finally, considered the feasibility of redistricting "to accomplish the alternative of school closing."

The subcommittee looked to the immediate future and possible reorganizations to adjust to declining enrollment in the coming five years. It recommended consideration of the following three alternatives:

Plan A. Close one elementary school in the school year 1977-1978. Close one additional elementary school in 1980-1981, with the middle school housing grades 5-8.

Plan B. Close one house of the middle school in the school year 1977-1978. Return sixth-graders to elementary schools, 1977-1978. Close one elementary school in the year 1980-1981.

Plan C. Phase out one house in middle school. Combine sixth graders into two remaining houses, school year 1977-1978. Close one elementary school 1978-1979. Close one house of middle school completely, 1979-1980.

The "houses" within the middle school operated as

separate schools within a school, serving to reduce the impact of the once-large enrollment there. Each house had its own guidance counselor, teaching teams, and secretary. Thus consolidation into two houses would not represent a reorganization of the school's program. The return of sixth-graders to the elementary schools, as recommended in Plan B, would seriously modify the conception of the midle school as providing a special environment to meet the unique needs of early adolescents. Furthermore, only a decade earlier the school district had committed itself to providing "greater stimulation, departmentalization of teaching, and special facilities and equipment" for sixth-graders.

The middle school's philosophy was very much a product of the 1960s, a period in which the baby boom's children were reaching the teenage years. As the proportion of youth grew, educational research foucused on early adolescence. An explosion of articles and papers recommended "a separate learning environment" for 11 to 13-year-olds, and school organization shifted from the junior high school ( grades 7, 8, 9 ) to the middle school ( usually grades 6, 7, 8 ). In Jamesville-DeWitt the change to a middle school launched Superintendent Baker's administrative career and provided the subject of his doctoral dissertation. Recognition given the middle school in educational circles reenforced its special place in the system. By the late 1970s research indicated that the middle-school organization made "no statistically significant difference in academic achievement," but the subcommittee on organization and facilities did not examine this reassessment.[30]

Not surprisingly, the subcommittee's three alternatives all called for elementary-school closings. The most drastic, Plan A, outlined **two** school-closings within a three-year period, at the end of which the elementary schools would include only grades kindergarten through 4, as the fifth grade was moved to the middle school. How the fifth grade would fit into the middle school's organization and program was not discussed in the report, which emphasized the cost-savings--largely through staff reductions--of each plan.

By closing two schools and moving fifth-graders, Plan A proposed a radical change, while Plan B repudiated the prized middle-school organization and program. The likely choice was Plan C, which merely consolidated houses in the middle school and closed one elementary school, but the final report stopped short of this conclusion. Instead, the subcommittee asserted (but did not show in its report) that it had made "a detailed study to establish the fact that the student population could be accommodated as suggested in **each** alternative."[31] Likewise, the feasibility of redistricting under each plan was asserted ("possible busing plans were actually laid out") rather than shown by redistricting maps and an accounting of the numbers of children involved in the possible closings, as other districts in the area and state did when planning school-closings.

The subcommittee on organization and facilities concluded that Plans A, B, and C produced about the same cost-savings over a five-year period, although they differed on a yearly basis. Because all plans were feasible and produced equal savings, the committee recommended that "the emotional impact of the various alternative plans on students, staff, families, and the community in general" be "seriously considered."

Although the subcommittee on organization and facilities used demographic data--in the form of the district's own system of enrollment projections--a separate subcommittee was charged with studying the demographic character of the school district. This committee concentrated on a community survey, also a useful strategem in developing public support. The administrators' handbook observed, "The major advantage of community surveys is that they build rapport, they say to the community, 'We are interested in your thoughts.'"[32]

In Jamesville-DeWitt some 2598 personal interviews were completed, as well as 275 mail interviews. In addition to gathering social-economic data, the interview presented a battery of other questions. Some asked for judgments, such as a rating of the school system. Others probed feelings: did the respondent feel his/her opinions mattered to school officials? Did he/she feel encouraged to use school facilities?

Finally, on the fifty-fifth question, the interview began to focus directly on pertinent questions. "Generally, how have you voted on past school budgets?" After this question came the following, "If you were to vote today, would you vote in favor of the budget or against it if the school tax remained the same?" Then on question 58, "Based on current trends and projections, our school population is expected to decline by approximately thirty per cent over the next five years.

In view of this information, would you support the closing of an elementary school?" Of those answering this question, 54 per cent replied in the affirmative, while 46 per  cent said no or unsure.

At this point the interview dropped the subject of school-closing, leading instead into a series of topics concerning the level of importance that the respondent attached to a pre-school program and opinions on how to finance it.  Then followed questions concerning a senior citizens' program, a summer school program, extensive adult education program, additional guidance service in the elementary schools, career counseling, and addition of staff to improve instruction in the three R's, all of which required tax increases.

On question 73, however--eighteen questions after the subject's first mention--the interview returned to school-closing. "With  reference  to  closing  an elementary school, would you be for or against closing the elementary school in your area?"  In reply to this question, 42 per cent of the respondents said "yes," while 58 per cent were opposed or unsure. Only in Jamesville did the question appear sharply and clearly. Residents there indicated decisive opposition to closing their own school.

The questionnaire did not solicit opinions about the  three  alternatives  that  the  subcommittee  on organization and facilities developed.  Nor did it seek a specific judgment on any form of reorganization other than  school  closing. Respondents  were  not  asked opinions on choices, such as returning sixth-graders to elementary school as opposed to closing a local school, for example.  Nor were they asked to state an order of preference.

The school administrators' handbook had offered the following recommendation:  "In questionnaire construc- tion, the reasons for conducting the survey should be clearly identified."  The handbook further advised that careful consideration be given to the order of questions in order to "move to the target areas logically and in sequential order."[33]  Instead, the demographic subcom- mittee offered a grab-bag of questions touching the concerns of all segments of the community.  As a result the survey offered a wealth of information but failed to reveal a public judgment or even a sense of direction on the critical questions of reorganization and taxation. According  to  the  National  School  Public  Relations

Association, the "right" questions are those that produce the information sought. "They are easily understood, logically sequenced, and there are just enough of them to direct the board and the administration into the course of action they intend to take."[34] The Jamesville-DeWitt survey had no such conclusive result.

Leading and dominating the fourth committee, the subcommittee on finance, was Paul Cummins, the board-appointed representative of senior citizens. Retired from the family fence-post business, Cummins had expressed his opposition to the 1976 budget in a letter to the local paper. By appointing Cummins to the Task Force, members of the administration and the board expected to produce a more understanding, sympathetic attitude, as their appointee grew better acquainted with the school system's problems and procedures.

Instead Cummins worked independently, producing figures that accentuated mounting costs and understated revenues. The school district's plight looked dismal in Cummins' forecast of the future. For example, although the local tax assessment base for the previous ten years, 1967-1976, had risen by an average of almost five per cent per year, the Cummins subcommittee projected an increase of half this rate for the years 1976-1981. Cummins also exaggerated expected increases in the school budget, projecting a 29 per cent increase per year. The situation looked doubly severe, for Cummins assumed no increased state aid, although state aid **had** increased by an average of 5 per cent a year during the period 1967-1976. Thus, concluded the finance subcommittee, the percentage of revenue produced by local property taxes would rise from 59 per cent to 75 per cent in a five-year period. The local tax per $1,000 assessed valuation would go from $112 to $169 within a five-year period, or a 51 per cent increase. By understating the local tax assessment base **and** anticipated state aid and overstating the rise in school budgets and costs, Cummins emphasized the need for critical decisions by the community.

The Cummins subcommittee generated figures that discomfited administrators as the budget vote approached. Increasingly frustrated with the unmanage-able Cummins, they quietly noted a yellow sheet separating the financial calculations from the rest of the final Task force Report. Nevertheless, Super-intendent Baker never publicly disavowed the Cummins forecast, and within the year he rebuffed criticism of

39

these projections. Accepted by some board members, Cummins' fiscal prognostications provided a justification for unwelcome changes in the future. Consequently, the school district's financial situation was never clearly described, the first of many intentional ambiguities to plague decision-making in the coming years.

While still serving on the Task Force, Cummins began to exhort the public to take action by supporting the newly-formed organization CASE, Citizens Advocating Sensible Education. During the time in which he prepared a financial report issued under the district's official imprimatur, Cummins also organized the first anti-budget group in Jamesville-DeWitt's history. CASE included a group of local doctors, dentists, small businessmen, and senior citizens, backed by Cummins' sense of mission and the printing facilities of a local graphics company, whose president joined forces with Cummins. By a series of newsletters printed on colorful paper, highlighted by cartoons and dramatic headlines ("J-D Taxes Soar"), Cummins publicized his financial projections. He contrasted rising costs and declining enrollment. "Budgets continue to accelerate and do not reflect any moderation in spending, even though 13% fewer students are now being served than five years previously," one newsletter observed. Voters were called upon to consider such questions as: "Are teacher salaries fair and equitable . . . how do they compare with my own?" or, "How long can we keep paying more for less student enrollment?"

As a member of the Task Force, Cummins answered questions about the district's financial prospects at school board meetings and budget hearings, while his organization's newsletter called for a defeat of the school budget. "A budget defeat now will make for a strong and better school system in the future," said a pink newsletter mailed to all residents in the district. "A creative and concerned Board of Education can do the job. . . it just needs a **public mandate** to get started. A defeated budget will provide that mandate a new starting point!"[35] When challenged as to the validity of his figures, Cummins simply explained that all numbers came from the Jamesville-DeWitt Needs Assessment Task Force. As an anti-budget organizer spoke for the school district, the administration recruited other residents to infiltrate CASE meetings. Consideration of the district's fiscal prospects had progressed very little indeed.

40

The final report submitted by the Task Force had other deficiencies as well. The bulky, unpaginated document had no discernible organization, and a major portion consisted of transcripts of interviews with principals and teachers concerning their attitudes on students, programs, and problems. The report carried no unifying theme or recommendation, no statement of long-range expectations, no convincing body of data to support any particular action. At most, the final report simply listed three alternatives for the immediate future and declared them to be equal in the amount of savings that they would offer in the coming five years. "Educational considerations, flexibility, and emotional impacts of each plan, therefore, can be the determining factors for the Board and the community in choosing from the three alernatives."[36]

The school district did not mail the one-pound document to residents but placed copies in the schools and the central office. In mid-March the board met in the high school auditorium to receive the published report before an audience of perhaps 150 residents and teachers who had followed the Task Force's activity. Seated together members of the board and the Task Force listened to comments from the public. A second meeting in late March drew a much smaller attendance, and members of the Task Force vigorously defended their work in response to several critical questions. At neither meeting, however, did board members weigh "educational considerations" or "emotional impacts" of the three plans before them. Not until April did the school district publish a newsletter summarizing the Task Force's findings, and press coverage of the final report was minimal.

On April 11, 1977--one month after the report's submission--after only short discussion, the board directed the superintendent to prepare "statistics on program implications, class sizes, financial implications, etc." to implement a modification of Plan C, phasing out one house in the middle school by combining sixth graders into two remaining houses. The board further requested an investigation of the "potential closing of one elementary school in 1978-1979, and the closing of one house in the middle school in 1979-1980."[37] By investigating **potential closing** the board members took precaution of calling their action a modification of Plan C rather than an outright commitment to a policy. But with a very few words the course was set.

Two months later, CASE's efforts to help older residents to the polls produced a record turn-out of 3168 voters. Again the budget passed by only 51 per cent, or 76 votes. The trusted circle of parents and school-supporters could no longer deliver a safe margin in the June vote. The electorate had grown to several thousand, and earlier murmurs of complaint now took the form of an anti-tax organization. The school district was changing. Figures from the 1980 census were to show that the percentage of residents over 65 more than doubled between 1970 and 1980, reaching 13 per cent. At the same time the school-age population had dwindled. The birth total for 1972--the children to enter kindergarten in 1977--was less than half of 1962's total. A continuing high birth rate and in-migration of young families no longer reenforced the school-age population, as optimistically predicted only fifteen years earlier. Across the nation school districts experiencing these conditions had seen budgets defeated, sometimes repeatedly. Facing a conundrum of rising costs and declining enrollment, administrators and board members arrived at a simple solution: close a school.

### NOTES

1. John K. Folger and Charles B. Nam, **Education of the American Population**(Washington, D.C., 1967), 66.
2. John W. Norton, **Changing Demands on Education and their Fiscal Implications**(Washington, D.C., 1963).
3. Harriett Fishlow, "Demography and Changing Enrollments," in Susan Abramowitz and Stuart Rosenfeld, eds., **Declining Enrollments: The Challenge of the Coming Decade**(Washington, D.C., 1978), 48.
4. Charles F. Westoff, "Marriage and Fertility in the Developed Countries," **Scientific American**, Dec. 1978.
5. Campbell Gibson, "The Elusive Rise in the American Birthrate," **Science**, Apr. 29, 1977.
6. **New York Times**, March 6, 1982; **Herald-Journal**(Syracuse), Oct. 8, 1981.
7. Ellen Bussard, **School Closings and Declining Enrollment**, (New York, 1981), 1.
8. Robert J. Dinkelmeyer and John J. Hudder, "Declining Enrollments: A Survey of States and Selected School Districts,"(Syracuse, 1977), 3.
9. Harriett Fishlow, "Demography and Changing Enrollments," 51.
10. Russell G. Davis and Gary M. Lewis, "The Demographic

Background to Changing Enrollments and School Needs," in Susan Abramowitz and Stuart Rosenfeld, eds., **Declining Enrollments: The Challenge of the Coming Decade**(Washington, D.C., 1978), 41.

11. Fishlow, "Demography and Changing Enrollments," 51.

12. National Center for Education Statistics, **The Condition of Education**(Washington, D.C., 1981), 58.

13. Dinkelmeyer and Hudder, "Declining Enrollments," 7.

14. U.S. Bureau of the Census, "Population Profile of the United States," 1976(Washington, D.C., 1976).

15. Peter J. Cistone, "The Recruitment and Socialization of School Board Members," in Peter J. Cistone, ed., **Understanding School Boards**(Lexington, 1975), 54; the civic accomplishments and qualifications of Jamesville-DeWitt board members Perkins, Carmen, Cargian, and Coit are described in Jamesville-DeWitt District Report, Sept. 1972 (Perkins); Report, Jan. 1973 (Carmen, Cargian); Report, Apr. 1980 (Coit).

16. Robert H. Salisbury, **Citizen Participation in the Public Schools**(Lexington, 1980), 74.

17. In 1959 Thomas H. Eliot described the long-observed taboo of politics in education. "School board members and school superintendents are engaged in political activity whether they like it or not." See Eliot, "Toward an Understanding of Public School Politics," **American Political Science Review**, Vol. 53(Dec. 1959), 1032-1051.

18. Quoted in Paul E. Peterson, **School Politics: Chicago Style**(Chicago, 1976), 123.

19. Katherine E. Eisenberger and William F. Keough, Jr., **Declining Enrollment: What to Do**(Arlington, Virginia, 1974), ii.

20. **Ibid.**, 11.

21. Dinkelmeyer and Hudder, "Declining Enrollments," 9.

22. Philip Meranto, **School Politics in the Metropolis**(Columbus, 1970), 38, for example.

23. Richard L. Andrews, "The Environmental Impact of School Closures," (Seattle, 1974); Eisenberger and Keough, **What to Do**, 11.

24. Robert C. Wood, **Suburbia: Its People and Their Politics**(Boston, 1959), 189; "Jamesville-DeWitt Statement of Philosophy," undated.

25. Eisenberger and Keough, **What to Do**, 16.

26. Cf. Evanston teachers described in **Time Magazine**, May 29, 1979; also Ellen Bussard, **School Closings and Declining Enrollment**.

27. Brian Powers, "Fitting Schools to Fewer Students," in Betsy Wachtel and Brian Powers, eds., **Rising Above Decline**(Boston, 1979), 5.

28. Eisenberger and Keough, **What to Do**, 20.

29. Jamesville DeWitt Needs Assessment Task Force, **Report**(Mar. 1977), 1.

30. Theodore C. Moss, Address to the Fayetteville-Manlius Concerned Citizens, St. Ann's Church, Manlius, Jan. 31, 1978; also see William Alexander, **The Emergent Middle School**(New York, 1969).

31. Emphasis added.

32. Eisenberger and Keough, **What to Do**, 13.

33. **Ibid.**, 23.

34. Quoted, Eisenberger and Keough, **What to Do**, 23.

35 CASE(Citizens Advocating Sensible Education), "Defeat J-D School Budget," Fact Sheet #3, undated; newsletter entitled "J-D School Taxes Soar," Fact Sheet #1, undated; newsletter entitled "Another J-D Tax Hike?" Fact Sheet #2, undated.

36. Jamesville-DeWitt Needs Assessment Task Force, **Report**(Mar. 1977), Section E-4.

37. Minutes, Jamesville-DeWitt Board of Education, Apr. 11, 1977.

## III.  How Not to Close a School

In the fall of 1977 opening-day enrollment was 3734,
a decline of 167 from the previous fall's 3901.
Declining enrollment was now affecting the middle
school, and the elementary schools lost only 61 students.
In the years since 1971, however, elementary-enrollment
in the district had declined by 549, or 28 per cent. The
severity of decline varied in the four schools. In a
six-year period Jamesville and Genesee Hills had lost
slightly more than one-third of their enrollment,
bringing both schools well below 350. Always smaller
than the other elementary schools, Tecumseh's enrollment
declined by 27 per cent, leaving a 1977 enrollment of 318,
almost identical to that at Genesee Hills. Moses DeWitt
showed a more moderate decline of 18 per cent but
nevertheless dropped to 412 students.

The district's September newsletter printed 1976
and 1977 enrollment figures without comment. The
superintendent's report called attention to changes in
the newsletter's format designed to "make reading easier
and highlight certain newswothy items," indicating a
response to the public attention given to the CASE
newsletter. A message from the president of the board of
education, Phyllis Perkins, stated, "We are elected and
selected to represent you, but we cannot do this unless
you are willing to openly confront us with your
concerns."

Sixth-graders entering the middle school in 1977
enrolled in two rather than three houses, in accordance
with the board's decision the previous spring. The
likelihood of the board's moving to carry out the second
part of the Task Force's Plan C, that is, closing of an
elementary school in 1978-1979 created little, if any,
public discussion. Neither newspaper reporters nor
parent-teacher groups anticipated a coming controversy.
Minutes of the Moses DeWitt Parents' Group, for example,
show business as usual, a succession of activities from
welcome coffees to Halloween parties but no discussion of
a prospective closing. Attendance at the board of
education's meetings remained low; only a handful of
regular board-watchers sat in on these sessions.

The board's procedures accentuated isolation from
the community.[1] Meetings followed an agenda that
permitted no public comment until adjournment. Although
some nearby New York State districts provided an

opportunity for questions after each item on the agenda, Jamesville-DeWitt procedures permitted no intrusions, a point firmly upheld by board presidents. Meetings normally took place in a small corporate-style board room in the high school, a room that had only about twenty chairs for residents. Seated around their board table most members presented only a partial profile to public view, while some were entirely obscured; only the board president and the superintendent faced the usually-small audience. Speaking in quiet, sometimes inaudible tones, board members addressed their comments to each other, alluding to information not presented to the audience. Meetings were interrupted only by board members rising to fill their coffee cups at a stand next to the table. When the board of education moved, albeit reluctantly, to larger rooms in the high school, poor amplification systems made it difficult for residents to hear. Conversations by residents, however, were likely to produce a reprimand or a bang of the gavel bringing the meeting to order.

A typical meeting in the late 1970s opened with an auditor's and treasurer's report, prepared by the school administration and presented by a board member for automatic approval. The agenda then included, for example, a report on programs for students with handicapping conditions, an announcement of the performance of Jamesville-DeWitt students on academic tests or in athletic or art competitions, and a discussion of heating or maintenance problems in the school buildings. Following these reports from administrators came a board member's account of a meeting of the New York State school boards' association. During presentations board members often glanced in their folders at reports or packets not distributed to the public. Rarely was there any sustained exchange of comments between board members and the superintendent. Not uncommonly the school board interrupted public meetings to recess into executive session to consider personnel questions.

During its many untroubled years the school system had functioned as what Paul E. Peterson describes as a unitary organization.[2] The district's administrators, board members, and trusted corps of school-supporters shared common interests, values, and routines. Although professional and amateur educational leaders played different roles, they held common objectives, such as enhancing Jamesville-DeWitt's prestige in the community, securing financial support, and guarding the schools from outside pressures. An overriding commitment to the system's excellence and future well-being limited conflict within a unitary organization. Procedures such as reliance on the agenda and the refusal to circulate documents and reports to the public served as defense mechanisms; these routines shielded school decision-makers from public opinion and protected their autonomy.

Board members and administrators were mutually dependent, but the professional educator held clear policy leadership. His activities masked by lengthy board meetings, detailed agendas, and countless public appearances, the superintendent held the initiative in decision-making, as described in many works.[3] In Jamesville-DeWitt as common elsewhere the superintendent's office not only prepared the board's agenda but produced reports and budgets with little involvement from amateur board members usually busy with other responsibilities. In communicating with the school board Superintendent Baker emphasized what was routine and non-controversial, as discussion frequently touched on "the way we have done it before." But, according to Peterson, "organizational behavior is prone to 'error' in crisis situations, those times when almost by definition routines are inappropriate for dealing with the problems the system faces."[4]

On November 14, 1977, the board of education met in what appeared to be yet-another routine session. Only a few residents were present to hear veteran board member Frederick Cargian move that "based on the information that the board has received from the Needs Assessment Task Force and the recent updating of our population trends and facilities usage, an elementary school be closed, starting with the 1978-1979 school year." Cargian then went on to request that "the superintendent and his staff project transportation routes and population shifts for each elementary school to enable the board to determine which elementary school closing will least affect the program and the students we serve."[5] Mallan seconded the motion, which produced only a brief exchange before it passed unanimously. Board members had not questioned the necessity of the measure or the process to be used in implementing it. The district's usual operating procedures were underway.

A "special edition" of the Jamesville-DeWitt newsletter gave an embellished account of the meeting to residents one week later. "At the November 14th Board of Education meeting, after the presentation of up-dated

47

figures and exhaustive discussion, the board voted unanimously to close an elementary school. There was NO decision about which one to close. This vote put into action the **1978-1979 phase** of the Task Force's alternative 'C'." The newsletter continued by reassuring residents that the board had found two issues "essential" in deciding upon the particular school to close: first, "the educational program for every child in the J-D schools must continue at least at the current level of excellence," and, second, "the disruption which always follows such a change must be kept to an absolute minimum." According to the newsletter, the board had found it clear that regardless of which school closed, "there would be adequate classroom and special space to accommodate all elementary students in the three remaining schools. Some elementary school attendance areas, of course, might have to be re-drawn to insure an appropriate distribution of students in the three remaining schools."6

The newsletter concluded by listing considerations to be taken into account in reaching a decision, including the present and potential use of buildings for other than regular school uses; the transportation of students; the number of extra classrooms available in 1978-1979; the acreage at each school site; the square-footage within each building; the enrollment projected for each school in 1978-1979; the district-wide age-range census; and the maintenance of buildings. The newsletter avoided setting these considerations in any kind of rank order or suggesting a system for evaluating each building systematically, although the experience of other districts recommended the use of explicit criteria.7 The administrators' handbook on declining enrollment, for example, had suggested a "facilities usage criteria test" to apply to each school, and one of the handbook's authors had written elsewhere, "A criteria/weighting system helps people make rational decisions about a highly emotional topic."8

Just as board members had never publicly discussed their decision to close a school, they did not explore the implications of the two stipulations stated in the newsletter: first, maintenance of the program's excellence, and, second, keeping disruption to a minimum. No topic relating to school closing and reorganization had been subjected to "exhaustive discussion," as stated in the district's special edition. Still remaining, however, was the question of which school to close. "Who will influence this vital decision?" asked the newsletter. The critical determination to close an elementary school had been quietly reached on the basis of a reading of budget votes, enrollment projections, and an opinion survey indicating that DeWitt residents felt ambivalent about keeping their local schools. Nevertheless, residents were assured that they had a part to play in the decision to be made on December 12. "Your schools, operated with your support, need your support, need your comment and suggestions in this important matter." To help make this possible the parent groups of the four elementary schools were to sponsor "information-opinion meetings" at each school.

At the information meetings board members and administrators presented the reasons for closing a school. Cost-savings, surplus space, and declining enrollment received emphasis. Using figures from the Task Force Report, school administrators cited cost-savings of $180,000, a figure later conceded to be high, or for the home-owner a savings of between $3.50-$4.00 per thousand dollars of assessed valuation. Although the savings would appear in the form of reducing prospective increases in the budget, some residents expected a school-closing to produce an actual tax rebate--a misunderstanding that was never clarified. Contrary to a 1976 recommendation from the New York State Education Department, school officials were not "very precise in presenting the analysis of the saving accruing from consolidation."[9]

Parents in the different school areas protested that the projected saving appeared insignificant in comparison to the value of local schools. In a time of rising inflation and school budgets little was to be saved and much lost. "Mrs. Perkins, don't be so anxious to save my money," said Thomas Maroney, a Syracuse University law professor living behind Moses DeWitt School. Board president Perkins asserted that to many senior citizens living on fixed incomes the tax savings of closing a school had great importance. She further contended that future passage of the budget required economies. "Fiscal responsibility" dictated that the board make every possible effort to save money.

No longer could the district afford the luxury of surplus space, said school officials, pointing to "excess rooms" amounting to 21 in all four schools: Tecumseh, 8; Moses DeWitt, 5; Jamesville, 5; and Genesee Hills, 3. District administrators showed floor plans in

49

which the "extra" rooms were blacked out. Extra rooms included those no longer used for classroom purposes, although some were now used for small-group instruction and remedial reading. Residents received assurances, however, that the schools' art and music rooms would remain unchanged and an average class-size of 22 would be maintained.

Questions from residents concerning alternatives to school-closings received short shrift. Board members, the public heard, had already considered all possibilities. The alternative of returning the sixth grade to elementary school was rejected. The middle school's program for sixth, seventh, and eighth-graders was one of Jamesville-DeWitt's finest accomplishments. Moreover, a grouping of grades seven, eight, and nine in a junior-high organization would be both socially and educationally undesirable, according to the superintendent.

District administrators depicted a Draconian drop-off in enrollment, a decline more severe and precipitous than that experienced in the previous five years. For example, the new district-wide age-range census showed only twenty-two babies within the 0-1 age group and seventy-two in the 1-2 age-group. Furthermore, it was asserted, whereas the 0-1 age-group had once increased by 300 per cent by the time the children reached school-age, this pattern--established over the period 1965-1975--was no longer holding. The kindergarten class size for 1982 could be expected to be exceptionally small. The presentations at the information meetings emphasized the extraordinarily low numbers of pre-schoolers, thus underscoring the presence of surplus space in the elementary schools in the years ahead. A once-growing community had become stable and middle-aged, and reproduction had virtually ceased.

At each informational meeting residents took the floor to defend the value of their own schools. (For attendance boundaries, See Figure 5.) Each school had drawn families to its area, and each had its partisans. Jamesville's elementary school provided an important institution in a small community, and DeWitt's three elementary schools offered focal points for the surrounding residential areas. Furthermore, despite Jamesville-DeWitt's many years as a central school district, the elementary schools had retained a great degree of autonomy, each having distinctive qualities in its educational program, administration, and involvement of parents.10

　　　　Residents from every area sought to elicit the
board's rationale in selecting a school to close.
Thwarted in this, parents simply urged board members to
spare their school or, as a second preference, not send
their children to another school. School-closing
created the first anxiety, followed by redistricting
explicitly stated as a concern that DeWitt children not
go to Jamesville. Parents in some areas called for
responsiveness and demanded that board members offer
their resignations if they failed to follow public
opinion. Stung by unaccustomed criticism, board
president Perkins rebuffed questions and her colleagues
rallied to her side. The early appearance of battle
lines was contrary to the newsletter's statement that the
school district needs "your comment and suggestions in
this important matter," as well as the board president's
own request that members of the public "openly confront
us with your concerns."

　　　　Consideration of long-range trends and projections
disappeared as the focus narrowed to which school to
close. Selecting and closing an elementary school
became an end in itself, a "bullet to bite," in the words
of board member Mallan, rather than a measure that was one
part of an assessment of the district's overall needs as
the Task Force was charged to consider. At no time in the
information meetings did board members discuss a second
school closing; nor did they consider the impact of
declining enrollment on the middle school. Furthermore,
within a decade decreased elementary enrollments would
reach the high school, carrying with them a serious
impact on programs and staffing at that level. But
school officials concerned themselves with only their
immediate objective.

　　　　By meeting at each elementary school, a public
relations gesture, the board of education inadvertently
reenforced local feeling and resistance to school-
closing. People in every area insisted upon the
importance of their school to their children and
neighborhood. Visiting the schools, board members and
administrators heard a variety of appeals and arguments.

　　　　In Jamesville, for example, residents cared about
their elmentary school, situated on a grassy campus of
twenty-three acres. The school had developed many
assets, including a senior citizens' room, a historical
museum, summer recreation programs, and a nature trail

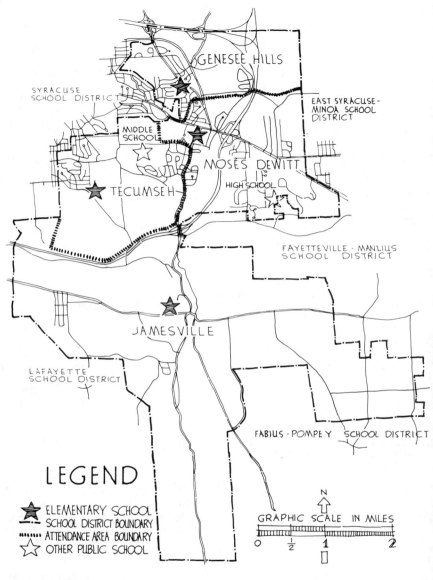

GENESEE HILLS

SYRACUSE
SCHOOL DISTRICT

EAST SYRACUSE-
MINOA SCHOOL
DISTRICT

MIDDLE
SCHOOL

MOSES DEWITT

HIGH SCHOOL

TECUMSEH

FAYETTEVILLE - MANLIUS
SCHOOL DISTRICT

JAMESVILLE

LAFAYETTE
SCHOOL DISTRICT

FABIUS - POMPEY SCHOOL DISTRICT

## LEGEND

⭐ ELEMENTARY SCHOOL
— · — SCHOOL DISTRICT BOUNDARY
••••••• ATTENDANCE AREA BOUNDARY
☆ OTHER PUBLIC SCHOOL

N
⬆

GRAPHIC SCALE IN MILES

0    ½    1    2

# ELEMENTARY SCHOOL ATTENDANCE AREAS 1977-1978

**FIGURE 5**

52

extending through the woods against a backdrop of the Alpha Portland Cement Company's smokestack. Answering the Task Force's opinion survey, only ten per cent of respondents in Jamesville had indicated a willingness to close their own school, in contrast to twenty-five to thirty per cent in every area of DeWitt. Jamesville residents, who once had their own K-12 system, expressed resentment at DeWitt's control of the middle and high schools. They felt determined to retain the last remnant of their educational autonomy.

The largest and newest of the elementary schools, Tecumseh was located in the only section of DeWitt that still included undeveloped areas, as well as extensive acreage used for golf courses. The building had twenty-six, rather than twenty-one or twenty-two, classrooms around a central courtyard. Academically, the school had an excellent reputation, confirmed by the Tecumseh children who won scholarships and prizes in high school. Working with small class-sizes and the principal's support, the faculty had introduced innovations, such as an activity room for children with learning problems. The special program for handicapped children offered at Tecumseh influenced the school's atmosphere and attracted some families to the area. Parents at Tecumseh described their school as one that offered children both academic excellence and acceptance of all kinds of people.

Like Tecumseh, Genesee Hills Elementary School had a site of about 10 acres, including fields and sledding areas. Both Tecumseh and Genesee Hills were the low-lying one-story buildings typical of modern school architecture, but Genesee Hills lacked adornment, even classroom cupboards and storage areas. Parents at Genesee Hills found that teachers gave individual attention to children who had problems, using a resource room and specialists who came to the school. The efforts for black children from nearby apartments received particular praise. Although these children represented less than one-tenth of Jamesville-DeWitt's student population, their needs deserved consideration in board decision-making. One resident called the board's attention to the lower real estate prices and greater social diversity in Genesee Hills, reflecting an income level below that in other parts of DeWitt. Past parents offered their support, as did a former president of the board of education who promised to do anything to persuade the board to preserve Genesee Hills.

At Moses DeWitt parents considered their school's central location an advantage. The school was ideally situated for "walkers" from surrounding neighborhoods, as well as for parents who traveled the former Genesee Turnpike either downtown or to other points in the eastern suburbs. The absence of a front lawn and a site less than half the size of those at Tecumseh and Genesee Hills drew no complaint, for the densely-populated area around Moses DeWitt had some characteristics of an urban neighborhood. Proximity and convenience took precedence over the grass and isolation of later suburban development. Teachers at Moses DeWitt escorted children to the edge of their schoolyard to see early nineteenth-century gravestones in the Orville Cemetery, and residents who lived near the school regarded their area as truly DeWitt.[11] Although Moses DeWitt antedated the district's other schools, all rooms but the original four were of 1950s construction. Like Jamesville Elementary, the building gave the appearance at the front of a one-story school but actually had two levels.

Parents described Moses DeWitt as academically strong. Children left elementary school well prepared for middle school and high school, and some returned to the area as adults to enroll their own children at Moses DeWitt. Furthermore, the school had withstood the ravages of declining enrollment better than any other. In 1977 Moses DeWitt's enrollment was 100 more than that at the three remaining schools, or about what Tecumseh's was in 1971. Nearby districts had often phased out schools with low enrollments, and the State of New York recommended that "any consolidation plan should have as a prime element the requirement of moving the least number of children the shortest distance possible."[12] Because Jamesville-DeWitt officials themselves had promised to make the "change that kept disruption to a minimum," Moses DeWitt parents felt reassured that the largest of the four elementary schools was safe.

Despite obvious differences in how residents saw the schools, district officials insisted that the four elementary schools be considered equal components of the system. Superintendent Baker assured the public that all schools had excellent programs and excellent results. That the academic performance of children varied from one school to another was never officially acknowledged in the discussion of closing. One year later a report on test scores for 1977-1978 presented at a routine board session revealed that parents had correctly perceived differences.[13] Children at

Tecumseh consistently led the district on standardized tests in reading, language arts, and math, achieving significantly higher scores than students elsewhere. Following but at a distance unknown by their parents were Moses DeWitt children. Not surprisingly, the children of the district's professional and upper middle-income groups generally established higher scores, especially in reading and language arts. Only in math did Genesee Hills children narrowly surpass those at Moses DeWitt, and Jamesville's results fell as much as twenty points below the Tecumseh scores. School administrators minimized the importance of these differences, however, pointing instead to the outstanding students at each of the district's schools.

In the weeks before December 12, many parents wrote and spoke to board members and administrators, attempting to learn how the closing decision would be reached. Some parents' groups exhorted their members to make their opinions known. A few residents went beyond this to marshal arguments as to why some school other than their own should be closed. Speculation centered on how the board would choose the school to close and the reshuffling of children expected from redistricting for three schools.

On Saturday, December 10, the board of education met in a "study session" to consider the closing decision. Less than a month later the Appellate Division of the State Supreme Court in Brooklyn ruled that the state's Open Meetings Law did indeed apply to study sessions as well as official board of education meetings.[14] But, in the meanwhile, the board deliberated all day without having to give prior notification or open the meeting to the public or the press.

Board members and administrators had earlier concluded that the district must economize by the conventional remedy of school-closing, described in one city as "service delivery system consolidation."[15] Most other districts in Onondaga County had already embarked on the prescribed course of closing, and some nearby suburban systems had closed several buildings. During an eight-hour discussion administrators agreed as the school board pinpointed Moses DeWitt for closing. According to later accounts, the board took "straw votes" showing the support for each school. Jamesville's three representatives stood solid for retaining that school. To close Jamesville Elementary would create considerable busing, particularly for those children in outlying

55

rural sections, board members agreed. Genesee Hills bordered the city, and a school closing might damage property values there. Moreover, the black children from the Springfield Gardens Apartments near Genesee Hills presented a special case; it seemed desirable for those children, whose families were often transients in the district, to have a school nearby rather than travel by bus to another area. Tecumseh served handicapped children in addition to being the school that administrators used for pilot programs and innovations in the curriculum. Supported by two members of the board of education, one elected from the Tecumseh area and recruited by the school's principal and the other elected as the district-at-large representative, Tecumseh also had a vocal parents' group, as demonstrated at the information meeting there.

In the end only board members John Luchsinger, Jr. and Frank Scibilia remained to support Moses DeWitt. Elected to represent the north-at-large area, Luchsinger had two young children, one enrolled in kindergarten at Moses DeWitt. Representing Lyndon, Scibilia had sent his children to his own school, Moses DeWitt, and his family's name was long identified with DeWitt's oldest area. Phyllis Perkins had received her appointment to the board at the recommendation of Moses DeWitt principal Ted Calver, and the biographical information about her issued in 1972 had emphasized her role in the Moses DeWitt and other parent groups. Now, however, Perkins presented herself as especially concerned with the needs of senior citizens, the representative of the district as a whole rather than the Moses DeWitt area. Among board members Perkins alone declined to support the school in her area.

In the week following the information meeting at Moses DeWitt on December 4, signs of apprehension first appeared in the cohesive neighborhood directly behind that school. This long-established residential section was regarded by its home-owners as special, if not exclusive. Children from DeWittshire had always walked to school at Moses DeWitt. United by neighborhood social events and previous civic battles, as in blocking the expansion of the nearby supermarket, DeWittshire residents could rally quickly, if necessary. When they learned that parents at other schools had spoken forcefully, even menacingly, to the board of education, DeWittshire residents began to wonder if Moses DeWitt parents had shown complacency in merely asking questions. In the words of one man active in previous

56

neighborhood issues, "Maybe we've been caught with our knickers down." DeWittshire residents set a meeting for Sunday night, the evening before the board was to reveal its decision.

Growing concern in DeWittshire prompted Perkins to appeal to the president of the Moses DeWitt Parents' Group to try "to keep the lid on" in that neighborhood. Meetings and activities would only interfere with the board's decision-making. Luchsinger, however, indicated that Moses DeWitt parents did have reason for concern. Following the school board's all-day meeting on Saturday, he answered the inquiries of several friends by saying that it was at least "very possible" that Moses DeWitt would be closed.

On Sunday night Luchsinger accepted an invitation to appear at a DeWittshire meeting as a guest in a private home, an action for which he later drew criticism from opponents on the board. In Jamesville-DeWitt as in other districts board members believed in keeping a solid front. "Unity is important," said a board member from another Onondaga County school district in a seminar for board candidates.[16] By even his discreet warnings to friends, Luchsinger had violated the orthodoxy of school board governance.

At the DeWittshire meeting Luchsinger attempted to balance his responsibilities to the board and to his constituents. He did not recount details of the school board's decision-making, but he did reveal pessimism about Moses DeWitt's prospects and indicated reasons why it would be "possible" for Moses DeWitt to close. Luchsinger urged residents to attend the board's meeting the next night. When questioned about the meeting, he simply said, "Be there!" DeWittshire residents responded by hastily drawing up a petition in behalf of Moses DeWitt and seeking a place on the agenda for Monday night. Most Moses DeWitt parents, however, did not know that an alarm had been sounded and continued to wait for the board to act.

On Monday, as phone calls and letters reached the district office, some board members and administrators began to wonder if they were ready to put the decision before the public. In the words of board member Carolyn Coit, "We had been told to expect criticism." Nevertheless, perhaps more time was needed to reassure the public and to develop the new school attendance areas. A school-closing had seemed inevitable, and it

57

could be expected to be painful. Superintendent Baker
told the press, "Closing a school is like a death in the
family."17 Another administrator, curriculum coordinator Ronald E. Osborn, remarked to parents, "No teacher
or administrator really wants to close a school." In
Jamesville-DeWitt administrators had come up from the
teaching ranks in the 1950s and 1960s during the system's
period of expansion. They had never taken an action that
signaled retrenchment. On Monday administrators
considered the possibility of delaying the decision, to
overcome divisions opening in the board and the
community.

The meeting of December 12 opened at 7:30 p.m.
before an audience of more than one-hundred persons,
scattered through the high school auditorium, including
a number of teachers as well as parents and other
residents. Board member William Hopkins of Jamesville
immediately offered a motion that there be no public
presentation regarding school-closing during the board's
discussion. Anthony DeBottis, representing Southwood,
then seconded the motion, which carried unanimously.
Thus even those DeWittshire residents forewarned of the
decision found themselves unable to register comments
before the board acted. Public comment was to be
restricted to fifteen minutes at the end of the meeting.

President Perkins opened by observing that "by law
the decision to close a school is determined by the board
of education." She noted that board members had spent
eight hours of arduous, exhausting effort on Saturday, as
they had narrowed the choices from the original twenty-
seven options presented by the administration--a number
that referred to a variety of attendance areas and bus-
routing plans rather than the immediate decision before
the board. Luchsinger commented on the administration's
options, concluding that until recently members had no
accurate reading of neighborhood feeling regarding local
schools. He then offered this motion: "Based on
hearings, correspondence, and other communications, the
board should take the opportunity to test the
neighborhood concept (example, maintain all four schools
and study other facts). All six schools should remain
open for one year while this study is made." Scibilia
seconded the motion.

In response to Luchsinger's motion, board member
John T. Mallan replied that Perkins had been correct in
stating that the entire district must be seen as one
neighborhood. He went on to recall that the board **had**

58

voted on November 14 to close a school. The school board had so acted because of twenty-one empty classrooms, he said,--a contention not supported by records of the board's public meetings. Further discussion simply wasted time, concluded Mallan. Luchsinger replied that information had recently poured in from a community that had not yet understood the options considered by the board. Certainly, said Joyce Carmen, the board should not act precipitously on this issue. On the other hand, if the school board did delay, it should investigate "new facts" and not buy time for nebulous reasons. Carmen expressed concern about what would be involved in redistricting and indicated this as an area for study. Speaking for the Southwood area in Jamesville, DeBottis declared that the children in his neighborhood had lost their school in 1965, and he did not see why this should be a problem to others. Coit, who represented the Tecumseh area, felt that the quality of the program could be maintained but the divisive attitudes of parents might be damaging.19

After listening to all of her colleagues, Perkins reiterated her previous opinions. Keeping all schools open would "simply be a response to emotional, social, and political pressure." This, she said, would be a "negative" action by the board. When Luchsinger's motion was called to a vote, it gained only four votes: those of Coit and Hopkins in addition to the "yes" votes cast by Luchsinger and Scibilia. If Luchsinger had simply moved that the board delay the decision by one month--as some board members expected him to--perhaps he could have gained a fifth vote as well. The administration did not seem averse to buying time, and board member Cargian's eighteen years of service made him receptive to signals from the superintendent. Then, too, Carmen had problems to consider. Many Tecumseh parents had gone on record at the information meeting and in letters as opposing any redistricting that removed children from the school, particularly a change that assigned expensive new neighborhoods to Jamesville. How could redistricting be handled so as to avoid this problem?

As it happened, however, the moment for delay had passed. Following the defeat of Luchsinger's motion, the board went into a five-minute recess to consider the next steps, to the dissatisfaction of the audience. This interruption indicated the board's obvious disarray and division over the next action to be taken. When the meeting resumed, Mallan moved that Moses DeWitt

Elementary School be closed; the motion was seconded by
DeBottis. Mallan explained that he recommended the
Moses DeWitt closing, because the school seemed to be
"the most risky" of the buildings to keep open. He cited
heavy traffic on Jamesville Road and further observed
that because the school had two levels, it could not offer
suitable facilities for the handicapped. Closing Moses
DeWitt, moreover, would not deprive any neighborhood of a
school. The high school would serve its surrounding
area including Lyndon, and the central part of DeWitt
would continue to have Genesee Hills and the middle
school on Randall Road nearby. The closing of Moses
DeWitt would not "collapse" any neighborhood; indeed,
its central location would facilitate busing the
children out to schools located along the edges of the
district.[20]

Luchsinger replied to Mallan's arguments by saying
that closing Moses DeWitt would greatly damage the
neighborhood around that school. Because more children
attended Moses DeWitt, he argued, more children would be
affected by closing that school. Rebutting Luchsinger,
Perkins and Carmen answered that they felt accountable to
all residents in the district, not just parents who had
children in school. Carmen remarked that taxpayers had
grown increasingly concerned with rising costs, and she
preferred that the district's dollars be spent on
maintaining and developing programs. "My primary
concern is that there be the best possible education for
all youngsters."[21]

Luchsinger then moved that the board table Mallan's
motion for one month. "I feel that to put off or to keep
open the six schools takes away from the task we should be
addressing," Mallan told the board.[22] Perkins added
that she could not in "good conscience" vote to delay a
school closing. Mallan held leadership of the board at
this point, and Luchsinger had not garnered support for
this motion to delay. His support ebbed to a 6-3 vote, as
only Hopkins and Scibilia, but not Coit, joined
Luchsinger in voting for a month's delay. If the motion
for a month's delay had been offered before a school had
been named, perhaps the outcome of the vote would have
been different. Once a decision had been outlined and a
possible majority had emerged, most board members were
ready to join ranks.

When Mallan repeated his motion and the vote was
taken at 9:15 p.m., the closing of Moses DeWitt drew the
support of all members except Scibilia and Luchsinger.

The 7-2 decision drew hisses and boos from the audience. The board then attempted to move into a discussion of potential plans to bus Moses DeWitt children to other schools, but it became obvious that this subject also carried political danger. Carmen moved that "redistricting be deferred until further input from parents and administrators can be obtained," a motion seconded by Coit. This passed unanimously, and the meeting was open to the public for comment.

Thomas Maroney took the floor, challenging Perkins's conviction that her conscience prevented her from responding to "emotional, social, and political pressure." Pressure from the public was to be expected in a democracy, Maroney asserted, and if she did not care for public pressure, why did she hold public office? The law professor further questioned the board's use of the agenda to silence the public until after a decision had been taken. Others also voiced resentment at this technique. William Stinchcombe, professor of history at Syracuse University, challenged the data upon which the decision had been made. "We have had three different sets of enrollment projections since March," he said. At the end of fifteen minutes, questions were abruptly cut off. A few board members lingered on the auditorium stage, attempting to justify to parents and other residents the decision that had just been made.

No one, even those who had voted for the closing, offered an accounting of the series of votes taken during the evening. At one point the board of education lacked only one vote to keep all schools open another year. Yet this 4-5 vote had quickly changed to a 7-2 decision to close Moses DeWitt. Most board members offered no explanation for their positions. Allotted only fifteen minutes at the end of the meeting, the public had yet to be heard from. The school district's long period of consensus was ending. In the months ahead Jamesville-DeWitt was to depart increasingly from the unitary model --the "autonomous, self-guiding, enclosed system" known in the past.[23]

## NOTES

1. Cf. Paul E. Peterson, **School Politics: Chicago Style**(Chicago, 1976), 118.

2. **Ibid.**, 113.

3. David B. Tyack, **The One Best System**(Cambridge, 1974); Raymond E. Callahan, **Education and the Cult of Efficiency**(Chicago, 1962); Roscoe C. Martin, **Government and th Suburban School**(Syracuse, 1962).

4. Peterson, **School Politics: Chicago Style**, 13.

5. Minutes, Jamesville-DeWitt Board of Education, Nov. 14, 1977.

6. Jamesville-DeWitt District Reports, Special Edition, Nov. 21, 1977.

7. See, for example, Ellen Bussard, **School Closings and Declining Enrollment**(New York, 1981).

8. Katherine E. Eisenberger and William F. Keough, Jr., **Declining Enrollment: What to Do**(Arlington, 1974), 38; also William F. Keough, Jr., "Enrollment Decline: The Dilemma from the Superintendent's Chair," in Susan Abramowitz and Stuart Rosenfeld, eds., **Declining Enrollment: The Challenge of the Coming Decade**(Washington, D.C., 1978), 355.

9. New York State Education Department, **Enrollment Trends: Programs for the Future, A Planning Guide for Districts with Declining Enrollment**(Albany, 1976), 40.

10. Comments made at the informational meetings held at the four schools are from the author's notes taken in Dec., 1977.

11. On the Orville Cemetery, "History's Silent Markers," **Herald-Journal**(Syracuse), Mar. 24, 1982.

12. New York State Education Department, **Enrollment Trends**, 38.

13. Administration report to the Board of Education, Dec. 11, 1978.

14. **Post-Standard**(Syracuse), Jan. 5, 1978; for convenience footnotes are to newspaper sources, but the author has extensive notes of all meetings.

15. New York City, described in **New York Times**, Feb. 7, 1982.

16. **Post-Standard**, May 1, 1980.

17. **Herald-Journal**, Dec. 9, 1977.

18. Minutes, Jamesville-DeWitt Board of Education, Dec. 12, 1977.

19. **Herald-Journal**, Dec. 13, 1977.

20. **Ibid.**

21. **Post-Standard**, Dec. 13, 1977.

22. **Ibid.**

23. Peterson, **School Politics: Chicago Style**, 112.

## IV. Moses DeWitt Militants

The school that the board of education closed on December 12, 1977, had first opened its doors in 1931. Once a modest square building, Moses DeWitt had grown into a modern facility as new construction followed the centralization of Jamesville-DeWitt. Moses DeWitt served DeWitt's original neighborhoods: DeWittshire, directly behind the school; the Cornwall Drive area on the opposite side of Moses DeWitt, directly across Jamesville Road; and Orvilton, to the north of East Genesee Street. Lyndon, which had closed its school after centralization, also sent children to Moses DeWitt; parents in this growing area began to think of the school as theirs by tradition and history, as one parent wrote to the board of education. In the 1950s residential development had extended southward along either side of Jamesville Road, bringing increased enrollment. First came the one-story houses in Andrews Heights, later split-levels built into the hillsides approaching the middle school and the new Tecumseh Elementary School, an area known as DeWitt Hills. In 1963 school attendance areas were redrawn to shift DeWitt Hills from Moses DeWitt to Tecumseh, a change at first resisted but later enthusiastically embraced by residents. Construction to the east in Lyndon and the Maple Drive area near the high school more than offset the loss of children from DeWitt Hills, however.

Located in the heart of a residential section, Moses DeWitt was always the district's largest elementary school. During the boom years between 1967 and 1971 enrollments ran into the 600s, about 50-75 more children than the number enrolled at Genesee Hills and Jamesville and often 175 above the total enrollment at Tecumseh. During the spring of 1969, for example, numbers at Moses DeWitt reached an all-time high of 630, at which time Tecumseh had an enrollment of only 454. Because of neighborhood identification with Moses DeWitt, school administrators did not reassign areas to Tecumseh or shift even peripheral neighborhoods to Genesee Hills or Jamesville. Long before the closing decision, allegiance to Moses DeWitt had precluded redistricting.

Presiding over Moses DeWitt was Theodore J. Calver, who became teaching principal in 1944. Calver had started his career at a one-room school on Tug Hill in Lowville, some fifty miles northwest of Syracuse. By comparison to these rural surroundings, DeWitt District

No. 10 was "already a great little community starting to grow" in 1944.[1]  As the nearby farmland was subdivided, the need for Moses DeWitt became even more obvious.  A member of the committee that advanced the Jamesville-DeWitt centralization proposal, Calver always considered Moses DeWitt a critical element in the district's centralization.  Even in 1950, he recalled, residents had made a "sizeable investment" in the school, which had both an "excellent program and a centralized location."[2]

Calver was to serve as principal from 1944 until his retirement in 1978.  In the fall of 1977 the longtime principal revealed that he would retire the following year but declined to submit his resignation until some months later the next spring.  During his thirty-four years as principal, Calver saw many changes in the school district, as new schools opened, new grade organizations were introduced--he opposed the removal of the sixth grade from elementary school--,new programs offered, and new administrators elevated to the central office.  At Moses DeWitt, however, Calver held sway.

In his school Calver initiated those changes he wanted and held firm against innovations urged by others. He recalled introducing "individualized instruction," the educational philosophy embraced by Jamesville-DeWitt as its own.  "The children began to move from classroom to classroom, with different groups in each classroom. As their skills developed, the groups kept changing," said Calver in describing changes made at Moses DeWitt.[3] The principal also emphasized music, art, physical education, and the library as important parts of a child's education but saw no need for resource teams or activity rooms such as those at Tecumseh and Genesee Hills.  The classroom teachers were to recognize and deal with problems, instead of sending them elsewhere. "For a lot of years we were used as a control group for the university as a school where a great deal of experimentation was **not** done.  And we've always had a very high level of achievement," the principal explained.[4]

Furthermore, in Calver's opinion, competent teachers could handle classes larger than the district's average, a view disputed by some faculty members and parents but accepted by the superintendent for Moses DeWitt alone.  In 1976-1977, for example, the average class-size at Moses DeWitt was 25, as opposed to 20 at the other three elementary schools.  The upper grades showed even greater differences:  Moses DeWitt's fifth-grade classes in 1976-1977 averaged 29, in contrast to only 19 at Tecumseh, 20 at Genesee Hills, and 23 at Jamesville. Individual principals, not the central office or "the district," established programs and class-sizes at the four schools.

At Moses DeWitt the principal defined what was expected of teachers, parents, and children. The atmosphere was serious; learning was encouraged but not by the intrusion of parents or other groups saying how the school should be run or used. Teachers were to do their jobs and parents to accept the school's verdicts as to their children's teachers, placement in groups, and progress. The school maintained discipline, and neither children nor teachers wanted to provoke Mr. Calver's disfavor. The principal was also known for his willingness to support his own teachers and his continuing interest in Moses DeWitt families. Calver knew his school, and successive superintendents found that he did not readily accept direction. While the principal set forth no-nonsense dictates, longtime secretary Iris Intrator radiated warmth to all callers, recognizing names and voices to give Moses DeWitt what one mother called "the feeling of a private school."

The parents' group at Moses DeWitt remained quiescent despite occasional efforts to stir discussion of curriculum or class-size. Although the organization had once held night meetings, Calver concluded that these did not inspire enough interest to justify the time. Instead, Moses DeWitt mothers met at noon to organize such events as welcome coffees, Christmas parties, teacher-recognition luncheons, and roller-skating for the children. Issues concerning the program and instruction at Moses DeWitt rarely arose. Parents felt generally satisfied that the staff at Moses DeWitt offered the children a good start in their education. Knowing or caring little about offerings at other schools, many felt satisfied that Moses DeWitt was the best, the district's "Ivy League," an attitude that created resentment elsewhere. Parents were not deeply involved in classroom activities at Moses DeWitt. Few worked in the school as aides or volunteers, and the educational program remained the prerogative of the principal and the faculty.

The parents' group functioned as an adjunct of the principal's office. Each year a fund-raising carnival produced substantial revenue, so that the parents' group treasury sometimes held amounts up to $5,000. Decisions as to how to spend this money usually emanated from the principal's office, producing new goods and supplies for the school. New parent-group officers also received Calver's approval, as he reviewed the names that one year's executive board nominated for the following year. Nomination assured election, rival candidates or tickets being unknown.

Neither the parents nor the principal had encouraged the use of Moses DeWitt for after-school or holiday activities, as was the practice at the other elementary schools. Moses DeWitt served a strictly educational function. The school did not have an evening gymnastics class, vacation movies offered by the Town of DeWitt parks and recreation department, square dancing, or a senior citizens' room. The school's traditional values and firm direction won the support of families that sent successive children to Moses DeWitt. Parents found the atmosphere predictable and secure--the school was a "cocoon from which a child can emerge as a butterfly," said a mother. Furthermore, neighbors in the immediate vicinity considered their elementary school a bulwark of residential DeWitt.

Traditionally a creature of the principal's office, the Moses DeWitt Parents' Group also received care and direction from the central administration. The parents' group at each school had a representative on the district's Parents' Advisory Council, a group nominally concerned with curriculum. The six parent-organizations also received official communiqués as well as gestures of interest from the board of education, as in the invitation to appoint one representative each to the Task Force. Before the board's decision to close a school, the presidents of the four elementary school parent-teacher groups had met with board president Perkins and district administrators, agreeing in advance to sign letters in support of the board's forthcoming action. But in the words of the Moses DeWitt president, "I never thought it would be Moses DeWitt!"

Parent-group officers did not act independently, even when their interests were at stake, and at Moses DeWitt the parents' group had never served a representative function. Indeed, many parents had not paid the $1.00 per family membership fee or even known of the group's meetings. When startled by the closing decision, parents did not turn to their official organization but gathered informally. On the night of December 13, a group assembled at the DeWittshire home of

66

Mary Jane and John Fennessey. A city planner who had both a professional and a personal interest in neighborhoods and communities, John and his wife Mary Jane, a former social worker, had useful experience in other causes. Recently they had led the successful effort to block expansion by a nearby supermarket.

Those seated at the Fennesseys' table and through the living room onto the floor again included mainly DeWittshire residents. They chose as their chairman Charles G. Mascott. A highly successful insurance executive, Mascott and his wife owned a five-bedroom house that faced one wing of Moses DeWitt and its playground. Having anticipated and feared a school closing since the time of the Task Force, Mascott eagerly took charge of the newly-forming protest organization.

The organizations's first task was to tell the community that parents would fight the closing; the second was to find an effective means for resisting. Taking out his typewriter, law professor Thomas Maroney began composing a statement to be issued to the local papers in time for the next day's editions.

> Residents of the Moses DeWitt School area are angry with the decision of the J-D Board to close Moses DeWitt. There is a feeling that the board, despite its protestations to the contrary, acted hastily in deciding to close the school, and acted without adequate factual basis or justification. . . .

> There was no legal reason why the board was compelled to act on Dec. 12. Board member John Luchsinger's attempt to keep the school open for one year and delay the decision to close the school was narrowly defeated. But his motion to table Dr. John Mallan's motion to close the school was defeated by a heavy margin, 7-2....

> The feeling is that factual data upon which the board relied is open to question; that realistic options presented by telephone and personal contact to the board, by citizens at various informational meetings were disregarded, and, finally that there was no rational explanation of why Moses DeWitt was

67

selected.

So read the statement hand-delivered to newspaper offices that night and carried in the next day's papers.[5]

To mobilize opinion against the closing, the parents' **ad hoc** committee also decided on December 13 to hold a meeting at Moses DeWitt on December 19 at 7:30, only one week after the board's decision. This timing appeared crucial, for the Christmas holidays would soon take many families out of town. The announcement of the meeting carried the notice:

Save Your School
Protect Your Property Value
You **Can** Change the Board's Decision

The reference to property value had created disagreement within the newly-assembled group. To home-owners whose property abutted the Moses Dewitt grounds or faced the school, the importance of Moses Dewitt to property value was assumed. To others the price of a house meant little in comparison with the conviction that the Jamesville-DeWitt Board of Education had made "a political decision rather than a practical one." One participant in the December 13 meeting told the press, "The community feels it had no input on the closing."[6] This feeling rather than immediate concern over the resale value of their houses rankled many protesters. They saw their cause as truly democratic.

Residents near Moses DeWitt did recognize the threat of commercial development along Jamesville Road, however. Nearby commercial establishments had already shown a zeal for expansion, and Moses DeWitt offered an ideal location, close to a major intersection. Residents speculated about Moses DeWitt's future use as cut-rate drugstore, supermarket parking lot, or as a block of taco stands and beauty shops. Neighborhood loyalists saw themselves as simultaneously defending residential DeWitt and a valued elementary school.

In other areas people worried less about the use of the Moses DeWitt building after closing and more about where their children would be sent: would children from the expensive residential enclaves of Lyndon and Maple Drive be bused to Jamesville--a community altogether different from Dewitt in its social-economic level and its pretensions? Parents could not imagine children who spent their vacations at country clubs or summer camps mingling with peers who lived in trailer parks. Genesee Hills, too, presented problems. Its enrollment included black and lower-income children from rent-subsidized apartments, a subject discussed **sotto voce**. At Tecumseh, Jewish and liberal parents were believed to push their children. Only Moses DeWitt had the right combination of reassuring characteristics. When social commentators criticized the suburbs as homogeneous, conformist, and conservative, they named those qualities that many DeWitt parents wanted in their children's elementary school.[7]

Why, asked parents, had the board of education not honored its promise to keep disruption to a minimum? Why did the children at Moses DeWitt, the largest school, have to bear the burden of redistribution to unknown schools? Moses DeWitt had always been **the** school for much of DeWitt, ever since that community was known as "the four corners." Now, having offered no explanation of its decision, the board of education had closed this school which suddenly seemed to mean much more than people had realized.

To show how much Moses DeWitt meant parents planned to circulate a petition, to be prepared for Monday's meeting. The petition was to call upon all residents to support the neighborhood **elementary-school concept**, not simply Moses DeWitt. Meeting the night after the closing, parents immediately recognized that they had to cast a wider net than simply defending Moses DeWitt but they had little idea how difficult this would be.

During the week Professor Maroney produced another academic, Michael Marge, dean of the College of Human Development at Syracuse University, to speak for Moses DeWitt. Marge had once presented complaints about the program at Moses DeWitt to the principal and the parents' group to no avail. He now appeared as a school supporter, however, and a television interview and newspaper coverage were arranged. Concerning the dangers of Jamesville Road near Moses DeWitt, Marge remarked, "I think a lot of parents are more concerned about the bus ride their children may have to take to other schools, like Jamesville." He then went on to say that Moses DeWitt parents would feel like "interlopers" at other schools following unpleasant treatment by board members. "My house and others are sort of lumped together as the rich guys and have been singled out for inconvenience." Marge's statement referred to the widely-held conviction that the board had taken a punitive action against the district's affluent families. In their study sessions board members had discussed breaking up pockets of wealth, or at least achieving an earlier social "mix" in the schools, as several revealed in conversations with residents.

In the days following Dean Marge's publicity, Mascott worked on the preparations for a meeting to be held on Sunday night. This meeting would make arrangements for the meeting scheduled at Moses DeWitt the following night. The **ad hoc** committee to defend Moses DeWitt would be sponsored by the Parents' Group, whose president was to announce the appointees to the Special Committee. Mascott secured the president's consent to this arrangement. Although resistance to the closing had not started within the Parents' Group, it rapidly moved to work under this name and, shortly, to draw on this organization's funds.

Mascott knew that the Special Committee must represent areas other than the neighborhood surrounding Moses DeWitt. A strictly neighborhood protest was certain to be dismissed as an obvious example of self-interest. Calls went out to draw supporters from all areas.

In the Sunday night planning session representatives of different neighborhood areas volunteered or were designated to serve on the Special Committee. Committee choices depended on those people who made their interest known. Using a large map of DeWitt, parents divided the Moses DeWitt area into sections. Each section was to have a representative on the Special Committee, charged with activating and reporting on that area. First, and of paramount importance, were DeWittshire and the Cornwall Drive area across from Moses DeWitt. These long-established neighborhoods were Moses DeWitt's obvious political stronghold. Farther south on Jamesville Road was the Andrews Heights section, a neighborhood that included some activist parents but many economy-minded senior citizens. North of East Genesee Street, Orvilton's long association with the school produced some true partisans, but a "swing vote" in this neighborhood was drawn to Genesee Hills, only a half-mile away. DeWitt Acres, one of the first postwar subdivisions, showed loyalty to Moses DeWitt, as did Lyndon. Parents in exclusive Maple Drive sections opposed sending their children anywhere but Moses DeWitt, although other residents there felt no indentification with the school's fate. Parents in the

Chapman Tract, a recently developed section of $100,000-
$200,000 houses accessible only by a private road, also
wanted their children to go to what was described as
DeWitt's "best" school, but population density in this
residential preserve was low.

Representatives on the Special Committee were not
chosen by a democratic canvassing of neighborhoods or by
a balancing of personalities, viewpoints, and abilities.
Nor did previous activity at the school indicate an
appointment to the Special Committee. Members of the
Special Committee came together hastily in a crisis, but
in the months ahead the group offered a focus to the
resistance. These parents chose to live in DeWitt not
only for the community but for the kind of education they
wanted for their children. They placed a high value on
education. Previously lulled by a false sense of
security, they now hoped to influence critical decisions
affecting the schools. Members of the group included a
doctor, lawyer, professor, self-employed businessman,
and planner; three women had been chosen, one a former
Junior League president described by the Syracuse papers
as a "civic leader" and "socialite," the second a faculty
wife who had a dusty Ph.D. and three children, and the
third a mother active in neighborhood and community
affairs. In many cases committee members worked jointly
with their husbands or wives.

Never did the Special Committee meet alone, either
at its origin or in subsequent occasions. Rather, it
formed the core of a group that volunteered to work. On
Sunday night this larger, informal group designated
corporate lawyer Gerald Mathews to act as Mascott's co-
chairman. The group then considered its strategy.
Whatever was to be done had to be accomplished by January
9, when the board of education was scheduled to hold its
next regular meeting.

At Monday's meeting at Moses DeWitt Mascott was to
speak on the urgency of the problem, and Mathews was to
outline the strategy to the audience. Near the doors
would be printed petitions reading:

> We, the undersigned, as residents of the
> Jamesville-DeWitt School District, hereby
> petition the Board of Education to
> continue the neighborhood elementary
> school concept, which has existed since
> the creation of the District, by keeping
> all four elementary schools open for the

1978-1979 school year. We urge the Board to consider and evaluate all fiscally responsible options and alternatives consistent with retaining the four neighborhood schools.

Also available at the door would be SAVE MOSES DEWITT bumper stickers for fifty cents. Parents had already paid for printing the petitions and bumper stickers. Monday night's program was to include two speakers, Dean Marge and Jean Stinchcombe, wife of a Syracuse University professor. Like the Mascotts, the Stinchcombes had followed school affairs closely since the time of the Task Force opinion survey.

An audience of 400 residents crowded the Moses DeWitt gym on the night of December 19 to hear the Parents' Group president announce the members of the Special Committee and turn the meeting over to Mascott. The closing of Moses DeWitt, Mascott told the audience, negated the concept of the neighborhood school; this policy represented a "total Jamesville-DeWitt School District problem and a landmark decision." The centralization of Jamesville-DeWitt had reflected an agreement that Moses DeWitt stay open. Perhaps that agreement no longer held, Mascott conceded, but at the least the board of education should have considered its past policy of maintaining neighborhood schools. To close a school is "precedent-setting. It's the beginning of the erosion of the neighborhood elementary school concept."

Marge then addressed the group, reviewing the board's decision the previous Monday. "The board has made an arbitrary decision, based not on facts, on objective factors--but on subjective factors." Moreover, the school board could not support the contention that the least number of children would be affected by closing Moses DeWitt, because that school's projected enrollment continued to be higher than that of the other elementary schools. The board had also overlooked the possibility of growth in the district. When pressed for an accounting of their decision, board members' "logic falls apart."

Jean Stinchcombe next addressed the group, describing the board's decision as not only profoundly "anti-social and anti-historical" but also "anti-educational." Moses DeWitt, she said, was a school that had roots in the community, a school that had

72

"established the reputation of Jamesville-DeWitt in elementary education." In regard to the economics of closing, Stinchcombe described savings drawn largely from utility bills and the principal's salary as trivial. "There is no reason for Moses DeWitt or any of our other elementary schools to be closed as a meaningless symbol of economy and efficiency." Greater savings could be achieved through other avenues, such as retirement and attrition of staff, or maintaining kindergarten through sixth grade elementary schools while reducing costs at the middle school.

Mathews then took the floor to outline what he called the "attack plan" for the next several weeks. In the first phase letters and a master petition would be sent to the board of education protesting the decision. Mathews hoped that at least 400 such letters would reach board members by Friday. In the meantime parents would circulate the petition through the entire community. In the second phase Moses DeWitt parents planned to appeal to other parent-teacher groups in the district for support. In the last phase the Special Committee would take the signed petitions and arguments against closing any school to the board of education at its January 9 meeting. Mathews reminded residents that "timing is critical" if the decision was to be reversed. "February would be too late to change opinions."

The meeting was then opened to comment from the floor. One resident suggested an economic boycott of the nearby service station operated by board member DeBottis, who had voted to close Moses DeWitt. Mathews answered cryptically that a boycott would only "compound a fester that had appeared on the board," and Maroney described the proposed action as "grossly unfair" and also illegal. Another resident recommended circulating a petition appealing to Moses DeWitt's principal to continue in his position for another year. If he were to do so the district would have four principals for three schools, and Calver's seniority could present a problem for other administrators. Dean Marge, a longtime critic of Calver, answered that the petition in behalf of the principal was "premature" and "could compound the issue." Furthermore, "let's not try and tell the school board how to run the schools," he stated, reaching a politic conclusion. Mascott again took the floor to emphasize concentration on the major goal, the petition and the concerted effort to persuade the board to delay the closing.

By the evening's end many parents had vowed to work and almost 400 had signed the petition. The cost of the bumper stickers was redeemed. Signers of the petition included parents and past parents. The area's professional character was seen in the more than 30 M.D.s following signatures. Not only doctors but lawyers, engineers, executives, and professors came forward to offer their support. Some Moses DeWitt faculty members expressed gratitude that parents had done what they felt they could not do. Only a few teachers who lived in the area gave open encouragement.

Television reporters showed interest in the growing controversy, giving the story coverage on the 11 p.m. news, and the morning paper gave the meeting a prominent place under the bold headline "Moses DeWitt Parents to Fight." A weekly suburban newspaper also turned to the subject. Normally filled with school district publicity releases, pictures of classroom activities and scouting troops, and bulletins from civic organizations and garden clubs, **Suburban Life** carried many columns of advertising. Now, however, this bland weekly had a real news item to feature on its front page. Young reporters covering eastside news for the morning paper's weekly suburban supplement also enjoyed a topic that gave them bylines and readers. Seeing the anger of residents and board members, alert novice reporters detected a controversy that offered more material than the usual complaints about hot lunches and bus runs. Although one critic has observed that newspapers treat education only by offering a "shabby analysis" of budgets and reading scores, local reporters rarely achieved even this level in Syracuse.[8] Indeed, school-closing presented exactly the sort of "conflict-oriented education issue" that this author has identified as a press favorite.[9] Turning first to their accustomed source, the school administration, and then to parents, reporters quickly produced record numbers of stories that publicized positions much beyond anything possible through the district's newsletter or parent-group propaganda. While reports and petitions entered houses only to be disregarded or forgotten, television pictures and newspaper headlines consistently demanded attention.

Meeting at the Mascotts' house the night after their December 19 meeting, parents took satisfaction in the impact of their activities. Bedridden at home, principal Calver knew only indirectly of the efforts in defense of his school. Parents had not sought recommendations from Calver whose illness and later convalescence in Florida came at a critical time. Nor did Scibilia or Luchsinger, the two school board members who had supported Moses DeWitt, attend meetings or offer direction. Although critics attributed the protest to master-minding by a pariah board member or a principal without honor, neither Luchsinger nor Calver had a significant influence on parents' discussions or actions. Even members of the Moses DeWitt Parents' Group board felt eclipsed by the free-wheeling militants who had taken up the school's cause. Nevertheless, within days the executive board of the Parents' Group authorized the Special Committee to spend up to $500 from its treasury in efforts to save the school. Two members voted against this authorization, and others had doubts about a parents' group acting as a political organization. But these reservations received little consideration in an atmosphere of crisis.

On December 21 Mascott prepared a letter to board president Perkins seeking a place on the school board's agenda for January 9. Members of the Special Committee began to circulate petitions in their neighborhoods and elsewhere in the school district during the Christmas vacation. Letters to the editor appeared in the newspapers almost daily, all but a few deploring the board's action. News-hungry local reporters gave close scrutiny to the unfolding situation, awaiting any change or development. In the midst of the holiday season parents had only a few weeks to gather signatures, refine arguments, and collect compelling evidence for their presentation to the board of education.

### NOTES

1. **Suburban Life** (DeWitt, East Syracuse), Apr. 12, 1978.
2. **Ibid.**
3. Lee Steinfeldt, "Ted Calver: A Man of Strong Ideas," **Post-Standard** (Syracuse) May 18, 1978.
4. **Ibid.**
5. **Post-Standard,** Dec. 14, 1977; **Herald-Journal**(Syracuse), Dec. 14, 1977.
6. **Herald-Journal,** Dec. 14, 1977.
7. David Riesman summarized the viewpoint of many social commentators, saying that they had come to regard the suburbs as "homogeneous, conformist, child-centered, female-dominated, anti-individualist," as quoted by D.W. Meinig, "Symbolic Landscapes," in D.W. Meinig, ed., **The Interpretation of Ordinary Landscapes**(New

York, 1979), 179.

8. Gerald Grant as quoted by Edward Wynne, **The Politics of School Accountability:  Public Information About the Schools**(Berkeley, 1972), 125.

9. **Ibid.**, 126.

## V.  Attacking the Census

Parents realized that simply reiterating their arguments to the board of education would accomplish little.  Board members had repeatedly said that they had already considered the points that parents raised.  A compelling argument would have to challenge--or at least cast doubt--on the underlying assumptions of the closing.  The argument would also have to look convincing to residents other than parents.

At meetings held just before Christmas, members of the Special Committee cast about for new evidence.  One possible avenue was a detailed analysis of the school district budget; a breakdown of expenditures suggested the possibility of attacking expensive programs in the middle school, where per-pupil costs exceeded those at the high school.  In taking their petition to the neighborhoods throughout Jamesville-DeWitt, Moses DeWitt supporters had found a general sympathy for local schools and a distrust of the middle school.  Many Jamesville residents supported a return to kindergarten through sixth-grade elementary school.  In DeWitt as well some parents feared that the middle school encouraged children to grow up early and allowed them a freedom they could not use.  On the other hand, the middle school's foreign language program had drawn approval from suburban parents, and the school's parent-teacher organization had a core of active supporters.  Even more important, the superintendent and some board members considered the middle school the centerpiece of the entire system.  Nevertheless, the Special Committee enlisted several parents to study K-6 schools, seeking information from other districts in the state that had changed their grade organization.

A criticism of the cost-savings of a school-closing did not immediately develop as a major concern.  After hearing of savings between $180,000-$200,000 to be expected from closing Moses DeWitt, one resident informed an administrator that he would "never again believe any figures from the district office."  Parents contended that any tax advantages gained by closing were negligible and other policies could produce greater savings.  Furthermore, Mascott developed the argument-- not appealing to everyone--that local businessmen were prepared to offer their services on a budget task force to solve the district's problems.  "We've got $100,000 worth of talent that we can donate free to the Board of

Education. We can cut the waste without interruption of school programs," he related to **Suburban Life**.[1] Having earlier upbraided this weekly's publisher for unsympathetic coverage and threatened a withdrawal of advertising, Mascott now found greater coverage given to Moses DeWitt positions.

But the argument that residents really wanted to pay taxes and were willing to offer valuable services free of charge had limitations. Board president Perkins and others could be expected to speak for those who did not want to pay. The budget had passed only narrowly for two years, so if residents had been eager to pay or to work, where had they been? The offer of free financial guidance to the school district seemed insulting to some members of the board.

Also self-serving was the conviction that Moses DeWitt residents offered a disproportionate share of the school district's local revenue. A small group studied the tax rolls to gather information on this subject, finding that the Moses DeWitt area produced under thirty per cent of the revenue raised locally. True, the Moses DeWitt section included some of the district's high-assessment areas, but discussing the amount paid in taxes reenforced the impression of a special interest asserting prerogatives based on wealth. People in other parts of the school district also paid high taxes and did not care to hear of the $3,000 to $4,000 paid annually by residents of what were called the "gold coast" neighborhoods.

Indeed, the overture to parent groups in other school areas, phase two of the attack plan, had foundered. The president of the Tecumseh parent-teacher organization indicated that "the majority of the Tecumseh executive board is on the side of the school board." According to Tecumseh's president, "The board of education made its decision on facts. . . . Once the decision was made, it's made. I don't think it can be changed." The president of the Genesee Hills parent-teacher organization announced that this group would also support whatever decision the Jamesville-DeWitt Board of Education reached. The Genesee Hills parent organization endorsed the school board's action the day after the decision to close Moses DeWitt. Only members of the Jamesville parents' group offered sympathy. Certainly that group could "understand and appreciate the concern of the Moses DeWitt people in asking for an attentive ear from the other PTO's," explained the

Jamesville president. But even Jamesville parents stopped short of public support. Few parents from other schools were willing to come to the aid of Moses DeWitt; most felt satisfied that their own schools remained open and their own children undisturbed. Closing Moses DeWitt meant that the other schools were safe.[2]

Thus parents found that they needed a new tactic to draw public attention and persuade the board to delay. In the days following the closing board members and administrators received scores of calls concerning the decision. Curriculum Coordinator Ronald Osborn fielded many questions and comments for the superintendent. In one conversation a resident questioned the district's census of pre-school children and enrollment projections, and Osborn acknowledged that the pre-school figures were extraordinarily low. Earlier board member Luchsinger had suggested to the president of the Genesee Hills parent-teacher organization that she count babies in her immediate neighborhood to see if the total was as low as the census indicated.

At a meeting just before Christmas parents first considered the possibility of challenging the census. Board members and administrators had used census figures to justify closing a school, and these numbers offered a vulnerable area that parents could feasibly attack. Unlike the question of cost-savings, the census did not require the use of technical information from the district or collaboration with administrators. Special Committee member Edward Sugarman, an orthopedic surgeon, suggested that by calling local diaper services he could get a quick impression of the number of children ages 0-2 in the Jamesville-DeWitt area. Although not all families use diaper services, the companies routinely calculate the percentage of the market that they serve; numbers could be easily obtained and discussed.

Protesting parents had seized upon a fruitful idea that transformed their strategy. Unknown to citizens, guides to school administrators consistently emphasized the importance of reliable information, particularly in presenting enrollment projections. "The administration must establish confidence in the historical basis for these projections and in the accuracy of the census figures, graphs, charts," advised the New York State Education Department in a 1976 planning guide.[3] Distrust of basic facts and figures often sparked divisive controversy that left administrators on the defensive.[4] Describing a superintendent's viewpoint,

William F. Keough, Jr. warned of a "potential pitfall" in the collection of accurate and complete data. "The importance of accuracy cannot be too greatly stressed; one inaccurate statistic will cast doubt on all others."[5]

As parents considered the census, school officials prepared their reply to the onslaught of public criticism received in the previous ten days. In a "special edition" report printed on a long green sheet dated December 22, 1977, board president Perkins and Superintendent Baker declared, "The decision to close a school was certainly neither capricious nor arbitrary." Replying to charges made by Moses DeWitt parents, Perkins and Baker explained that far from being precipitous, the closing followed long-range planning. "Last year, the Needs Assessment Task Force--representing a broad cross-section of the J-D community--studied the District's past, present, and future in depth." Furthermore, "the idea of the neighborhood school was considered," they stated in reply to Mascott's allegations to the contrary.

"Why Moses DeWitt?" asked the "special edition." Rebutting claims that Moses DeWitt held any special historical or academic position in the district, Baker and Perkins wrote, "There are no program or historical reasons to justify the closing of any particular school." Continuing with the rationale for closing Moses DeWitt, they explained:

> Therefore, disruption for students, both immediately and in the future, has to be a prime consideration. Moses DeWitt now has the largest enrollment and the largest building (sic). In view of the continuing decline in enrollment, closing any of the other three elementary (schools) would require, by 1980, the closing of a second elementary school. A second closing so soon would lead to disrupting many of the same students again. On the other hand, closing the largest school now will delay, by at least two years (until 1982-1983), the need to close a second school. By that time, those disrupted now will have moved beyond the elementary level. If the enrollment decline continues at all grade levels, total district reorganization for the 1983-1984 school year will be an important issue for thorough consideration.[6]

This rationale had never before been presented to the public, in district newsletters, board meetings, or at the informational sessions held at the four schools. Board members had not discussed delaying a second closing in conversations with parents. Administrators had explicitly referred to keeping "disruption at a minimum," but they had not drawn attention to the possibility of "total district reorganization" by the period 1982-1983. The justification for choosing Moses Dewitt was an **ex post facto** argument that merely papered over the board's action but did not account for it.

Reading the "special edition," members of the Special Committee planned a newsletter that would follow but improve upon the new format of district reports. This newsletter was to be published under the title "SAVE OUR SCHOOLS," or SOS, carrying on its masthead the ram's head of Jamesville-DeWitt athletic teams. Mascott, Maroney and Joseph Jerry, a lawyer whose clients included the Town of DeWitt planning board, contributed ideas for the new publication, financed under the $500.00 appropriation voted by the Moses DeWitt Parents' Group.

Drawing on his experience in local affairs, attorney Jerry drafted a simple question-and-answer text that raised critical points about closing. The newsletter cited the Task Force Report for money-saving alternatives to school-closing, such as the early retirement of staff or the retention of existing fifth grades in the elementary school. Then the SOS newsletter posed a critical question: "Are the enrollment projections reliable?" "No!" came the answer, citing a timely article in a recent Sunday supplement magazine carrying carrying the headline "It's Beginning to Look Like a Baby Boomlet." In 1977 total births in Onondaga County rose dramatically after a seven-year downward spiral.[7] Jamesville-DeWitt followed the same trend. Instead of 94 children ages 0-2 in the school district as listed in the census, "the Moses DeWitt committee has gathered solid data showing that there are 331 children 0-2 in the district." The diaper services had supplied figures making a rough total of 301, incorrectly typed as 331 in the newsletter's printed version. The figure was a rough one--not in the form of "solid data" as described in the newsletter. Much later, however, live-birth figures gathered from the county's bureau of vital statistics also showed a total of close to 300 children born in the years 1976 and 1977.

The SOS newsletter next asked, "Will the closing of

Moses DeWitt adversely affect other schools?" The authors found that it would indeed, causing crowding at Tecumseh and leading inevitably to redistricting of the three remaining schools. "It was stated categorically at the December 12 School Board meeting that **all** districts (of elementary schools) would have to be changed," an issue that board members had actually sidestepped on that occasion. The newsletter then played on the school district's rationale for closing Moses DeWitt. "In the December 22 District letter it was stated that the closing of Moses DeWitt would only **delay** the closing of another elementary school." The prospect of a second closing might stir questions, if not opposition, from complacent parents in other school areas.

By December 28, Moses DeWitt supporters had collected 1,000 signatures for their petition. Members of the board, however, showed no sign of changing their judgment of the situation. Interviewed by **Suburban Life,** board members echoed the opinion that closing Moses DeWitt in 1978 would preclude another school closing in two or three years. Perkins explained that her major concern was the future. "When we referred to moving the fewest students we didn't mean just now, but in three or four years," she said, elaborating her new position. Carmen indicated that her primary consideration was "what's best for all the kids in the district from an educational standpoint," a tenet of district ideology that served many purposes. Board member Coit saw the closing as an attempt to provide the "best possible education for the most children," but she said she understood the feelings of Moses DeWitt residents. Only Luchsinger and Scibilia saw any reason to examine alternatives other than closing Moses DeWitt.

The argument about the census offered the best prospect for shaking the board from its commitment to close Moses DeWitt. Members of the Special Committee and other supporters, now including Paul Brunner, president of Crouse-Hinds, a local manufacturing company, and Donald J. Weiner, professor of electrical engineering and systems analysis at Syracuse University, met to discuss plans for the next few days. Sugarman argued that statistics from the diaper services alone would undermine the district's figures, but others insisted that names, birthdates, and addresses of children would bolster the argument. In the next few days several mothers organized a street-by-street survey of the Moses DeWitt school area, so that the Special

Committee could present exact numbers and details when it appeared before the board of education in a private session scheduled for January 4.

In the meantime parents attempted to probe Superintendent Baker's sentiments. They urged their elected officials in town and state government to speak to school administrators. Mascott and Sugarman met with the superintendent to tell him that they considered the situation serious. Later Mascott told the local press that if "administrative alternatives" to the closing did not develop, the Moses DeWitt committee "has already thoroughly researched the legal action it has as an option." After January 9, parents would have only two days within the thirty-day limitation for appealing to the State Commissioner of Education after a closing decision. "We're cutting it close," Mascott said. But it could be done. Up to sixty days could be taken to file a suit to stop the closing, if necessary.[8] Accompanying arguments and persuasion was the likelihood of parents' resorting to legal action.

On Wednesday, January 4, the district office informed parents that the board would not meet with them, as previously scheduled. Instead, the school board conducted a study session of its own, attended by no district residents. This meeting occurred a day after a New York State appeals court had ruled that the state's Open Meetings (or "Sunshine") Law applied to school board "study sessions." According to the Open Meetings Law, the public and the media were to be notified "at least 72 hours" or "a reasonable time prior" to meetings. In this last-minute clandestine meeting, board members and administrators attempted to stake out their position.

An alert newspaper reporter appeared at the meeting, however, and related in the morning paper that Superintendent Baker had discussed maintaining the four elementary buildings as K-8 schools, while closing the middle school.[9] At the board's December 12 meeting Baker had said that he would feel "personally hurt" by removing even the sixth grade from the middle school, a school that made Jamesville-DeWitt a "leader." Now the proposal to **close** the middle school served to rally board members rather than offering a subject for serious consideration.

Board member Mallan, for example, opposed moving students from the middle school. "We've got a gorgeous facility out there. That seems a big price to pay. I just don't think it's worth it." Only Luchsinger, who at an earlier study session had discussed placing all elementary-school children in the middle school, showed interest in considering the new proposal. At this meeting he proposed examining the district to see how strongly residents wanted to keep the elementary school in their neighborhood. Board member Carmen countered that "it seems a poor time to pull into little neighborhoods" in light of the problem of declining enrollment in the district; meeting children from other neighborhoods would be good for pupils. "If you don't close an elementary school now, you're never going to be able to close an elementary school," said Southwood's representative DeBottis. The board recognized the importance of the community's reaction to closing. "If it (the neighborhood school concept) is weak, and we close an elementary school, then we're home free. If it's strong--look out," concluded the superintendent, leaving his own position unclear.[10]

The next night members of the Special Committee appeared at an informal meeting of the board of education. Although the meeting was announced and attended by some residents, Moses DeWitt supporters did not encourage a turn-out for this presentation. A show of public support was to come on Monday, January 9, while the informal session served to persuade board members. Mascott organized the presentations, speaking of Moses DeWitt parents' willingness to support the district and offer help in passing the budget. William Stinchcombe presented arguments in behalf of keeping Moses DeWitt. A chart produced by the graphics department of a local manufacturing company showed that enrollment at Moses DeWitt had declined the least of any of the four schools during the years between 1971 and 1978. (See Figure 6.) "For the decade 1971-1980 Moses DeWitt will have declined the least. In 1980 Moses DeWitt will still have more students than any of the three other elementary schools have today," said Stinchcombe.[11] A map showed the concentration of 200 elementary-school children living within a one-mile radius of Moses DeWitt.

Board members received a table contrasting the findings of the school census and the district's projections with the parents' finding for the Moses DeWitt area. In the 0-1 age group for Moses DeWitt the school census had found only four babies, from which the district had projected 11. Parents, however, had found 36 children in this age group. "These figures have significance for the entire district, and we believe the

84

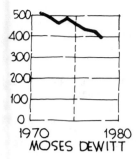

MOSES DEWITT

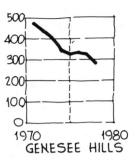

GENESEE HILLS

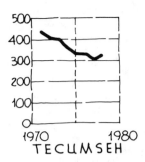

TECUMSEH

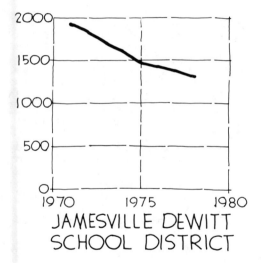

JAMESVILLE DEWITT
SCHOOL DISTRICT

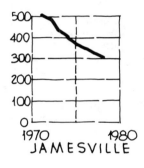

JAMESVILLE

ELEMENTARY SCHOOL ENROLLMENT TREND

1971-1978

**FIGURE 6**

85

need for more accurate information is apparent,"
Stinchcombe concluded.12 For example, the district's
projected kindergarten enrollment for all four schools
in 1982 showed 35 children, but Moses DeWitt parents had
already found 36 children that age in their area alone.

Members of the board showed interest in the
presentation. Residents attending the meeting also
asked questions. A Moses DeWitt parent, not then
involved in the Special Committee or Parents' Group,
James Carroll, questioned the financial savings of the
closing. "If the financial figures are not firm and the
enrollment projections are open to doubt, what data base
are you using?" asked Carroll, director of the public
administration program at Syracuse University's Maxwell
School. After the meeting, two board members showed
sympathy for the position presented by parents. But as
Maroney concluded, "We don't want to move them to tears--
We want to move them to action."

Most board members did not appear moved. Mallan
did not think the challenge to the board's data presented
a problem. Sometimes, he remarked, you don't know if the
sun will come up, but you do the best you can; would the
revised figures make any difference? In any event, he
said, parents had presented numbers for only one area.
Board president Perkins indicated that she did now know
if a re-vote would be taken. Most of the letters and
calls that she received came from residents who wanted to
have Moses DeWitt closed in order to keep the educational
program of the entire district sound. Carmen said that
she would reconsider the decision only if verified and
substantial facts were presented to the board. "I'm
always open to new fact, but it must be verified fact,"
she declared. "I've never boxed myself into a
situation." Although open to new facts, Carmen added
that if there were a good argument to keep the school
open, "it would, in good faith, have been presented"
already.13

Because their figures still failed to receive
serious consideration, Moses DeWitt parents decided to
extend their census to the entire school district.
Three women organized and directed a system whereby every
street in Jamesville-DeWitt was canvassed for the
birthdates, names, and addresses of pre-school chidren.
Callers emphasized the child's birthdate rather than age
to make the parents' group census comparable to that of
the school district. The school district used a
December 1 cut-off for kindergarten entrance, and that

86

had to be taken into consideration in arriving at totals for each year. In areas unfamiliar to Moses DeWitt supporters, census takers walked the streets; near Genesee Hills they went door to door at the Springfield Gardens Apartments. Closer to home they did telephone checks. Local nursery schools provided class lists, so that parents could cross-check their findings. The effort was undertaken and completed within four days.

In the meantime another "SAVE OUR SCHOOLS" bulletin took form. "While the administration thought there were only 94 children in the 0-2 age group, we have counted over 300!" exclaimed the newsletter, using the figure from the diaper services rather than the census now in progress. "Jamesville-DeWitt is experiencing a 'Baby Boomlet,' NOT declining enrollment," announced the second issue of SOS, introducing a confusion that long clouded discussion. Even if the number of babies was greater than that cited by the district, enrollment would still decline. The birthrate had dropped sharply during the 1970s, as administrators knew but failed to emphasize. Unlike many districts, Jamesville-DeWitt did not routinely collect birth data, which later showed that 1963's birth total of 376 had fallen to 1973's total of 143. In 1977-1978 both school officials and parents focused on the census, not birth totals. Because of the discrepancies between district figures and their own census, many parents did not acknowledge declining enrollment, a position that reenforced their opposition to school-closing. Thus "denial or disbelief that changes will really happen" fueled community controversy, as described in one treatment of declining enrollment.14

In addition to announcing a baby boomlet, the second issue of SOS declared support for the middle school. Distributed by Special Committee representatives to every house in the Moses DeWitt area, the newsletter announced, "The Moses DeWitt Parents' Group DOES NOT SUPPORT the K-8 option." Seeking to deflect criticism from middle school supporters, Moses DeWitt organizers now spoke of **temporarily** retaining fifth-graders in the elementary schools, and they soon dropped even this recommendation from arguments presented to the board. Immediately following the newsletter, parents canvassed neighborhoods by telephone to assure attendance at the board's January 9 meeting. The weekend before the meeting Special Committee members told the press that they estimated an attendance of anywhere from several hundred to a thousand residents.15

An aroused public and daily scrutiny from newspaper reporters presented a new experience for Jamesville-DeWitt board members. These officials adhered to the principles of "conflict avoidance and nonpartisanship" characteristic of suburban schools in the era of expansion.[16] "School district politics tends to maximize the search for consensus," wrote the authors of another study of educational decision-making.[17] In Jamesville-DeWitt school politics took place in what has been called a "sacred community." Established verities had not been shaken and social behavior served to maintain group and community solidarity. Officeholders had no acquaintance with the public confrontation and open debate characteristic of the "secular community."[18] Instead, small talk governed by the "etiquette of gossip" allowed criticism to circulate privately but not publicly.[19]

Before the public members of the board presented a united front. Differences of opinion remained concealed or resolved in executive sessions. As civic leaders, not experts in education, board members deferred to the superintendent. The challenge to the census not only threatened the administration's technical authority but jeopardized the comfortable relationship between the board and the superintendent. As in the small town described by Vidich and Bensman, board members normally dealt with "minor problems of administrative detail."[20] In most cases Superintendent Baker reached his own solution to the problems presented to the board while appearing to defer to its judgment. Quietly, Baker worked to make his views mesh with those of board members and to gain public acceptance for his goals. Like his counterpart in Vidich and Bensman's small town, he recognized divergent interests as well as differences of power within his district.

> While giving due weight to these various
> interests he must at the same time try not
> to alienate any one of them. As a result
> he publicly tends to try to agree with
> everyone and his public statements are of
> sufficient generality to be satisfactory
> to all groups.[21]

Until the school-closing controversy Superintendent Baker satisfied all groups. He held the respect not only of board members but of teachers and parents. At his urging teachers in Jamesville-DeWitt refrained from employing union negotiators and parents' organizations willingly accepted leadership from the administration. Baker not only had the right credentials, he was boyishly handsome and meticulously dressed, presenting the image of a successful young executive. Considered a leader among county school administrators, he used his knowledge and position to influence board members and residents at meetings and indirectly through personal persuasion. But as superintendent at Jamesville-DeWitt, Baker was not an "alien expert." A former teacher in the system, he lived in Jamesville and had family ties making him a part of the community rather than an outside authority. Most administrators as well as board members were local people, longtime residents who represented community rather than cosmopolitan values. To question the administration's competence in handling the census required self-criticism, opening a fault line in the unitary organization in which all parts were interdependent.

Thus the crisis over Moses DeWitt presented a unique problem. Never before had school board members dealt with a major controversy. Never had they acknowledged failure. For years residents had taken pride in the school system and officeholders had basked in the glow of having "one of the leading school districts in New York State and, in several regards, in the United States."[22] The board of education had not provided a forum for dissent or loyal opposition, from its members or from the community. Board members had the stark alternatives of accepting administrative recommendations or condemning their professional staff. Residents faced the narrow choice of embracing the system's excellence or appearing as anti-education. Neither school officials nor citizens had established a tradition of discussing educational issues. Only the appearance of CASE in 1977 had indicated a rupture in the system, ominous but short-lived. The district had been solid. The board had not hired administrators with the expectation of firing them if policies failed or public opinion shifted, as happened in many districts. Now, however, board members, administrators, and residents faced a crisis that threatened to destroy the school district's solidarity--what one board member referred to as the "euphoria" of a successful, close-knit system.

# NOTES

1. **Suburban Life** (DeWitt and East Syracuse), Jan.4, 1978.
2. **Ibid.**, Dec. 22, 1977.
3. New York State Department of Education, **Enrollment Trends: A Planning Guide for Districts with Declining Enrollment**(Albany, 1976), 6.
4. Ellen Bussard, **School Closings and Declining Enrollment**(New York, 1981), 5. William F. Keough, Jr., "Enrollment Decline: The Dilemma from the Superintendent's Chair," in Susan Abramowitz and Stuart Rosenfeld, eds., **Declining Enrollment: The Challenge of the Coming Decade** (Washington, 1978), 363.
6. Jamesville-DeWitt District Report, Special Edition, Dec. 22, 1977; Tecumseh was the largest building.
7. **Herald-American**(Syracuse), Dec. 25, 1977.
8. **Suburban Life**, Dec. 28, 1977.
9. **Post-Standard** (Syracuse), Jan. 5, 1978.
10. **Ibid.**
11. **Suburban Life**, Jan. 11, 1978.
12. **Ibid.**
13. **Post-Standard**, Jan. 9, 1983.
14. Bussard, **School Closings and Declining Enrollment**, 5; all issues of SOS and other Moses DeWitt publications are in the author's possession.
15. **Post-Standard**, Jan. 9, 1978.
16. Louis H. Masotti, **Education and Politics in Suburbia: The New Trier Experience**(Cleveland, 1967), 33.
17. Laurence Iannaccone and Frank W. Lutz, **Politics, Power, and Policy: The Governing of Local School Districts**(Columbus, 1970), 29.
18. **Ibid.**, 31-32.
19. Arthur J. Vidich and Joseph Bensman, **Small Town in Mass Society**(Princeton, 1968), 41-45.
20. **Ibid.**, 192.
21. **Ibid.**, 196.
22. Jamesville-DeWitt District Report, Special Edition, Dec. 22, 1977.

## VI. The Big Night

On the night of January 8 Moses DeWitt supporters gathered at the Mascotts' to make final preparations for the meeting the next evening. Board president Perkins had requested a presentation shorter than the one given at the informal meeting on January 5. To the contrary, Mascott thought that the presentation should be longer, to exploit the advantage of what was expected to be a large and sympathetic audience. This meeting offered the opportunity--the only one--to make the case and make it dramatically. The program would include four speakers, Mascott, Crouse-Hinds president Brunner, Jean Stinchcombe, and law professor Maroney.

To emphasize the seriousness of the question, Special Committee Co-Chairman Mathews had recommended that a court stenographer produce a record of the meeting. A lawyer himself, Mathews arranged for a stenographic reporter to appear at the board meeting. The transcript of the board's discussion would form part of the record if parents decided to go to court. The decision to hire a court stenographer caused no objection, although most parents had never seen one at work. Many supporters had expressed a willingness to go to court if necessary, but the implications, procedures, and costs of such an action had yet to receive full discussion. Lawyer-supporters thought that Moses Dewitt parents might pursue several avenues, ranging from procedural to Constitutional arguments, challenging the district's apportionment of board positions as a violation of one man, one vote as upheld by the United States Supreme Court. Hiring a court stenographer was simply an easy first step. Attention still focused on the atmosphere and effect of the presentation to the board.

Brunner suggested that a large overhead projected to the audience would show the findings on the census more effectively than numbers read from a sheet distributed to board members. Parents did not want their presentation to have the appearance of an "amateur hour." Materials were to be professionally prepared and complete. In addition to tables and numbers, members of the board and administration would receive lists of the names, addresses, and birthdates for children 0-2 in each elementary-school area. Although their census had included all pre-school children, parents decided to emphasize the 0-2 age bracket, because it presented the greatest contrast with the district's figures.

Strategists studied the petitions, attempting to determine how many signers had and did not have children and where these residents lived. The petition's purpose was to show district-wide support for maintaining all four elementary schools, an argument that otherwise had drawn a disappointing response. The over 2,000 signatures could be seen as an unprecedented expression of public sentiment--a sentiment that could translate into votes for and against the budget.

Before leaving Sunday night's meeting, the four speakers reviewed their arguments: the Moses DeWitt parents' commitment to education and helping the school system; the inaccuracies in the information the district had used in reaching a decision; public support for keeping all schools open; and preserving the district's excellence by avoiding an injurious, unnecessary decision.

The bitter winds and cold of January 9 did not prevent an overflow audience of 600-700 residents from crowding the high school's auditorium and hallway. Setting up his equipment, the court stenographer immediately complained that the arrangement of the table on the stage prevented his making an accurate record. The table had been placed perpendicular to the audience rather than facing it, because as board president Perkins explained, "it is sometimes hard for us to hear each other." Members of the audience called out their objections to an arrangement that did not allow a full view of the board. After this protest the table was turned full-face to the audience, as the stenographer aggressively approached board members and asked for the spelling of their names "to make sure I get them right." As the meeting started an administrator remarked, "This looks like one we could go to court on."

The board first conducted some routine business before turning the meeting over to Mascott, who began by saying:

> I feel it's important right from the onset
> to state that our Committee and group are
> totally supportive of a unified
> Jamesville-DeWitt district.

The audience responded with applause as the speaker went on to present the board with a petition "that has

92

2,207 names." Of the signers 65 per cent had no elementary-school or pre-school children. Furthermore, some 568 signers lived outside of the Moses DeWitt area. "It was an army of people out there who helped with the petition and were concerned about the elementary school process and the entire district's educational program that's been so excellent for so many years since the founding of this district in 1950." The petition reflected "a good cross section" of attitude and feeling throughout the district, Mascott concluded, as he turned the floor to Jean Stinchcombe for a discussion of the census.

Describing the parents' census, Stinchcombe reported, "For every baby zero to one year of age that the official Jamesville-DeWitt census listed for Moses DeWitt, we found ten babies." She continued by describing similar discrepancies in the other elementary-school areas.

> In Genesee Hills, the school district census taker found no babies, zero to one, whereas we have found 23. I believe that figure must now be revised. In the few hours since I recorded it, six more zero to one babies have come to light.

The audience laughed and applauded as other figures were read out. "In Tecumseh seven appeared on the census rolls, but we found 23. In Jamesville, the census listed only one, but the parents found 16." After discussing the graph showing these findings, Stinchcombe observed that the school district had counted only 12 babies and projected an enrollment of 35 for the 1982 kindergarten, whereas the parents had an "actual count" of 102. (See Figure 7.) "The urgency of school closing must now be discounted," she concluded before introducing Paul Brunner.[2]

Referring to the petition Brunner asserted, "In just three weeks 2200 votes have been received, and I emphasize votes, because everybody who has signed this petition is at this point aware of the issues, is following them, as evidenced by tonight's attendance, and will continue to follow them to the time of the budget." Brunner continued, again linking the petition to support for the budget, perhaps to the surprise of some signers.

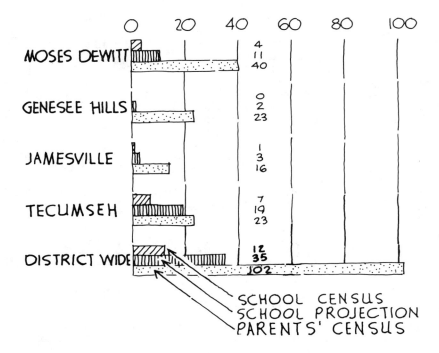

| | 0 | 20 | 40 | 60 | 80 | 100 |
|---|---|---|---|---|---|---|

MOSES DEWITT
4
11
40

GENESEE HILLS
0
2
23

JAMESVILLE
1
3
16

TECUMSEH
7
19
23

DISTRICT WIDE
12
35
102

SCHOOL CENSUS
SCHOOL PROJECTION
PARENTS' CENSUS

COMPARISON OF THE SCHOOL DISTRICT CENSUS & THE PARENTS' CENSUS OF 1978 FOR PROJECTION OF 1982 KINDERGARTEN ENROLLMENT

**FIGURE 7**

94

Please put in context 2200 votes compared to 3100 that voted in the last budget elections. Therefore, if I had to qualify the signatures, I would qualify it as a groundswell, grass roots landslide for keeping all schools open.

Brunner then emphasized the importance of constantly gathering and analyzing new data. His organization made monthly forecasts despite having five computers and twenty comptrollers. He suggested that independent businessmen establish a committee to review budgetary figures, to look at statistics and arrive at "a decision that allows everybody to, in effect, have the best system that New York State can command." The businessmen's committee would tap such talent that the school district would probably "go bankrupt" if it tried to hire it. In concluding Brunner appealed to the board of education to "help us" and "we will help you in June (budget vote)."[3]

Thomas Maroney then took the floor, summarizing the arguments presented to the board. He emphasized Moses Dewitt parents' support for "every single one of the present schools in this district." We petition you, he appealed, "to continue the neighborhood elementary school concept which has existed since the creation of this district by keeping all four elementary schools open for the 1978-1979 school year."[4]

Board president Perkins then opened the floor to comments from residents. One parent spoke in behalf of the middle school's program and the danger of dismantling it, to which Perkins replied that the issue before the board was "merely keeping all six schools open as they exist at the present time without any change in program." Another mother supported the board's decision to close Moses DeWitt but referred to her impression that "closing Moses DeWitt was merely a first step of a hidden agenda, that the board had in mind to eventually close another school and eventually lead to a counterplan." To this Perkins answered that "there is no hidden agenda and never has been." She did not discuss consideration given to closing a second school, or to delaying a second closing. The board-selected chairman of the Task Force declared that he did not think that the board could "just willy-nilly decide not to do anything in the future."[5] Other parents spoke in behalf of keeping all schools open, showing emotion at the prospect of having their children's education disrupted.

In the previous ninety minutes school officials and residents had witnessed events new to Jamesville-DeWitt. Normally the superintendent controlled the information presented to the board of education. The facts needed for a decision came from administrators, who had the technical knowledge and resources that board members lacked; administrators acted as the "gatekeepers" of information for the public as well as the board.[6] Now, however, indignant parents presented new facts and demanded a response.

In the past parents' groups had always been among the reliable, good organizations, such as the Rotary and the League of Women Voters. These were the groups that administrators used to mobilize opinion for the school program, quietly and indirectly. The PTAs included those individuals, primarily women, whose interest and loyalty could be counted upon to serve the administration's purposes. Administrators knew their PTA-mother. The staunchest school supporter, according to Eisenberger and Keough, is the mother "who has spent long years building a good reputation in the local schools."[7] Another author wrote:

> PTA meetings furnish opportunities to escape from the home for a few hours, meet neighbors, make new friends, gossip, talk about children, partake of coffee and pastry, and achieve a fugitive sense of social purpose.[8]

"It is a rare PTA that ever opposes the wishes of a principal," concluded political scientist Robert A. Dahl.[9]

The new Moses DeWitt Parents' Group departed from past experience and extended into the community in alarming fashion. This organization included more than the usual known "troublemakers" seeking favorable treatment for their own children. Men bearing respected names and titles had joined women in an effort to resist the district's policy and promised to do so in the future if thwarted. Although this group had emerged as independent of Moses DeWitt principal Calver, he did not oppose their activities. He, too, opposed the board's decision, athough he made no public statements or appearances following his return from Florida.

Board members found themselves in a vulnerable

position. Those most committed to the "sacred community" as upheld in Jamesville-DeWitt responded by "rigid adherence to policy statements regardless of the situation involved," a reaction characteristic of decision-making in a closed community.[10] For others the experience of facing hundreds of angry constituents was disquieting. In responding to the crisis, board members had only past practices and their own instincts as a guide, for the board's role had never been sharply defined. As described by one author, "Many school board members move in a sea of confusion about their powers."[11]

Before the January 9 meeting began, a board member remarked to the superintendent, "What is going to happen? What can be done?" Guiding board members indirectly, Baker answered, "Well, why don't you do something about it?" Although some board members repeatedly emphasized their legal authority to close a school, the superintendent still held the key to power in the school district. As David Minar wrote, "If anyone lurks behind anyone else, making 'real' decisions, it is the superintendent lurking behind the board."[12] The superintendent had led the board to the precipice and he would lead it back.

Unknown to the audience, a decision had already been negotiated when president Perkins returned the meeting to the board. Taking the microphone board member Coit stated, "I feel that Boards of Education are noticeably slow moving and I personally would rather err in the area of being overly conservative than being overly anxious to make change where children's lives are concerned." She went on to move that the board defer the closing set for the 1978-1979 school year "until the 1979-1980 school year to provide this Board with an opportunity to verify the data that has been given us, and to study additional alternatives to such a closing."[13] Luchsinger seconded the motion and other board members then offered their comments.

Board member Carmen expressed concern about "the numbers of youngsters who do not appear on our official census." She continued:

> Indeed, I have great faith in the people from Moses DeWitt who have done obviously a monumental task, but I really must address the questions in a very official manner. I would respectfully request that our administrators please see to it

that another census is taken, going door to door, with no residence left untapped.[14]

Cargian declared that he was also "upset at the head count," adding that he appreciated "Mr. Brunner's remarks about the hundreds and thousands of dollars' worth of talent we have out there." But "we have talent here on the board," Cargian asserted before recommending that the census be redone by an "independent service."[15]

Mallan found that it was still feasible to close a school.

As a matter of fact, it was feasible this year. . . .So we know it's feasible. We know we don't need the space, and I know it's not a choice betwen space, and I agree in program, but if I had, not saving money but cost benefit--I'd rather put that money in the programming staff, program development and staff.[16]

If anything, Mallan reasoned, the parents' figures simply showed that a second closing could be delayed and thus their census might be a "godsend in disguise." Mallan concluded his argument as his words trailed off, "In other words, the fear of having the second closing would be--I'm not arguing, please. I feel the same way you do, Carolyn--30 years in this game, I don't like to see education shortchanged. I also know we have to play with cost benefit."[17]

To this comment Coit took the microphone, explaining the rationale for her motion. "I'm willing to spend a year convincing these people, because I think that it would be money well spent." DeBottis then expressed a similar feeling. In the weeks since voting to close a school he had learned that "this is a very powerful seat I hold. It can affect the lives of a lot of people." Concluded Debottis, "An appeal has been brought to me by a large majority of this community and I feel I must respond in a positive reaction here tonight."[18]

Hearing two local representatives reply to the feeling of their community, Mallan, an education professor and former school administrator in the midwest, tried to redirect the discussion. He referred to keeping a "district perspective" and considering experiences in areas other than New York State, contending that one of the board's responsibilities was "to pull back from the gut level of things."

Taking the microphone for the first time, board member Luchsinger said that board members should be responsible, representative, and responsive. On the basis of his colleagues' comments, Luchsinger found that "we are trying to be responsive." After reviewing his experience of the closing issue, Luchsinger concluded that the board should honor two responsibilities: first, to "verify the enrollment pattern in our community so there can be no mistake and no questions, so that the community and the Board can agree on the figures; secondly, it must test the wishes of the district residents and the strength of the neighborhood concept."[19] Scibilia, the second of Moses DeWitt's two supporters, agreed with Luchsinger's position. Looking into the audience, he found that "the grass roots are certainly talking."[20]

Board president Perkins did not agree with Scibilia's interpretation.

> I don't like to be intimidated. I don't like to be subjected to pressure. I'm concerned about some of the names on the petitions because I have been told that people have had to sign that petition because they lived next to their neighbors.[21]

Perkins continued, "My bottom line for education was the very best education for all of the children in the district irregardless of their neighborhood, their race, or religion, or whatever creed they might be." She then tallied the 131 letters that she had received by January 2, finding public opinion to be "heavily in support of the board's position."

Because of efforts in behalf of Moses DeWitt, some parents "are afraid for the welfare of their children," asserted Perkins. In response to questions called from the audience the board president went on to say:

> I have received phone calls from parents who have children at Moses DeWitt School at the present time who have indicated their willingness to have those children transferred to other schools but their

concern has been if Moses DeWitt is kept
open, and they have publicly stated their
position, that there will be harm to their
children.[22]

Again replying to the audience's dismay at this startling
allegation, Perkins moved on to criticize political
activities by the Moses DeWitt Parents' Group. "I am
concerned that money from a parent-teacher organization
was in use for this kind of purpose." Some people
expressed concern, she said, about money raised by all
being used "for a cause in which they do not necessarily
agree."

According to the president, board members voted
their own consciences. She did not discuss her
decisions with other board members, for this "is not my
way of operating." Suddenly dropping her previous tone,
the board president declared, "This is democracy."[23]

Perkins and Luchsinger then had a brief colloquy in
which they discussed the letters received by board
members and their significance. After board member
Carmen had asked Osborn to reiterate the differences
between the parents' census and the district census and
Perkins had called for a reading of the motion, a voice
from the audience rang out, "Can we hear from the
superintendent?"

Making a belated appearance in the evening's
proceedings Superintendent Baker stated:

I'm not concerned with the census figures.
I'm not afraid to be out 900 per cent. I'm
concerned with the number of students that
are coming in next year and the following
year. I'm very concerned with the emotion
that is present in our district at the
moment.[24]

Baker continued by saying that the next three to five
years would see "some changes in this district which have
major impact." If enrollment continued to decline, the
superintendent explained, "we either lose the
neighborhood concept or the middle school concept or the
high school concept." Nevertheless, because of the
emotion present in the district, he found it only fair to
"postpone any decision for at least a year."
Furthermore, "I think the board has always listened to
the community. That's why we're a Class A district,"

Photograph 1.  **Superintendent Lansing G. Baker**
did not mind being 900 per cent off on the census, but he
was "very concerned with the emotion that is present in
our district."

concluded Baker. But a decision favorable to Moses DeWitt would require parents to honor their commitment to "support the board every way you can, budgetwise and programwise."[25]

When the roll was called, the board voted 6-3 to defer closing Moses DeWitt for one year. Joining Perkins and Mallan in opposition to the motion was Jamesville representative Hopkins, who said he voted "for the 8,000 eligible voters who did not sign the petition to make a change in our decision."[26]

Only days earlier school officials had shown determination to close Moses DeWitt. Sometime before the January 9 meeting, however, administrators decided that the closing decision was ill advised. A determined, well-organized opposition threatened to undermine the district's political system as it had developed over almost thirty years. In this system the chief school administrator had great resources; he sat at the "peak of an internal political power pyramid."[27] The superintendent not only drew respect for his specialized knowledge, he had gained the community's trust by his service in the Rotary, the United Way, and appearances at countless school concerts and gym demonstrations. The board and the administration had not diverged on public issues. Rather, the superintendent publicly deferred to the board's wishes, sitting quietly through many meetings, and the board gave the seal of public approval to the administration's policy. A unified board served a presumably monolithic community.

Local organizations had used their resources for purposes other than influencing school district decisions. Administrators knew that "parents are more interested in the current education of their own children than in enduring problems of the educational system as a whole."[28] The political system offered a great deal of "slack" in the system. These citizens showed growing political skill, as they gathered information, published propaganda, and successfully presented their own viewpoint to an interested press. People formerly content to confer with their child's teacher or accompany the third grade on a field trip now felt motivated to acquire political skills and apply them to the school district. As parent-organizers spent more time on the subject, they learned more. And as they extended their political activities, these protesters seemed increasingly likely to shatter the district's consensus, perhaps irrevocably.

By providing the board of education with inaccurate information, Superintendent Baker had jeopardized his own reputation as an expert. More than his reputation as an authority was at stake, however. The superintendent had what he himself described as a "reservoir of trust."[29] Board members had placed their confidence in his ability to do what the district needed. Now in the face of public criticism, board members did not know how to justify their decision except to say that they believed in "the best possible education for all of the children." Inexperienced in making or defending policy, board members also felt uncomfortable in publicly disagreeing among themselves. "I'm not arguing, please," interjected Mallan as he contradicted Coit's position during the January 9 meeting.

Board members saw themselves as trustees serving on a board of directors for a philanthropic or cultural institution rather than as delegates of the people. Hence Perkins' sentiment "I do not like to be intimidated. I do not like to be subjected to pressure." Responding to public opinion was difficult, for board members did not consider themselves politicians. Overt political action and demands were unfamiliar, alarming. According to one analysis, a board of education often "feels threatened when anything but harmless group activity flourishes, because that has come to mean that all is not well in the district, that the natives are restless."[30]

Even before hundreds of emotional residents crowded the high school auditorium, administrators had sensed a clear and present danger, a problem that could not be alleviated by referring to the fine reputation of Jamesville-DeWitt, its outstanding educational program, or the support always given by the community. In a classic study of school decision-making a suburban superintendent was described as follows: "His resistance to change never reached the point of intransigence which would have resulted in the demise of his political system," a sentence applicable to Superintendent Baker in the days before January 9.[31]

Although some board members believed devoutly in their closing decision, the administration decided to draw back. Faced with adversity and opposition, school leaders would not charge ahead anyway. To proceed despite public outcry would inevitably create a divided community and board. "There is a very delicate balance in board-community perception between a strong administrator and a dogmatic one," wrote one superintendent.[32] Baker and his staff decided that the costs of proving themselves right by implementing the decision were too great.

Administrators cited emotion as the reason to delay, thus avoiding the issue of their own errors in preparing for school-closing. The superintendent admitted that he did not even mind being off "by 900 per cent" on the census, for only the enrollment in the next two years was critical.[33] Discrepancies in the census figures now served a purpose: they gave board members a pretext for delaying--not reversing--their decision. A year's delay could be interpreted as a prudent measure, needed to gather new "official" census information to quiet critics and to spend time "convincing" parents that the closing decision was right. Even those board members who opposed deferring the decision agreed on the need for new information. Board member Hopkins called for a new census of pre-school children and "the total school population." Mallan did not "like to work from a poor data basis because everything else becomes kind of ludicrous," and board president Perkins felt "very concerned about the credibility of our census." Thus, although board members were still divided, they could grasp at a thread of unity in seeking new facts.[34]

Revealing his position to the board, Superintendent Baker had sufficient influence to produce a 6-3 margin for deferring the decision, from what had been a 7-2 vote to close a month earlier. Politically sensitive to his board members, Baker could usually produce the results he wanted. By persuading the board to wait a year he avoided "the appearance of loss of power even when forced to yield," in the manner of the classic superintendent.[35] But the course has been perilous, "the boat almost careening out of control," in the words of one administrator.

Why, then, had the school district reached this strange and unprecedented state of affairs? The closing of a school had been anticipated for several years, as the Task Force and administrators prepared the way. Little attention focused, however, on how to choose which school to close. This critical subject was not discussed until two days before the board's December 12 meeting. In a day-long study session board members made the decision to close Moses DeWitt, the choice that Superintendent Baker

104

accepted only later to describe as the one "most likely to guarantee that all schools stayed open." The board's study session was a private meeting at which board members could present their views, an occasion at which administrators could "size up the strength of opposing forces" without public observation or conflict.[36] In allowing board members to make their preference known, Baker probably did not expect to be caught in an irreversible or politically dangerous decision. Study sessions often presented the appearance rather than the reality of decision-making; the superintendent could usually develop tactics to change board members' positions if necessary. But in this instance a nervous community learned of the choice. Once the school had been publicly named, the room for maneuver decreased markedly. And the Open Meetings Law enforced this effect, as the public appeared at board meetings, petitioned officeholers and applied pressure to their elected and appointed officials.

Having secured a year's delay Moses DeWitt parents found that they still had their work ahead of them. Board members had given few, if any, signs of changing their original positions on closing. The administration had conceded only time; it had not modified its objective, acknowledged errors, or altered its approach to decision-making. "Well, they called our bluff. Now we have to prove that we were right," Mascott told **Suburban Life** immediately after the board's decision.[37]

## NOTES

1. Quotes are from a court stenographer's transcript of the Jamesville-DeWitt Board of Education's Meetin, Dec. 9, 1978 (Vito Lentini, CSR, Machine Shorthand of Syracuse). Transcript, 6.
2. **Ibid.**, 12-15.
3. **Ibid.**, 22.
4. **Ibid.**, 26.
5. **Ibid.**, 34.
6. L. Harmon Zeigler and M. Kent Jennings, **Governing American Schools**(North Scituate, Mass. 1974), 191.
7. Katherine E. Eisenberger and William F. Keough, **Declining Enrollment: What to Do**(Arlington, 1974), 11.
8. Robert A. Dahl, **Who Governs?**(New Haven, 1968), 156.
9. **Ibid.**
10. Laurence Iannaccone and Frank W. Lutz, **Politics, Power, and**

Policy: **The Governing of Local School Districts**(Columbus, 1970), 65.

11. James D. Koerner, **Who Controls American Education?**(Boston, 1968), 122.

12. As quoted by Iannaccone and Lutz, **Politics, Power and Policy**, 68.

13. Transcript, 43-44.

14. **Ibid.**, 45.

15. **Ibid.**, 47.

16. **Ibid.**, 49.

17. **Ibid.**, 50.

18. **Ibid.**, 51.

19. **Ibid.**, 63.

20. **Ibid.**, 68.

21. **Ibid.**, 69.

22. **Ibid.**, 72.

23. **Ibid.**, 74.

24. **Ibid.**, 79-80.

25. **Ibid.**, 80.

26. **Ibid.**, 83.

27. Iannaccone and Lutz, **Politics, Power, and Policy**, 67.

28. Dahl, **Who Governs?**, 158.

29. Interview with author, Mar. 6, 1980.

30. Zeigler and Jennings, **Governing American Schools**, 158.

31. Daniel E. Griffiths, et al., **Organizing Schools for Effective Education**(Danville, Ill., 1962), 225.

32. William F. Keough, Jr., "Enrollment Decline: The Dilemma from the Superintendent's Chair," in Susan Abramowitz and Stuart Rosenfeld, eds., **Declining Enrollments: The Challenge of the Coming Decade**(Washington, D.C., 1978), 362.

33. Transcript, 79.

34. Mallan on data base, **Ibid.**, 49; Perkins on credibility of census, **Ibid.**, 68.

35. Griffiths, et al., **Organizing Schools for Effective Education**, 225.

36. Iannaccone and Lutz, **Politics, Power, and Policy**, 65.

37. **Suburban Life**(DeWitt, East Syracuse), Jan. 11, 1978.

## VII. Playing Politics in Jamesville-Dewitt

After the board's decision to defer the closing, Moses DeWitt parents attempted to strengthen their organization for the year ahead. "What have we gained?" asked a new issue of SOS. "A final decision? No--only a reprieve." Board members Perkins, Mallan, and Hopkins had voted against the resolution to defer closing, while other board members continued to consider a closing necessary and desirable. Moses DeWitt parents urged supporters to continue their interest in school issues. "We must stay organized," said the newsletter. The Special Committee attempted to enlist parents in task forces to study such questions as legal and political issues, curriculum and program, district census and data, parent-teacher group reorganization, and the budget.

The new task forces took form to "help in any way" the school board's consideration of closing and budget issues. "We think we are very lucky to have some of the talented business people that we do, who are willing to bring their knowledge to bear on school district problems," Mascott again observed to the press.[1] The new task forces would help collect ideas for saving money and increasing revenue, as well as study grade alignments and staffing.

While attempting to involve greater numbers of parents in task forces--an effort that never succeeded--leaders of the Special Committee moved to take positions as officers of the Moses DeWitt Parents' Group. Instead of continuing to seek approval from the Parents' Group executive board for expenditures and support for political action, the Moses DeWitt militants took control of the organization and its purse strings. In March a new slate of officers including leading activists gained election and immediately assumed office rather than waiting for the end of the school year, as had been the previous practice. Although the Mascotts soon moved out of state, equally militant parents moved into the presidency and vice-presidency. The Special Committee was now absorbed into the Parents' Group, which intended to "demonstrate the need for the neighborhood school concept."[2] Moses DeWitt principal Calver told the insurgents now controlling his once-sedate parents' group that the superintendent considered their election "big trouble."

Meanwhile, the school district needed to redeem its reputation after being caught "900 per cent off" on its census. First came verification of the list of babies ages 0-2 in the Moses DeWitt area. "We're calling the names to verify each child's date of birth," said Superintendent Baker on January 16. "So far, we've found an awful lot of new children."[3] But this cursory check did not suffice. Board members called for a new, official census, and they wanted an effort that would allow no possibility of doubt or dispute.

The board also considered doing an "attitude survey" of district residents as well. Board members wanted to know the degree of support for neighborhood elementary schools and for the budget. How much would voters be willing to pay to support four elementary schools in the future? Would they be willing to sacrifice aspects of the program to maintain these schools? How large a tax increase would the voters be willing to approve? The board speculated on the direction that the community wanted to take. Considering the four elementary schools, board member Scibilia said reassuringly, "The community has always backed us," a statement that drew Coit's rejoinder, "Yes, backed us to the wall."

Residents reacted quickly to the board's prospective opinion-survey. "I think we have to be interested in this questionnaire's purity," stated one Moses DeWitt parent. After showing initial interest administrators discouraged the idea of an opinion-survey, doubting that residents clearly understood terms such as "program" or the context of possible questions. Board members also saw problems in conducting an opinion-survey in an emotionally-charged climate. Noting the possibility of bias in any set of questions, board members Mallan and Coit concluded that conditions were not conducive for a survey. Coit felt that the board's time could be better spent "visiting at the schools, talking to people." Thus, the board abandoned the opinion-survey, to concentrate on the census and enrollment projections.

The school board decided to have the census conducted by teams of parents organized by principals at the four elementary schools. In the past the district had employed only several census-takers, often students, who worked in the summer--a practice that had left the board open to its recent ordeal. The new census, however, would require a door-to-door visit at every address in the school district. To verify the accuracy of the findings, the board employed the accounting firm of Price Waterhouse and Company. Upon completion of the census, Price Waterhouse and Company planned to survey 300 Jamesville-DeWitt residents "to validate census information."[4]

After Price Waterhouse offered its seal of approval, the accounting firm forwarded the information to the Jamesville-DeWitt administration. Only administrators--not board members--examined the census results before they were sealed and sent to Syracuse Research Corporation in May. A local "think tank" once part of Syracuse University, SRC had agreed to project enrollment at no charge to the school district. Using SRC "will boost our credibility," curriculum coordinator Osborn explained to the press.[5] The board's original timetable had called for completing all work on the census before the budget vote and election of school board members. Residents wondered when the census and projections would be released to the public. Would the board use this new information to close a school by fall, as it had originally desired?

During the months that administrators and board members concentrated on a census that would be irrefutable, Moses DeWitt parents considered the forthcoming election for two positions on the board. A strong, although silent, supporter of Moses DeWitt held one of these seats, and possibly he would seek reelection, as he did, running unopposed. The other position, however, belonged to Joyce Carmen, a board member eager to close Moses DeWitt.

The Parents' Group had established a task force to study legal and political questions, and this group, led by three lawyers, began to consider the question of challenging Carmen's reelection. Changing the composition of the board of education offered a direct, effective way of protecting Moses DeWitt. Parent activists had reason to expect that they could elect a candidate. Only recently they had gathered 2200 signatures for their petition and turned out a largely sympathetic audience of well over 500 people. Thus, parents viewed the election as a promising opportunity. By contesting the board position, they would use the democratic process to advance their cause.

By mid-February the legal-political task force had concluded that Dr. Edward Sugarman was the best candidate for the board position held by Mrs. Carmen. An orthopedic surgeon, Sugarman had an impressive record of community service. Since 1972 he had been police and fire surgeon for the Town of DeWitt, a position that he filled by actually "rolling" with the men and equipment rather than acting as only a "paper surgeon." He was also a past president of the Onondaga County Medical Society, a past chairman of the Physicians' Division of the United Way, a consultant to the Shriners' Hospital for Crippled Children, and a DeWitt Rotarian.[6] The father of three children, Sugarman had an active interest in the schools. Furthermore, he and his wife had been among the first to protest the closing of Moses DeWitt. Sugarman had spoken to the superintendent and to the local press on the subject, in addition to providing data used in challenging the board's closing decision.

Another consideration figured in the decision to select Sugarman as the candidate. The board position held by Joyce Carmen had become known as the "Jewish seat." Residents, board members, and administrators spoke of an unwritten rule guaranteeing one "Jewish seat" on the Board. Although Jewish children represented almost one-third of the students enrolled in Jamesville-DeWitt schools, only rarely had Jews gained election, or appointment, to the board of education.[7] Even on executive boards of parent-teacher groups, Jewish parents were under-represented. Moses DeWitt, particularly, had a reputation for maintaining a conspicuously Christian atmosphere in the observance of holidays as well as excluding Jewish parents from leadership positions. One critical parent who nonetheless opposed the closing remarked, "Moses DeWitt is run as if it is a parochial school." Jewish residents sometimes voiced resentment at the celebration of Christmas or claimed that Moses DeWitt parents looked forward to the holiday season in which "they dance around their Christmas trees." Some militants accepted the validity of these statements; most agreed that a Jewish candidate would be necessary to avoid losing the "Jewish vote" in the election. Sugarman met this qualification in addition to having other assets.

Several members of the Special Committee questioned the wisdom of running a man against a woman. "Why write off 300 women's votes?" asked one skeptic. But most parents felt so confident of victory that this question did not appear serious. No other candidate had expressed interest, and attention focused on Sugarman. A large group of leading activists gathered to appeal to him to

110

run. Not only did he seem the most electable candidate, his future role on the board was described as indispensable. He could expect continuing support both before and after the election from parents dedicated to saving Moses Dewitt. Board member Luchsinger appeared briefly at the meeting to describe to Sugarman the duties and life of a board member. Ostracized by most board members for his part in the school-closing crisis, Luchsinger clearly wanted company, but he recommended that Sugarman run as independently of him--and of Moses DeWitt--as possible. Within a few days Sugarman accepted the entreaties of his friends and supporters and agreed to run.

The as-yet unannounced candidate then set out to plan his campaign. Members of the legal-political task force of the Parents' Group now became part of the Sugarman for School Board Committee. No longer did this task force, consisting of two businessmen and three lawyers, have any official connection with Moses DeWitt. But because one lawyer had served as co-chairman of the Special Committee and another had been among the school's most vocal advocates, the new division of forces seemed a formality, not a reality, to Moses DeWitt partisans and later to the community. Nevertheless, to develop the impression of an independent organization, Sugarman named a campaign director and treasurer.

The campaign opened poorly. Appearing at a meeting of the Parents' Group for the "last time," Sugarman observed that news of his candidacy had been "leaked" to the administration by a member of the group's executive board. Consequently, he developed a strategy that would not provide the Parents' Group with details as to his campaign. Officially the candidate severed his ties with Moses DeWitt. Nevertheless, he still needed the resources of the Parents' Group, including supplies for his campaign and financial support for a proposed mailing. Moses DeWitt supporters, moreover, planned to distribute literature, make telephone calls, and assure his election. Publicly, Sugarman intended to shirk any connection with the controversial Moses DeWitt militants, while relying heavily on their efforts to elect him.

Despite the already-strained relations between Sugarman and Moses DeWitt supporters, most parents continued to be confident of victory. No other parent-teacher organization had the political experience gained by Moses DeWitt parents in the previous three months.

Moses DeWitt not only had experienced, dedicated activists, it had a sizeable treasury, a non-profit postal sticker, and the largest population base in the school district. Having more at stake than other groups as well as more zeal, Moses DeWitt partisans failed to anticipate the circumstances that could contribute to possible--even inevitable--defeat.

The school-closing issue had temporarily disrupted the prevailing culture of Jamesville-DeWitt. Local residents, however, soon reasserted the norms long accepted in the community. "The culture of school boards holds that education is too important to become a political affair," wrote one scholar.[8] Not only board members but residents had accepted the board of education as an elite system of decision-making. To challenge this system, as did Moses DeWitt parents, was to question the "sacred, protective nature of local school governance,"--to call into doubt the whole set of beliefs by which residents upheld the high quality of their officials and their schools. Board members were not to vote as the people wished but as they thought best, thus protecting the quality of education for all. The culture's norms further instructed the "board member to avoid representing any group within the school district," and to concentrate on "good education."[9]

Openly political in their use of the press and their own printed newsletters, as well as their repudiation of the school district's information and rationale for closing, Moses DeWitt parents had rebuffed the aristocracy of school decision-makers. They had effectively represented a particular interest, using politics to do so. But now they had skated near the edge of what the public was willing to tolerate, although they did not realize it.

Jamesville-DeWitt officeholders abjured the term "politics," denying anything political in their election or later actions. "I don't ever want to hear the word 'politician'!" exclaimed one board member. Often described by his board members as "the professional," the superintendent nevertheless had to "deal with and through political forces to accomplish his ends."[10] While denying any political role, the school administrator must "constantly make concessions to the dominant interests behind school policy and attempt to implement his program through more indirect and subtle means."[11] Indeed, the superintendent provided the focal point for a system whose intensely political character

112

was denied by all participants.

Although he, too, considered himself a civic leader rather than a politician, Sugarman did not realize the importance of the non-political ethic. Soon after the announcement of his candidacy, Sugarman's campaign chairman mailed one hundred and fifty letters to selected supporters. After extolling Sugarman's qualifications for office, the letter concluded, "Contributions should be made payable to Dr. Ed Sugarman Campaign," noting the name and address of the campaign treasurer. By this apparently innocuous statement, the candidate had taken an irrevocably political action.

Residents, moreover, associated Sugarman's name with a particular group, and the school district culture "denigrates any board member who attempts to represent a group of citizens, labeling such board members as low-level politicians uninterested in 'good' education."[12] The incumbent board member, on the other hand, could not be disentangled from a system widely agreed to be excellent. In the words of two scholars, "the public, the board, and the superintendent view the board and the superintendent as one impregnable decision-making system."[13] Moses DeWitt parents could not easily isolate their opponent for criticism.

By campaigning for Sugarman, parents had opened themselves and their candidate to an effective opposition strategy. Sugarman himself sensed the problem, not knowing whether to repudiate his connection to Moses DeWitt or exhort the school's partisans to greater efforts in his behalf. Criticized for being a Moses DeWitt candidate, Sugarman recoiled from activist parents. Needing their manpower and commitment, he turned to them once more--a cycle repeated several times before the election.

In May, acting with Sugarman's approval, the Moses DeWitt Parents' Group published an election edition of their newsletter SOS, mailed to every resident in the school district. This document outlined the chronology of the closing issue and emphasized the errors in the district's census. After urging voters to support the budget in June, the newsletter concluded that "the survival of the neighborhood elementary school remains an important issue in this school district." Quotations from local papers highlighted Sugarman's support for "all six schools" and Carmen's vote to close Moses DeWitt but stopped short of an explicit endorsement of Sugarman.

113

Carmen reacted immediately, contending that her opponent "appears to be the candidate of one special interest group." She reminded voters that she was campaigning for a **district-wide** position. The incumbent continued, "I am not a one-issue person. My priority has always been the best educational interests of all the children in the district, coupled with fiscal responsibility and integrity."[14] Effectively invoking the school district culture in her own interest, Carmen observed that she had never solicited financial backing for her candidacy and would accept none. "To ask for funds is precedent-setting in the district."

Sugarman now attempted to answer this ideological assault on his candidacy, but he remained on the defensive. As the incumbent, Carmen had stated her commitment to the entire district and to the "best educational interests of all the children." Sugarman's efforts to demonstrate that he, too, shared this commitment failed to carry conviction. He had **not** held office on the board of education to serve the entire district; indeed, he had come to public attention as a Moses DeWitt parent, part of a "special interest group." Sugarman's criticism of Carmen as a "no issue" candidate did not answer the allegation that he stood for a special interest or issue, a charge that hurt, as the candidate conceded. "I was one of the residents who gathered the original information on the census ," he explained. "But I hate being painted as a one-issue candidate." As for the criticism about raising money, "It's just so much nonsense!" Elaborating, Sugarman asked, "Should we limit the board to people who can afford to print brochures and distribute them?" But even on this question, the challenger failed to dispel criticism.[15]

While attempting to raise several other issues, such as physical fitness and programs for students not bound for college, Sugarman repeatedly returned to the underlying question of his connection with Moses DeWitt. He had severed ties with residents, he told the local press. "I'm not a member of the group's executive committee," he explained. "Sure, I'm a Moses DeWitt parent," the candidate acknowledged. "In September, when my daughter goes to middle school, I will be a middle school parent." A Sugarman campaign statement distributed throughout the district anticipated the time when the candidate would have a child in each level of the school system:

I mention this to clarify that I am a one-group candidate--that group is comprised of four elementary schools, one middle school, and one high school, as well as special education and adult education programs.[16]

To rally their supporters Moses DeWitt activists again emphasized the inaccuracy of the district's census. In their election-issue of SOS, Moses DeWitt parents had asserted that the new, official census "will reveal over 300 more children age 0-5 than in district figures," a figure drawn from an administrator's comment at a board meeting. But because school administrators declined to release figures from the new census, Carmen successfully deflated this argument. "We don't know where they're getting these figures," she stated to the press. "No official report on the census had been made to the board of education by the administration to date."[17] The administration refused to confirm that Moses DeWitt supporters had contributed sound information, thus weakening the impact of their arguments in other parts of the school district. Sugarman's campaign statement that the parents had been accurate and the new, official census unnecessary seemed unconvincing to residents who distrusted a "special interest group."

Frustrated in their efforts to gain acceptance of the census figures, parents sought new ways of presenting their arguments. In May they invited a professor from the Massachusetts Institute of Technology to speak on the issue of school-closing. Professor Robert Rotberg, a former school board member in Lexington, Massachusetts, discounted the conventional wisdom that school closings save money. "Savings are illusory at best," he told an audience of 150 residents, including several board members and administrators. In school districts in which salaries account for 75 per cent of the budget, one elementary school represents only a fraction of that budget, he explained. Small schools, according to Professor Rotberg, "are valuable in terms of something intrinsic to the small corridors, the small rooms, the neighborhood locations."[18]

Although extensively covered by the local press, Professor Rotberg's presentation failed to stimulate any comment by the incumbent candidate. In a campaign statement circulated shortly before the election, Carmen stated:

> I have dedicated my work as a member of the
> Board of Education to the best educational
> interest of each child in the entire
> Jamesville-DeWitt School District, to
> open communication between Home and
> School, and to fiscal responsibility and
> integrity.

When voters questioned Carmen about school-closing at a "meet the candidates night," she adeptly sidestepped the issue, saying that she could not comment until she received official figures from the new census. She repeatedly emphasized her service to the entire school district and to "all of the children." Invoking all of the tenets of school board ideology, she concluded her campaign appeal by asserting that "public education is the strength of our country," and "the quality of our schools is enhanced by the support of our community."

As the election approached, Sugarman campaigners grew less optimistic. The local school board, wrote two political scientists, typically enjoys reserves of untapped support. Furthermore, "the ability of an incumbent school board member to mobilize this potential support has important consequences for the process of decision-making within the district,"-- a consideration not immediately recognized by Moses DeWitt partisans but increasingly apparent as the campaign advanced.[19] Thinking of themselves as the district's most cohesive political organization, Moses DeWitt parents had failed to reckon with the power of incumbency. Nor had they considered the disadvantages of working within an at-large electoral system.

"Circulation in office and turning incumbents out of office are also discouraged by at-large systems," according to political scientists Zeigler and Jennings. Ward officeholders have a specific clear-cut constituency that can turn them out of office. In the at-large electoral district, by contrast, "specific group reprisals" often become "lost in the common balloting."[20] Attempted reprisals against incumbent Carmen not only became lost in the campaign, they were turned against her challenger. Carmen forces stigmatized the Sugarman campaign as a divisive influence designing to "pack" the board with Moses DeWitt supporters.

By keeping her campaign general ("I am dedicated to maintaining OPEN COMMUNICATION between Home and

School."), Carmen appealed to the heterogeneous interests in the rest of the school district. Identifying herself with the cause of good schools, she raised doubts that her "one-issue" opponent shared the same commitment. Despite Sugarman's constant assurances that "I do believe in one issue--sound education for all," his candidacy threatened the accepted political culture. Both directly and indirectly Carmen repeatedly emphasized her opponent's connection with Moses DeWitt, effectively casting doubt on his support for other schools. Voters in school areas other than Moses DeWitt could rally to the cause of "the best possible educational interests of each child in the entire Jamesville-DeWitt School District" and at the same time protect their own school by voting for the incumbent.

Administrators did not intervene to allay voters' fears about the goals of Moses DeWitt parents. Although both the Parents' Group and Sugarman urged passage of the budget, this support for the school district received no acknowledgment. When the election issue of SOS stated that the tax rate offered the voters in 1978 amounted to only "one seventh of what the Task Force predicted," board president Perkins angrily asserted at a budget hearing that she found this argument "highly misleading." Superintendent Baker offered no comment at the hearing, although he knew Moses DeWitt parents were the budget's most vocal supporters as well as a traditional source of "yes" votes. Candidate Carmen also termed the newsletter's arguments in behalf of the budget "misleading."[21] Supporting the budget had not given Moses DeWitt parents legitimacy in the system. To acknowledge Moses DeWitt support for the budget would give that group the status of a loyal party rather than a "special interest" group.

Likewise, school administrators resisted pressure to release or discuss figures from the new census. By postponing discussion of these figures, they would not "interfere with the election," they said, and at the same time avoid further embarrassment before the budget vote. As Moses DeWitt claims about the number of pre-school children went unverified, Carmen found herself free to dismiss the subject as "premature" and any discussion of enrollment numbers "speculative."[22] Administrators did not wish to confirm Moses DeWitt parents' contributions in this controversial area.

As the campaign progressed, administrators perhaps

117

concluded that an incumbent's defeat could produce "drastic policy changes (that) might upset the whole delicate balance" in the district.[23] Even before her appointment in 1972 and first election in 1973, Carmen had long attended board meetings, and she and the coterie that eagerly campaigned for her in coffees throughout DeWitt made a known, familiar group. Her re-election would thwart the ascendancy of the sometimes rancorous Moses DeWitt activists, whose future role in the district remained unpredictable. Furthermore, administrators knew that an incumbent's defeat often came as the prelude to a replacement of the superintendent. Various segments of the public saw Carmen and Baker as having a united stand. Whether accurately or not, many residents believed the incumbent board member and the superintendent carried out a common policy.

Certainly, Superintendent Baker recognized that he and his administration had provided the centerpiece in the controversy concerning school-closing. Although Sugarman promised his support to the district and did not criticize the superintendent in his campaign, the challenger was of the opposition party. Like it or not, the superintendent knew that his fate and the incumbent's were "not independent of each other."[24] Scholars have observed that an incumbent's defeat often leads to conflict on the board, especially between the new member and the superintendent. As Iannaccone and Lutz explain, "The political effect of one incumbent's defeat is much greater than the one new school board member's voting power would suggest." New alignments develop among board members, and "the new man usually becomes the center of a new series of struggles with the established leader of the old power structure."[25] Perhaps fearing that possibility, Jamesville-DeWitt administrators offered Sugarman only Rotarian friendliness but not support. Hinting that the theatrical Carmen did not please them entirely, they did nothing to tip the balance in Sugarman's favor.

On election night, Moses DeWitt supporters found that their candidate carried only 43 per cent of the vote, losing to the incumbent by 373 votes.[26] Moses DeWitt activists had failed to convince other residents that their candidate represented the interests of the district "as a whole." By their very organization-- which they had regarded with pride--they had alienated and frightened voters in other areas. Although the budget passed handily by 63 per cent, Moses DeWitt efforts for the budget ("Vote for a Responsible Budget.

Vote 'Yes'," said the SOS) received no credit. Indeed, board member Mallan found it "preposterous" to conclude that Moses DeWitt parents had had anything to do with passing the budget.

Greatly chagrined, parents found playing politics in the "sacred community" very difficult. In this community, interactions and discussion follow clearly delineated patterns. Behavior reenforces community solidarity, just as the school district's ideology supports the incumbent as a symbol of that system. Thus Moses DeWitt parents learned that the path to the board of education was not easy, as they first anticipated. In fact, substantial--if not insuperable--obstacles stood in the way of achieving that goal.

## NOTES

1. **Post—Standard**(Syracuse), Feb. 12, 1978.
2. **Suburban Life**(DeWitt and East Syracuse), Mar. 29, 1978.
3. **Ibid.**, Jan. 18, 1978.
4. **Suburban Life**, Apr. 26, 1978.
5. **Ibid.**
6. **Herald—Journal**(Syracuse), May 19, 1978.
7. Percentage is based on the absence-rate on Jewish holidays; interviews at schools and temples; and interfaith survey (1965); in recent years Jewish representation on the school board has increased.
8. Frank W. Lutz and Laurence Iannaccone, "Beyond Operational Indicators--Toward Explanatory Relationships," in Frank W. Lutz and Laurence Iannaccone, eds., **Public Participation in Local School Districts**(Lexington, 1978), 102.
9. On politics in the "sacred community," see Laurence Iannaccone and Frank W. Lutz, **Politics, Power, and Policy: The Governing of Local School Districts**(Columbus, 1970), 29-39.
10. Arthur J. Vidich and Joseph Bensman, **Small Town in Mass Society**(Princeton, 1968), 186.
11. **Ibid.**
12. Lutz and Iannaccone, "Beyond Operational Indicators," 107; the Sugarman campaign was inescapably political both in its connection to Moses DeWitt and in the appeal for money, in Martin A. Yenawine, Chairman, Ed Sugarman for School Board Committee, Letter, Apr. 30, 1978.
13. Lutz and Iannaccone, "Beyond Operational Indicators," 107.
14. **Herald—Journal**, May 22, 1978.

15. **Herald-Journal**, May 31, 1968.
16. **Ibid.**; second quote is from Dr. Ed Sugarman campaign flyer, June, 1978.
17. **Herald-Journal**, May 22, 1978.
18. **Post-Standard**, May 25, 1978.
19. On the school board's reservoir of latent support and the power of incumbency, see L. Harmon Zeigler and M. Kent Jennings, **Governing American Schools**(North Scituate, Mass., 1974), 13.
20. **Ibid.**, 59.
21. **Herald-Journal**, May 22, 1978; other statements concerning communication between home and school come from Joyce Carmen campaign flyer, June 1978.
22. **Herald-Journal**, May 22, 1978.
23. See Zeigler and Jennings, **Governing American Schools**, 66-71.
24. **Ibid.**, 67.
25. Iannaccone and Lutz, **Politics, Power, and Policy**, 104.
26. Voting statistics are from the Jamesville-DeWitt District Office.

# VIII.  Doing it Again:

## Census and Task Force Once More

Following the passage of the budget and reelection of Joyce Carmen, administrators reassessed their situation. Although their authority remained intact and the district's academic reputation untarnished, administrators had been through a disquieting year. Instead of the usual discussion of internal issues, such as teachers' study sessions, personnel changes, or building maintenance, school officials had faced six months' continuing scrutiny from a newly-awakened public and an interested press. Residents had not only challenged administrators' monopoly of information, they had held public attention for a half-year. The closing issue had offered one of those rare occasions when, in Roscoe Martin's words, "public politics forces its way onto the stage." Faced with unexpected external pressure, "the board of education advances (or is pushed) to the fore as the spokesman for education, and the schoolmen retire to the wings until the hubbub has subsided," according to Martin's interpretation of politics in suburban education.[1]

In Jamesville-DeWitt the board of education had been first pushed to the fore and then rescued by administrators, who decided to defer the controversial closing for a year, in which to consolidate their control of the system. By denying Moses DeWitt parents access to the new official census figures and thus injuring the Sugarman campaign, administrators' efforts had been directed toward "destroying the credibility or at the very least limiting the role of 'outside' organizations." The presence of an organized citizens group limited administrators' discretion. An unstructured public, as known in the past, had allowed school officials to organize support for policies of their own choosing. In political scientist Martin's judgment, "the educational bureaucracy has achieved notable success in driving the public school structure toward a monolith under oligarchic control."[2] If this control had been shaken during 1978, administrators could renew it in the weeks following the defeat of Sugarman and the long-awaited retirement of Moses DeWitt principal Calver.

Although administrators expected principals to have "personal concerns in regard to school closings," Calver had gone beyond this.[3] Principal for thirty-four years, he gave neither support nor lip service to the closing decision. He did not subordinate personal concerns for "his" school to district policy at a critical time. Instead of "setting the stage for positive understanding of the declining enrollment problem," as recommended by the American Association of School Administrators, Calver had directly and indirectly encouraged public resistance. Circumspect in his statements at public meetings, Calver refused to justify the closing in press interviews. "Actually," he told **Suburban Life**, "closing Moses DeWitt was the farthest thing from consideration in my mind. I was surprised to hear it suggested."[4] Just as Moses DeWitt was needed at the time of centralization, it was still needed, he concluded. To parents resisting the closing, he offered neither direction nor control but advice as to how to be more effective. Certainly he had not instigated the parents' insurrection but neither had he played "a vital role in all phases of a district-wide contraction effort," as expected for one in his position.

Calver's retirement offered an opportunity to remedy this situation and redefine loyalties. "School administrators rather than teachers are the elite of the American public school system," wrote Robert A. Dahl in his study of New Haven.[5] An ambitious teacher moves into administration, seeking to obtain a "school of his own" as principal.[6] But loyalty to this school and its parents and teachers should not supersede a principal's commitment to "the system" and to his superiors in the central office. To insure dedication to the district as a whole, Jamesville-DeWitt administrators decided to move against the feudal baronies that had developed in the elementary schools.

Through many years Calver had resisted the central office's directives, but he was not alone in developing political independence. In Jamesville, too, a much younger principal had created a network of community support that made him equally confident that he knew and controlled "his" school. A resident of Jamesville, principal Dr. Robert T. Catney organized the summer recreation program there, led Catholic Youth Organization basketball, and helped establish a senior citizens' room and a historical museum within the elementary school. Active in church and civic affairs, Catney showed a willingness to resist central administrators.

When administrators first proposed to Catney that he accept the vacancy at Moses DeWitt, he declined to leave his fiefdom in Jamesville. Catney's refusal led to a decision to transfer all principals, thus affecting each of the four schools. The change will work to "help bring the district together as a whole, rather than having a district of individual schools," explained curriculum coordinator Osborn.[7] Although Catney had criticized Moses DeWitt Parents for "threatening" the district with the prospect of a budget defeat, he now began to orchestrate his own parents' group in resistance to district policy.

At the board of education meeting following public announcement of the principals' transfers, Jamesville residents presented a petition of 703 signatures asking that Dr. Catney's transfer be reconsidered. Again, strong local attachments and loyalties within "individual schools" showed themselves. Acting with Catney's knowledge, a Jamesville spokesman criticized the board for "implementing policy changes without notifying the public," and wondered aloud if the board had "learned its lesson since the Moses DeWitt issue."[8] Jamesville residents had responded to news of Catney's transfer with "shock, disappointment, disbelief, and utter frustration."[9] After completing paeans to Dr. Catney for both educational and community leadership, the Jamesville spokesman assured the board that residents would make no demands. Nor would they challenge the board's decision, he said, implicitly drawing a comparison between Jamesville residents and those from Moses DeWitt. Instead, "we urge that the transfers be reconsidered."[10]

After several minutes discussion, the board thanked the Jamesville residents and upheld the transfer of principals. Superintendent Baker explained to dis-gruntled Jamesville residents that all principals were being shifted, rather than one or two, "to make every area nervous...."[11] Parents in each school now had a new, unknown administrator, not a familiar advocate of their interests. Whatever their private reservations, principals accepted the changes. Transferred to Moses DeWitt after twenty years as principal at Genesee Hills, Pauline Clair admitted that she was anticipating her own retirement. Nevertheless, Clair remarked--despite evidence to the contrary--"In this district, unlike others, it really doesn't matter where you're working." She then added, "The moves also show that no one is tied down to a brick building," the goal that administrators had in planning the transfers.[12]

Having accomplished a shuffle of principals, the school district moved ahead to the much-delayed report on the validated census. Although census figures had been available for six weeks, administrators had safeguarded the information until the budget had passed and the new principals had taken charge. Only when they had strengthened their own position did administrators permit renewed discussion of the census. Even on the day of the board's meeting, Baker told the press, "We're not releasing anything until the meeting. SRC will be there to explain it."[13]

Figures finally released by the district were "quite close to the census data provided by the Moses DeWitt Parents' Group," a local reporter observed.[14] (See Figure 8.) After a six-month interlude and an expenditure of $7,000, the official census confirmed the report made by parents in January.[15] While the parents had found 102 infants in the 0-1 age-group, the new "validated" census found 103; Moses DeWitt parents had actually undercounted the children between 1 and 2, finding 100 in contrast to the new census report's figure of 106. The original district census had counted **only** 35 babies between 0-1, and 56 between 1-2, and parents had effectively exploited these errors. Although discrepancies certainly did not offset declining enrollment, administraors saw it demonstrated that "one inaccurate statistic will cast doubt on all others."[16] Because of this, school officials had attempted to withdraw the subject from discussion during the many months spent on official census figures "given a 98 per cent accuracy rating by Price-Waterhouse,"--figures virtually identical to those that parents had collected in four days.

During the protracted consideration of the census, both school officials and residents became more concerned with the accuracy of their numbers than with the significance of these numbers. As the school district refused to confirm their census report, parents grew adamant about its importance. Knowing that the district's first census had seriously undercounted children 0-2, some parents expected the schools to be filled, if not overflowing, within several years. Seeking to sidestep errors that allowed both board members and citizens to question their "professional expertise," administrators insisted that Jamesville-DeWitt **did** have declining enrollment, "And you better

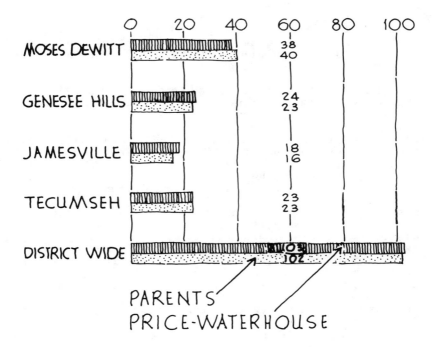

PARENTS
PRICE-WATERHOUSE

COMPARISON OF PARENTS'
& PRICE-WATERHOUSE 1978
SURVEYS OF PROJECTED 1982
KINDERGARTEN ENROLLMENT

**FIGURE 8**

believe it, kids!" Baker exclaimed to one group of Moses DeWitt parents in a rare display of exasperation.[17] Administrators compared the sizes of the entering kindergarten class and the graduating high school class, and in the fall drew satisfaction that enrollment projections made in June were "right on the mark" for September opening-day figures.[18]

But these officials failed to explain that the whole system--not simply elementary schools--would sharply contract in the next decade. Following the administration's lead, board members predictably associated declining enrollment and elementary-school closing. At the board's July meeting, however, the Syracuse Research Corporation social scientist called upon to "explain" the census figures and projections observed that the birth rate had remained constant in the years between 1973 and 1977. Kindergarten class-size was expected to remain at about 150, instead of plummeting to 90 pupils in 1981 and then to 35 in 1982, as district officials had first forecast. Disregarding even the new census figures, SRC researcher Robert Dinkelmeyer turned to county health department records of live births and related birth totals to kindergarten enrollment five years later. Studying this comparison over several years, Dinkelmeyer found the kindergarten enrollment figure slightly higher than the birth total. By multiplying the birth total by 1.04--to account for children moving into the district--he produced an enrollment projection qute different from that presented at the "information meetings" preceding the closing of Moses DeWitt.

Dinkelmeyer's techniques showed 1981 and 1982 kindergarten classes far exceeding the figures cited in December. Furthermore, his projections were above the numbers of around 100, as reported in the "98 per cent accurate" verified census. Explaining his method the SRC researcher said, "It's a relatively simple technique, but it's widely accepted."[19] Although the American Association of School Administrators outlined this approach as a standard technique, Jamesville-DeWitt officials had used their own rule-of-thumb system whereby they saw a 300 per cent increase between the number of children counted in the 0-1 age bracket and the number ready to enter kindergarten five years later. When they realized that this increase no longer held true --indeed it never did--they mistakenly expected elementary-school enrollment to drop precipitously. But instead of the expected depletion of young children,

126

SRC projections showed elementary "enrollment leveling off in the next few years."[20]

"Watching the presentation of the long-awaited Jamesville-DeWitt census results was not unlike waiting breathlessly to hear the announcement of a Miss America Beauty Pageant or an Oscar for Best Motion Picture of the Year," ran a headline in the weekly suburban paper.[21] If so, the presentation drew little comment from board members or administrators. "The board will determine at a later time how we will use this information," said board president Perkins. Superintendent Baker struck the same attitude. "We're digesting the information now," he said, adding incongruously--considering the long delay in releasing the report--"At this point, there's nothing that can be said."[22]

The 150 residents in the room were not to hear either board members or administrators explore the "long-awaited" census results. At this meeting as at others, those residents who spoke merely entered their opinions in the public record. Rarely did public comment stimulate discussion by board members. Just as Jamesville residents had gone unanswered in their appeal to keep their principal, so did Moses DeWitt parents who sought confirmation or at least discussion of their efforts on the census.

SRC researcher Dinkelmeyer, rather than Jamesville-DeWitt officeholders, weakly fielded questions on the census and projections. Clearly surprised by the board's request that he address the public, Dinkelmeyer showed hesitancy but at least saved board members and administrators from facing their critics. As some Moses DeWitt parents found satisfaction in the forecast of kindergarten class-size, others assailed the "theoretical assumptions" in the SRC projections, describing them as "fraught with future errors."[23] Unprepared, as he later admitted, for the intensity of public interest in the question, Dinkelmeyer conceded that he was "unsure of what level of accuracy I'd give to these predictions." The next day Baker told the press that the school district planned "to get the state education department to look at" some of the new enrollment information, a step that if taken produced no public results.[24] Periodically, the superintendent referred to the state education department as a source of information and advice, a tactic giving an appearance of professionalism and diverting attention from local issues. Rarely, however, did he report on data supposedly gathered. In the case of the census the impact of the new report was muffled, just as administrators desired.

The only acknowledgment of public interest generated by the closing issue came when board members Coit and Mallan proposed that the board of education devote its second meeting of the month to "communication with the public." In this second meeting the board agreed to abandon its usual lengthy agenda, whereby residents were barred from speaking until after adjournment. In the "communications" meeting residents could offer comments and questions in the course of an informal board session. Coit and Mallan thought these sessions could provide for a better exchange of opinion and relieve public frustration with the board's approach to decision-making.

Other board members had their own idea of how the public might be redirected toward the goal of school-closing. At a study session early in the summer board members had seen a "30-minute color and sound film strip on declining enrollment" produced by the American Association of School Administrators to accompany its booklet on the same subject. Again they heard that "the establishment of a Task Force of lay citizens as an advisory group is an essential ingredient of any school closing effort." Of course, Jamesville-DeWitt had already tried a task force, but a second effort might demonstrate board members' open-mindedness and at the same time help guide parents by involving them in the forthcoming decision.

At a study session on July 31, Perkins--newly elected to her second term as board president--proposed the establishment of four committees to study declining enrollments and "how to cope with them."[25] In the following three meetings Perkins took the lead in designating the committees, their composition and objectives. She first outlined the four committees: demographic, to study the new census report, "update" the original Task Force Report, and examine mobility in the school district; planning, to reach long-range predictions based on a study of new building and projections made by town and county planning agencies; facilities and program, to "update" the information on available space in the schools--a question that had been disputed in the original closing effort--and possibly examine "alternatives to the present curriculum;" and lastly, finance, to examine the local economy and school district budgeting.[26]

Not only did Perkins have the committees' purposes in mind, she had a plan for choosing their members. Two board members were to chair each committee, which would also include two administrators, two faculty members, and a member designated by each of the six parent-teacher organizations in the school district. "The way in which the committees are composed gives the community an opportunity for increased input," said Perkins.[27] According to her plan, board members and administrators were to direct public "input," also assuring that the four committees worked together instead of acting "as isolated units." Perkins depicted the possible closing of Moses DeWitt, or any school, as a mutual problem for board members, administrators, teachers, and parents. This way "we can reach a decision that is best for the entire district."[28]

Having chaired the committee to establish the first Task Force, Perkins intended to guard against unexpected criticism or delay. She wanted goals, procedures, and dates to be clearly established from the outset. The four committees had the assigned task of "reviewing and updating data gathered by the Task Force; reexamining a school closing and/or alternatives, including educational impact upon students, emotional impact upon the community, and fiscal impact upon the budget," and, lastly, revising "the five-year plan of the District in accordance with state mandates," said a memorandum dated August 29. The committees' first meeting was scheduled for September; by January their assignment was due. The board expected the committees' reports by January 8, to reach a decision in February.

Board members asked few questions about the Perkins plan, although Mallan found that the January deadline "leaves little time to discuss and synthesize information." Always the board's advocate of philosophical discussion, Mallan wanted the closing issue to spark a review of program, too. "Are we overlooking a chance to spread our wings a little bit?"[29] Other board members disagreed. Carmen proposed that curriculum and program be distinguished in committee discussions. "Curriculum is a way of delivering program," she explained. Hopkins, who with Carmen was to co-chair the facilities and program committee, agreed, "Yes, we have guaranteed that closing a building will not affect programs. That was one of our commitments." Carmen then reiterated her opinion that "people want quality. People will pay for value received, not empty seats." DeBottis drew a different conclusion, saying that people liked the district's quality and the committee should indicate "what the community out there is willing to spend." Coit asked about the effect of committee reports that answered "maybe" to the question of school-closing. But those board members most committed to school-closing felt certain that the new study committees would lead to this end.[30]

Members of the community at first drew the same conclusion. "Are we to hear the words 'Task Force' in perpetuity?" asked one irate resident who lived behind Moses DeWitt. Further questioning board president Perkins, this parent asked, "How independent will the community members be of the administrators serving on these committees? Where will the public be in this hierarchy? Will this arrangement give full vocalization to community response?" Board president Perkins assured parents that they would indeed have "input."[31]

In this and other instances board members and administrators publicly emphasized the importance of parents' involvement, while privately grumbling about the problems created by meddlesome or wayward individuals. According to James D. Koerner, "the most persistent piety about local control of education is that it gives parents a direct and active role in management of their schools."[32] In this author's judgment, ninety-five per cent of parents with children in public schools have "never tried to make a single change in the local schools." A Stanford University study further noted that many voters actually "despair of their own ability to do anything" about schools.[33]

By turning to the district's six parent groups as a source of public opinion, board members now felt doubly reassured. Most parents in Jamesville-DeWitt were not "troublemakers." Indeed, in the opinion of one board member, parents in school areas other than Moses DeWitt were "nice people." They preferred to support board decisions, or in any event did not relish quarrels with authority. Furthermore, each school now had an administrator removed from familiar associations and committed to the district as a whole. Under the principal's direction the PTA could be expected to function "as a creature of the local administration." In normal times, wrote Koerner, the PTA is "chiefly useful to the administration for raising money for special projects and persuading parents who are interested enough to attend meetings that the local

130

schools are in the front ranks of American education."[34] In establishing committees consisting of board members, administrators, and parent-group representatives, Perkins did not solicit divergent viewpoints.

Moses DeWitt parents, however, saw an invaluable opportunity to advance their case once more. The new study committees offered a way of restating the issues and perhaps shifting the focus from Moses Dewitt. Even the board's formal guidelines to committee members called for reexamination of school-closing **and/or** alternatives. And committee members were specifically asked to consider a policy's "emotional impact upon the community." The new committee reports would provide the basis for board discussion and action, just as the first Task Force Report had set the stage for the original closing decision.

Realizing their stake in the four committees, executive officers of the Moses DeWitt Parents' Group carefully considered their prospective appointees. These committee members were not only to participate in sessions but to shape the views of others, significantly influencing--if not writing--the final reports. Thus, the appointees had to be knowledgeable, committed, and willing to work. In making the appointments, Moses DeWitt officers turned to themselves for two of the committees. To the demographic committee they named Jean Stinchcombe. After the successful attack on the district's census, she had developed an interest in enrollment projections and demographic trends in Jamesville-DeWitt. Appointed to the planning committee was John H. Fennessey, co-president of the Moses DeWitt Parents' Group. A founder and partner in an upstate planning and development firm, Fennessey held a master's degree in planning as well as membership in the American Institute of Planners. For the finance committee, Moses DeWitt parents recruited James Carroll, a political scientist and lawyer who directed the program in public administration at the Maxwell School, Syracuse University. The fourth appointment, to the facilities and program committee, was John E. Hayes, Jr., president of a laboratory supply company and an engineer who held a master's degree in operations research.

Fennessey and Stinchcombe had played leading parts in the Moses DeWitt resistance from its inception, while Carroll and Hayes had taken an active interest. Carroll, for example, had attended the informal session that Moses DeWitt parents held with board members before

131

the formal presentation made in January 1978. At this informal meeting, Carroll had challenged the financial and enrollment data that the board had used in reaching the closing decision. A resident of the DeWittshire neighborhood behind Moses DeWitt, Hayes had also attended board meetings, taking an increasing role in the summer of 1978, when the superintendent first told him that the deferred school-closing would have saved only $70,000.

In September Perkins called together all forty-eight committee members. She instructed the new appointees that their goal was to be "an honest, objective appraisal of all facets of the subject." Committee members received deadlines for their work, so that the board could act in February, to make any changes effective for the coming September. Periodically the committees were to report back to the board for discussion of their findings to date.[35]

Moses DeWitt parents wondered if Perkins' planning would permit their take-over of the committees. The board president was clearly determined to mastermind the process that Moses DeWitt supporters also wanted to turn to their own ends. At first the Perkins direction held. In October the board of education refused to allow the demographic committee to be chaired by two parents after board members Coit and Luchsinger desired to relinquish this role.

Despite Perkins' determination other board members showed less zeal about committees. Accustomed to accepting rather than providing direction, they usually waited for administrators to supply information. For most board members the study committees offered no exception to this practice. Only in rare instances did board members contest the administrative pattern of "oligarchic control."

Early in the committees' deliberations, teachers' participation diminished and virtually ended. In return for high salaries and benefits, Jamesville-DeWitt teachers had foregone a union, or any public role. Only a few teachers, usually residents of the district, had the temerity to take an active part in any public meeting. Most had little desire to enter into a potential controversy with their employers. "As bureaucrats," wrote Martin, teachers "close ranks behind the superintendent for the furtherance of educational policy and the solidification of public school doctrine."[36]

132

Likewise, only a minority of representatives appointed by parent-groups other than Moses DeWitt showed sustained interest. Despite some noteworthy exceptions, most appointees from other schools did not have sufficient motivation to study the question of school closing and/or alternatives. If a school were closed, they did not expect it to be theirs. The day after the board voted to defer the closing decision, Perkins had said to the press, "If an elementary school is closed, there is no reason to believe it would not be Moses DeWitt."[37] Other board members' opinions were equally well known.

Thus, instead of 48 members only a few board members, administrators, teachers, and parents remained to participate in the second task force. But this time public representation did not come primarily from safe PTG leaders and school supporters but from Moses DeWitt partisans, who in the eyes of board president Perkins had practiced intimidation and coercion, and, in Superintendent Baker's opinion, meant "big trouble."


**NOTES**

1. Roscoe C. Martin, **Government and the Suburban School**—(Syracuse, 1962), 100.
2. **Ibid.**, 99.
3. Katherine Eisenberger and William F. Keough, **Declining Enrollment: What to Do**(Arlington, 1974), 29.
4. **Ibid.**; **Suburban Life** (DeWitt and East Syracuse), Apr. 12, 1978.
5. Robert A. Dahl, **Who Governs?**(New Haven, 1964), 152.
6. **Ibid.**
7. **Post—Standard**(Syracuse), July 20, 1978.
8. **Suburban Life**, July 19, 1978.
9. **Post—Standard**(Syracuse), July 20, 1978.
10. **Ibid.**
11. **Suburban Life**, July 19, 1978.
12. **Ibid.**
13. **Herald—Journal**(Syracuse), July 17, 1978.
14. **Post—Standard**, July 20, 1978.
15. Expenditures discussed at the Jamesville—DeWitt Board of Education meeting, Mar. 13, 1978.
16. William F. Keough, Jr., "Declining Enrollment: The Dilemma from the Superintendent's Chair," in Susan Abramowitz and Stuart

Rosenfeld, eds., **Declining Enrollments: The Challenge of the Coming Decade**(Washington, D.C., 1978), 363.

17. Jamesville-DeWitt Board of Education meeting, Feb. 13, 1978, author's notes.

18. **Suburban Life**, Sept. 27, 1978.

19. **Post-Standard**, July 20, 1978.

20. **Ibid.**

21. **Suburban Life**, July 19, 1978.

22. **Herald-Journal**, July 18, 1978.

23. **Suburban Life**, July 19, 1978.

24. **Herald-Journal**, July 18, 1978.

25. **Suburban Life**, Aug. 2, 1978.

26. **Ibid.**

27. **Post-Standard**, Aug. 3, 1978.

28. **Ibid.**

29. **Ibid.**

30. Jamesville-DeWitt Board of Education meeting, Aug. 28, 1978, author's notes.

31. **Ibid.**

32. James D. Koerner, **Who Controls American Education?** (Boston, 1968), 146.

33. Richard F. Carter, **Voters and Their Schools**(Palo Alto, 1960), 135.

34. Koerner, **Who Controls American Education?**, 148.

35. Jamesville-DeWitt Board of Education meeting, Sept. 18, 1978.

36. Martin, **Government and the Suburban School**, 62.

37. **Post-Standard**, Jan. 10, 1978.

# IX. New Reports and a New Policy

The committees met throughout the fall, making periodic progress reports to the board. A number of weeks passed before any direction became evident. Members of the planning committee "are just trying to get a data base so we can decide what questions we should be asking," said Mallan in late September.[1] The facilities and program committee conducted tours of all six buildings to enable committee members to list "those rooms used for academic purposes." Committee members were looking for "surplus space," according to Co-Chairman Hopkins. The study of room-use delayed consideration of that committee's second objective, "to review a sampling of programs at all grade levels." In September the finance committee broke into subcommittees, as a graduate student in public administration began an analysis of the school district budget under the direction of Professor James Carroll, a Moses DeWitt committee member. The demographic committee concentrated on different ways of projecting enrollment and studying residential mobility.

By mid-fall the finance committee had identified various options before the board. The committee listed a number of possibilities, the first being to close one or two elementary schools. Or the board might consider closing two elementary schools and placing the fifth grade in the middle school. Other choices involved more sweeping changes in the schools and grade organization. One such change would be closing all elementary schools and placing grades K-6 in the middle school and grades 7-12 in the high school. Another drastic change called for closing the middle school and moving the sixth and possibly seventh grades into the elementary schools, while shifting the eighth grade to the high school. If the board wanted to avoid school-closings or reorganization, it could examine and possibly cut programs not mandated by the state, or it could cut the budget "five per cent across the board." Lastly, the board could leave the system as it was.

The finance committee next reported to the board on the costs of operating each building, citing utility, custodial, and non-instructional costs by school. These figures showed the middle school to be the most costly on a per-student basis. In its next statement the committee offered an analysis of instructional costs by school, costs that included primarily salaries and small amounts for supplies. Again, the cost per student was highest at the middle school, according to finance committee figures. Among the four elementary schools, the cost per student was lowest at Moses DeWitt. Instructional costs and fringe benefits made up seventy-five per cent of the district's budget, reported board member Cargian.

In November the finance committee advised the board that some of the choices mentioned would not be feasible in the coming year. Because of projected enrollment and "school capacity limitations," in 1979 the board could close one elementary school, eliminate or cut programs, or plan to reorganize school facilities in 1981-1982, when enrollment would allow greater flexibility. In two more years the board could make a more thorough reorganization than simply closing a school. The finance committee decided to make no recommendation concerning the different options from which the board would choose. As the committee's chairman, Cargian observed that the "board was not excited about postponing the decision."

The demographic committee also offered detailed reports to the school board during the fall. In October and November committee members reported on the location of the district's elementary and pre-school children and presented enrollment projections for the next five- and ten-year periods. (See Figure 9.) The committee developed different methods to project student enrollment. One method used the number of live births and cohort-survival, or the ratio of children retained in a class from year to year. The other used a regression curve. The two different methods produced enrollment projections that were almost identical for a five-year period.

Addressing the board, committee member Jean Stinchcombe explained that "looking at live births is a simple, sound way of anticipating what later kindergarten enrollment will be,"--a more accurate approach than a census of pre-school children.[2] A comparison of birth figures and kindergarten enrollment over six years showed a slight increase from families moving into the school district. But once a group entered school, its size remained about the same.

Stinchcombe presented projections showing elementary enrollment dipping to below 1,000 by the year 1982, and then remaining level during a period in which middle

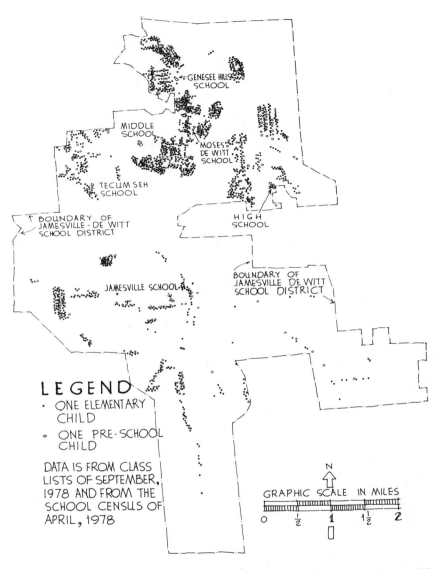

LEGEND

· ONE ELEMENTARY CHILD

○ ONE PRE-SCHOOL CHILD

DATA IS FROM CLASS LISTS OF SEPTEMBER, 1978 AND FROM THE SCHOOL CENSUS OF APRIL, 1978

GRAPHIC SCALE IN MILES

0    ½    1    1½    2

LOCATION OF ELEMENTARY AND PRE-SCHOOL CHILDREN IN 1978

FIGURE 9

137

and high school enrollments would drop markedly, as
smaller birth groups moved into these levels of school.
The middle school would drop from 761 students in 1979-
1980 to 473 in 1987-1989, while the high school would
decline during this period from 1,344 to 782, according
to these projections.

Also speaking to the board for the demographic
committee was Philip Schuls, an engineer appointed by the
Genesee Hills Parent-Teacher Group. Instead of
continuing to dispute the district's census and past
projections, members of the demographic committee had
reached an understanding of enrollment trends after
lengthy discussion of different forecasting methods.
Schuls explained several mathematical models for
projecting enrollment, describing the exponential curve
as the most satisfactory. When the live-birth
projections are superimposed on exponential regression
curves, "the result agrees very well."

A critic of the board's decision-making in 1977,
Schuls then observed that "the interpretation of data is
more important than the data itself." If enrollment
decline persists, the school district may reach a point
at which it must close a school. This point may not be
reached for several years, or at all. In the meantime
the demographic committee and the board of education
should decide what future level of elementary enrollment
would lead to a school-closing. The community would
then be informed that if and when a "critical enrollment"
is reached, a school should be closed.[3] The board
received this suggestion silently.

During the fall the facilities and program
committee offered little beyond a report that members had
toured school buildings. Even these tours were
inconclusive, because "we found that each group saw a
different view of the subject building," reported
committee co-chairman Hopkins.[4] Board member Carmen,
who also served as co-chairman, stated that the committee
planned to focus on the size of school grounds, use of
rooms, maintenance costs, and renovations necessary for
the handicapped.[5]

Hopkins said that the facilities and program
committee also intended to list mandated and nonmandated
programs to indicate the district's offerings above and
beyond state requirements. When questioned by residents
about a further examination of program, most board
members faild to see this as part of the committee's

charge, its title to the contrary.  In November a listing of "surplus" rooms in each school failed to draw public acceptance or even agreement within the committee.

Board member Mallan told his colleagues that the planning committee was holding meetings with local planners and bankers.  As a result of these conversations, Mallan could foresee "no substantial changes that would influence the number of children in the community."[6]

Initial committee reports did not contradict the board's, or the community's, assumption that a school would be closed.  Headlines such as "Reports Indicate Future Closing at J-D," "School Closing Feasible," and "J-D Board Told Possible Effects If School Closed" pointed in the direction of what many considered inevitable.  Moses DeWitt parents hoped at most to persuade the board to re-examine its rationale for selecting their school.  If board members publicly discussed the criteria for closing schools, perhaps a different outcome would result.

During meetings in the fall, however, board members offered few comments on any of the possibilities before them.  Alternatives such as closing all elementary schools and placing these grades in the middle school, or closing the middle school and enlarging the elementary schools never became a topic of board discussion.  Business as usual continued, as board members heard auditor's reports and comments on the school year's usual activities.  Even board members' reports from their committees often emphasized mundane rather than policy considerations.  In successive meetings in October and November, for example, board member Mallan described a tour of the bus garage and extolled the fine staff and quality of work done there.   Thus even when charged with reaching important decisions, the Jamesville-DeWitt Board of Education showed what one scholar called "the customary failure to distinguish between fundamental policy and housekeeping details."[7] In Koerner's judgment, "school boards typically get bogged down in trivia and leave the most important decisions to somebody else, most often to the superintendent of schools."

In Jamesville-DeWitt, however, reconsideration of school-closing and alternatives involved more than board members and administrators.  By mid-December the four committees began preparation of their final reports.

The finance committee approved and submitted to the board an eighteen-page document drafted by Professor Carroll's graduate student. The report did not concentrate on school-closing. To the contrary, the finance committee found that "there appears to be no compelling financial consideration which suggests that closing a school is the best way to reduce expenditures."[8] Instead, the report emphasized the "great potential" for reducing expenditures by eliminating or cutting non-mandated programs. In 1979 the school district allotted close to a million and a half dollars, or 12 per cent of the budget, to programs not mandated by the state or above the level required by the state. Such areas included guidance counseling and foreign languages in the middle school and different levels of course offerings in language, art, music, industrial arts, and business at the high school. The report noted that the reduction of counseling at the middle school could save as much as $100,000 a year and still meet state requirements.[9]

The finance commmittee found it impossible to attach any definitive figure to the cost savings of school-closing. Instructional costs "will not be significantly altered due to a school closing," the report noted. Moreover, unless an empty building is rented, "additional expenditures for maintenance, security, and closing preparations will be incurred."[10] If the closed building were not sold or rented, the school district could achieve only minor savings from heat, light, and reduction in salaries for administrators, custodians, and secretary. Robert I. Rotberg described such reductions as "trivial savings" in his consideration of school-closing in Lexington, Massachusetts.[11] In Jamesville-DeWitt, the assistant superintendent for finance estimated in 1978-1979 that a school closing would save between $70,000-$80,000.[12]

The finance committee examined evidence from other school districts that supported this conclusion. In a survey of school-closings Richard L. Andrews found that a majority of districts found no savings, or even increased costs in closing a school.[13] The finance report referred to indirect costs incurred at the time of closing, such as expenditures for moving, scheduling new bus routes, and revising school assignments. The report explicitly noted that another indirect cost--"the financial impact on neighborhoods or the community as a result of school-closing"--was not analyzed.

The finance committee forecast a budget increase of

about three-quarters of a million dollars, or a tax increase of $6.50 per thousand dollars of assessed valuation if the board were to take no action. The cost savings of a school-closing would not offset the projected budget increase in any case.

The demographic committee offered an analysis of the closing question and a recommendation as to how to deal with it in the future. The committee concluded that no school should be closed until elementary enrollment dropped below 1,000 students, possibly in 1982 or 1983. The committee adopted an 85 per cent utilization figure as a cut-off mark for closing. The 85 per cent utilization figure provided a safe margin for errors in projecting enrollment, in addition to guaranteeing a class size of 22 and the continuation of program rooms for art, music, reading, and other purposes "now currently accepted" in Jamesville-DeWitt. The demographic committee recommended that "the preferred course of action is to wait until enrollment declines to 990, the capacity that can be accommodated in 3 elementary schools. When that occurs an elementary school shall be automatically closed."[15] The report added that the choice of which school to close is the prerogative of the board of education.

The demographic committee not only attempted to establish generally-accepted enrollment projections, it set forth a standard of enrollment capacity, based on the number of buildings, classrooms, and special rooms necessary to preserve the program offered in the existing four schools. Led by board members Luchsinger and Coit, the committee defined a point at which a school could be closed with no loss of program rooms or increase in class size. Because it considered both enrollment and capacity, the demographic committee readily agreed that it was "premature to reorganize into three elementary school buildings in 1979." Nevertheless, the question of closing could be expected to arise in the future. Having a clearly-defined formula to answer questions about class size, enrollment, program, and flexibility would not only save the board from again facing these issues but prepare the community for an eventual closing.

The voluminous demographic report also took into account other considerations, such as the age and number of children of incoming residents, potential real estate development, and increasing numbers of children in a recently-renovated apartment complex. Acknowledging the difficulties of closing, one part of the report

141

Photograph 2. Board member **John F. Luchsinger, Jr.**, co-chaired the demographic committee with Carolyn Coit; they recommended that a school be closed when elementary enrollment fell below 1,000.

stated, "Preserving the sense of community and the constituency for the schools' future welfare is as important as any other consideration." Instead of risking a repetition of the experiences of 1977-1978, Coit and Luchsinger took the board a recommendation that summarized the committee's findings and offered a basis for future policy.[16]

The facilities and program committee shared the demographic committee's conclusion that a school-closing was premature in 1979. Board members Hopkins and Carmen acquiesced in a statement of committee "consensus" recommending that all schools stay open but later opposed this position. The committee agreed that each school should have a separate room for art, music, and remedial reading, and it found "a multi-purpose room for educational support in each building very desirable." This committee also urged an average class-size of 22. If the board adopted these standards, the district would be very close to 100 per cent utilization if a school were closed in 1979. Surplus space would consist of only one-half a classroom.[17]

The planning committee made no specific recommendation on school-closing, but it noted an area for potential development in Jamesville that could eventually add 350 houses. Because of the availability of public utilities and an accessible site, the proposed residential tract could bring new families into the school district, although development might be delayed by "insufficient demand." Except for the Jamesville area, the planning report observed that land available in the school district for housing is "limited and quite expensive." But the committee cited a local real estate authority's statement that "potential buyers in Jamesville-DeWitt are willing to spend $10,000-$15,000 more for a home than elsewhere largely due to the desirability of the school district."[18]

When the reports were officially presented to the board of education on January 8, 1979, residents learned that none of the four committees recommended closing a school in 1979. As hoped, Moses Dewitt committee members influenced the reports, but board members and representatives from other schools had joined in reaching a consensus. Having established the committees for the purpose of settling the school-closing question, board president Perkins expressed her displeasure. "I am personally disappointed in the effectiveness of the committees," she told the audience. Furthermore, in

143

her opinion, many members of all four committees lacked "objectivity and cooperation," and some had failed to attend meetings.[19] She criticized the lack of commitment by some committee members, particularly in comparison to the participation in the Task Force, created under her direction in 1976. The second try at the task force had clearly failed. The board president alleged that the four committees had lacked leadership, although board members served as their co-chairmen. Rather than blaming her colleagues for the unsatisfactory reports, Perkins took responsibility for inadequate leadership, explaining that she had "tried not to interfere" in the committees' work.

Perkins then reviewed past history to justify her position. The decision to close Moses DeWitt had been based on data and commitment to educational program. The board had a standing motion to close Moses DeWitt, which had been deferred. Now it was time to settle the question in what the board president hoped would be a unanimous decision. Perkins explained that the final vote on whether to close Moses DeWitt could come within the next four scheduled meetings, leaving no doubt that her focus had not changed during the previous six months of committee work.

At its next meeting the board attempted to discuss four committee reports. Was it now premature to close a school in 1979, when the board had voted 7-2 to close Moses DeWitt in December 1977? Mallan said that he found no problem in closing, for "you look at the elementary decline, and you see it is there." But could the three remaining schools accommodate the children? Administrators, as well as some board members, had changed their view of capacity and surplus space. In 1977 the administration had referred to twenty-two extra classrooms. When residents and committee members insisted that the so-called surplus space served an educational purpose, administrators agreed. In the fall of 1978 administrators assured the public that whatever the reorganization, elementary schools would continue to have program rooms for art, music, and reading, and in at least two schools a resource room for special purposes. In 1977, by contrast, administrators had never publicly discussed how art, music, reading, and other special programs would be affected by moving from four to three elementary schools.

Mallan did not see space or program rooms as a problem. For him closing was a question of "are we going

144

to bite the bullet or not?" Coit and Luchsinger acknowledged declining enrollment but asked that the board establish the number of children at which a school can be effectively closed. Coit thought this approach served to prepare the community and avoid the emotion of naming a school, as Luchsinger had agreed in drafting the demographic report. Even Scibilia, who himself attended Moses DeWitt, agreed that a formula for automatic closing meant that "if a school closes, it is Moses DeWitt." Other board members gave little attention to an enrollment threshold or the value of an already-designated school for closing, perhaps because they expected to accomplish the closing of Moses DeWitt without waiting. Mallan thought that an enrollment cut-off simply served "to keep the pressure on," and it would be better to keep the closing "clean."[20]

Moses DeWitt principal Pauline Clair, however, supported the demographic committee's recommendation. Once an exponent of closing, the veteran administrator regarded the issue more cautionsly after six months as principal at Moses DeWitt. "It is my opinion that all elementary schools should remain open until we reach a student population of 1,000," she wrote the board. If Moses DeWitt were closed, Genesee Hills, where she had served as principal for twenty years, would be at almost 100 per cent capacity and have a class size larger than that suggested for the district. Now approaching retirement, Clair alone among Jamesville-DeWitt principals made her opinion public.[21]

Coit again joined the issue when she, too, asked that the board not jeopardize class size or prematurely "jam" children into three schools, a statement that drew an angry retort from Mallan. Mallan also disputed Superintendent Baker's comment that residents should not look for significant savings in school-closing. The money saved could be used to improve program, argued Mallan. Perkins opposed any reduction in nonmandated programs as recommended by the finance committee, saying that she had been on record for more than a year as opposed to any proposal to "scrap" programs to save a facility.[22]

When the board opened the meeting to discussion from the floor, some of the 125 residents, largely Moses DeWitt parents, asked why it was necessary to close a school. "How can you be planning to do this? How can the board inflict a substantial amount of pain on a group of citizens who obviously don't want their school closed?" asked finance committee member Carroll. "I

145

don't see political logic, and I don't see financial logic, and I don't see educational logic."[23] Because the budget had passed by a two-thirds vote in June, residents repeatedly questioned the urgency of saving money by a measure that could alienate community support.

Superintendent Baker explained that a closing was first considered as a way of cutting costs after the budget passed only narrowly in two successive years. A school-closing that saved between $70,000 and $100,000 could mean between $1.50 and $2.00 per $1,000 assessed valuation. "You people are willing to spend that. Okay, you're telling us that, and we're listening," said board member DeBottis. Luchsinger agreed, saying that support for the budget meant that the board could take "at least another year" to look into the problem. Coit thought "we can afford the time" to seek a "creative solution," a viewpoint disputed by Mallan and Perkins, who believed enough time had been spent. Finally, in reply to a direct question from a Moses DeWitt parent, Superintendent Baker said that he favored keeping all schools open, provided the district could pay for this.[24]

Other residents continued to question the board's long-range policy. "The Jamesville-DeWitt school district does have a serious problem which must be solved within the next five years," stated Moses DeWitt parent Donald Weiner, as he described shrinking middle and high school enrollments, underutilized elementary schools, and increasing educational costs. "The board has yet to face these issues squarely. Closing an elementary school has only a negligible impact in solving these problems," the engineering professor concluded. Demographic committee member Schuls sought in vain to stimulate further board comment on the idea of an enrollment threshold for closing. Again, a majority of board members refused to entertain the question.

After this inquiry failed, another parent urged the board to consider the four schools as more than buildings. A resident of the DeWittshire neighborhood who served on the facilities and program committee suggested that Jamesville Elementary offered an example of community involvement in a school. Jamesville's experience shows that "people can and will emotionally, intellectually, and financially identify with the school if it meets their needs."[25] Again, board members offered no comment. At the meeting's end most residents assumed that the board would soon act to close Moses DeWitt despite committee recommendations to the

146

contrary. As in the past only a few board members had exchanged views with each other or with members of the public. Of the nine members only four had indicated any willingness to delay the closing.

At the next week's meeting, however, Cargian astonished the audience by reading a prepared statement in which he said that the closing issue had been the most difficult in his nineteen years of service on the board. "After last week's meeting, I felt strongly that all schools should remain open," read Cargian, who had previously said nothing to reveal this sentiment. "At the meeting with the public, I heard more people say, 'Don't close my school,'"[26] Cargian then moved that "all six schools remain open and the issue of school closing be set aside until the quality of programs we are able to offer in Jamesville-DeWitt is seriously jeopardized." DeBottis quickly seconded the motion, which was tabled so that the board could take action at next week's meeting, now considered the date for the final decision.

Assuming that all four schools would stay open, Mallan posed some questions that "a citizen of our community and a supporter" might ask the board. Despite the recent, sustained outcry over an actual closing decision, he cited evidence from the 1977 Task Force questionnaire indicating that a majority of respondents favored elementary school closing when decline exceeds 30 per cent. Mallan further questioned whether the board had explored the value of $70,000-$100,000 in, for example, hiring five additional teachers--a suggestion at odds with his own frequent references to declining enrollment, which produces staff attrition.[27]

After the board's meeting on January 22, Jamesville-DeWitt residents realized that a new policy had taken shape. The Tecumseh Parent-Teacher Group belatedly informed its members that at recent board meetings "most of the views presented have come from parents of school children from the school slated to be closed." According to a newsletter from Tecumseh PTG officers, "the easy answer in the short run is to keep all four schools open, thus encouraging silence." The Tecumseh newsletter urged readers to contact school board members prior to next Monday's meeting.[28] During the previous year Tecumseh parents had showed complacency, expecting the board to implement the anticipated and, in their opinion, much-deserved closing of Moses DeWitt. By moving to action only on January 24,

Photograph 3. **John T. Mallan** pondered questions that might be asked of the board and wondered aloud about the "problem we are being asked to solve."

they were too late to influence policy.

Nevertheless, residents arriving at the board's fourth meeting in January still wondered if the five votes apparently behind Cargian's motion would hold. Before voting on the motion, board members had a brief exchange of views. Making one of her rare public statements of the month, Carmen wondered if sharing special teachers among four elementary schools would affect or jeopardize program, to which Cargian replied that it would not.

After recalling the original decision to close Moses DeWitt, Coit promised that she would not again vote without giving reasons. In the past year she felt that the community had reached a greater understanding of the meaning of local schools and at the same time she saw a sympathy for the "eventual loss of a building in one area." She found a willingness on the part of Moses DeWitt parents "to cooperate in what must be done, if it can be accomplished fairly, with long-range planning that assures only one move per child, no loss of program, and within the community in which they reside"--a set of conditions which few board members or administrators were willing to discuss or accept. Answering Tecumseh critics who urged an immediate closing, she stood by the board's original designation of Moses DeWitt but reiterated her belief that the district should not crowd a building or jeopardize class size by a premature closing.[29]

Reacting to Coit's remarks, Carmen argued that by closing a school the district could produce more class sections per grade and, hence, smaller classes, a point not supported by either of the redistricting plans to be implemented in the event that Moses DeWitt closed. Board member Mallan wondered aloud "what the problem was" in closing a school. He did not expect a school-closing to add considerably to bus travel, to cause "massive" overcrowding, to hurt teacher-parent communications, or to reduce the program's quality. "What is the problem we are being asked to solve?" asked Mallan, apparently mystified.[30]

"The problem is the community--They don't want the school closed!" answered board member DeBottis as a standing-room audience of 200 applauded and cheered.[31] Luchsinger remarked that three of the four committee reports favored keeping all schools open and no report contained "negative comments" on this policy. Scibilia

Photograph 4.  **Carolyn Coit** thought the public accepted
the "eventual loss of a building in one area."  She saw
Moses DeWitt parents as willing to cooperate in school-
closing if it was "accomplished fairly."

supported Cargian's motion, adding that he had also liked the idea of an enrollment cut-off.[32]

Hopkins countered that he had heard from people who wanted to close a school right away. Perkins also argued that many residents wanted to close a school but hesitated to come forth at a meeting where such a viewpoint would be at odds with Moses DeWitt residents. Again evoking the image of intimidation that she used the previous January in depicting Moses DeWitt activities, she referred to people who were "afraid to speak up at meetings" and instead called her. Perkins concluded that althought $70,000 might not look like much to some, it was a great savings to others.[33]

The board then voted 5-4 to keep all schools open until programs were "jeopardized." Two Jamesville representatives, DeBottis and Cargian, two Moses DeWitt supporters, Scibilia and Luchsinger, and Tecumseh board member Coit made a new alliance. Despite her call only weeks earlier for a unanimous decision, board president Perkins did not cast her vote for the new policy. Nor did Carmen, Hopkins, or Mallan. The Moses DeWitt minority that had drawn criticism for its refusal to "go along" with the 1977 decision was now in the majority. The new minority included board members who had previously denounced internal divisions and denied legitimacy to opposition within the board.

But did the new majority create the policy? Three board members had clearly supported the demographic committee's recommendation, but this did not emerge as the board's policy. Again, the superintendent made the critical decision, and the board responded to his initiative, although by only a one-vote margin. A determined minority wanted a contrary policy, but these board members assumed the success of their goal and thus failed to plan strategy or mobilize support.

Judging the community's direction once more, Superintendent Baker had stated that he supported keeping all schools open. Despite deep conflicts in the school district, he still possessed resources that others lacked. Generally silent throughout the January meetings, Baker faithfully gave the impression of being the board's servant, while shaping the policy he wanted. Many scholars have written of the superintendent's decisive influence in internal, or school-centered, issues. According to Roscoe Martin, "Concerning public issues, the superintendent's influence is less in

151

Photograph 5. Board member **Frederick P. Cargian,** a weathervane of the superintendent's policy.

evidence but scarcely less effective, for he defines the issues, proposes acceptable alternatives, and provides ammunition for school spokesmen."34

Cargian advanced the motion that superintendent Baker found to be an "acceptable alternative." All schools would remain open until program was "jeopardized," a qualification that allowed the superintendent more flexibility and discretion than an automatic enrollment cut-off for closing. According to Cargian's motion, the superintendent could act without explicit constraints established by the school board, waiting instead for events to dictate any change in policy.

The superintendent had preserved his own authority. Moses DeWitt parents took satisfaction in the outcome, too. The four committees had changed public discussion of the subject, and their meetings and reports had affected the outlook of some board members. The open-ended motion adopted by the board perhaps gave more freedom of action and a longer future than did an automatic closing when elementary enrollment fell below 1,000. Just as the superintendent felt that he had preserved his opportunities to influence future policy, so did Moses DeWitt parents.

### NOTES

1. **Post–Standard**(Syracuse), Sept. 21, 1978.
2. **Post–Standard**, Nov. 2, 1978.
3. Philip G. Schuls, Report from the Demographic Committee to the Jamesville-DeWitt Board of Education, Oct. 31, 1978.
4. **Post–Standard**, Nov. 2, 1978.
5. **Ibid.**
6. **Ibid.**
7. James D. Koerner, **Who controls American Education?** (Boston, 1968), 124.
8. Jamesville-DeWitt School Finance Committee, Report to the Board of Education, Dec. 18, 1978, 6.
9. **Ibid.** 5.
10. **Ibid.** 4.
11. **New York Times**, June 3, 1976.
12. Jamesville-DeWitt Board of Education meeting, July 31, 1978; Jan. 4, 1979.
13. Richard L. Andrews, "The Environmental Impact of School

Closures," (Seattle, 1974).

14. Jamesville-DeWitt School Finance Committee, Report, 7.

15. Jamesville-DeWitt Demographic Committee, Report to the Board of Education, Jan., 1979, 1-2.

16. **Ibid.**

17. Facilities and Program Committee, Report to the Board of Education, Jan., 1979.

18. Planning Committee, Report to the Board of Education, Jan., 1979.

19. **Suburban Life**(DeWitt and East Syracuse), Jan. 10, 1978.

20. Jamesville-DeWitt Board of Education meeting, Jan. 15, 1979.

21. Letter by Pauline Clair, Principal, Moses DeWitt Elementary School, to the Jamesville-DeWitt Board of Education, Jan. 11, 1979.

22. **Post-Standard,** Jan. 18, 1979.

23. **Suburban Life,** Jan. 17, 1979.

24. **Post-Standard,** Jan. 18, 1979.

25. **Ibid.**

26. **Post-Standard,** Jan. 25, 1979.

27. **Ibid.**

28. Tecumseh Parent-Teacher Group, Letter, Jan. 24, 1979.

29. Carolyn Coit, Statement to Jamesville-DeWitt Board of Education, Jan. 29, 1979, 1-2.

30. **Post-Standard,** Feb. 1, 1979.

31. **Suburban Life,** Jan. 31, 1979.

32. **Post-Standard,** Jan. 30, 1979.

33. **Ibid.**

34. Roscoe C. Martin, **Government and the Suburban School**(Syracuse, 1962), 61.

# X. The New Dogma: Keeping Everything Open

After January 1979, Jamesville-DeWitt officials embarked on a course that seemingly denied the importance of the previous three years' consideration of school-closing. A February district report explained that the decision to maintain all schools reflected a "thorough consideration of the best interests of all students **and** the expressed opinions and wishes of District residents." Following the January vote, "all board members agreed it was important to immediately resume consideration of steps necessary to continue the excellent educational program for which Jamesville-DeWitt is noted."[1]

The newsletter acknowledged that there had been "strong differences of opinion" concerning the decision. Nevertheless, perhaps the time-honored goal of providing "the best possible educational program for every J-D student" might again unite the board and the community. Those board members who had voted against the new policy had repeatedly insisted that program was their primary interest. "My overriding priority has been and always will be for the best education for all youngsters in our school district," Carmen had said.[2] Cargian's motion provided that all schools remain open only until program was "jeopardized." Thus Perkins did not yet see a sacrifice of the "quality programs" that in her opinion have "made us a leader."[3] The school district did not plan to "scrap" programs "for our children" in order to maintain facilities, as Perkins and others of the board minority feared. Instead, Jamesville-DeWitt would have both programs and buildings until further notice.

By Cargian's motion, Superintendent Baker hoped to chart a policy that fell within the public's zone of tolerance, or "the area of maneuverability granted (or yielded) to the leadership of the schools by the local community."[4] Battle-weary board members also wanted to minimize controversy. "We all have too much in common to accept an adversary posture among ourselves," Coit had said on January 29.[5] She expressed confidence that "solutions can be found, short of community strife" if united support were given to the board's decision. Despite their past travail board members still upheld the ideal of unity. At the first meeting of January, Perkins herself had urged her colleagues to help implement the forthcoming decision, so that the board could return to "important matters deferred for two years." These

155

important matters related to educational program and course offerings "based on children's needs."

As educational program instead of school-closing became the focus of the board's and the community's attention, administrators found their influence strengthened, as they intended. In a survey of eighty school districts Zeigler and Jennings found that boards seldom opposed their superintendents on educational program questions. Only 38 per cent of board members felt that their board **ever** disagreed with the superintendent about the content or nature of the educational program, and over 50 per cent of board members expected the superintendent to get his way even if the board did disagree.[6] Educational program offered the subject on which administrators received greatest deference. This was the realm in which their professional authority held intrinsic value to the community as well as to the board. "The claim that only professionals can make competent judgments has been accepted by the public," wrote one political scientist who described "overblown professionalization" as the single greatest influence on school decision-making.[7]

By withdrawing from the arena of public conflict and returning to supposedly-deferred educational issues, both the board and the superintendent hoped to resume business as usual. Board members could expect relief from public interrogation, and the superintendent could exercise authority in his acknowledged area of "expertise." Superintendent Baker had successfully deflected the public as well as the board from pursuing cost savings by program reductions as an alternative to school-closings. He had prevented public attacks on programs that not only fell within his jurisdiction but made his reputation. Better to close a building if necessary than to concede control of educational program. But in the meantime the public's zone of tolerance dictated a careful course of action. To reduce conflict, the superintendent attempted to give the community what he thought its then-dominant interests wanted.[8] When program was adversely affected, a school could be closed; programs would not be cut for the purpose of preserving a school.

Having put the closing issue behind them, board members returned to subjects that some believed neglected during the many months of crisis. Among the topics discussed at the first meeting in February were National School Lunch Week, a tax-exemption policy for new businesses, and a drug-abuse instruction program in the high school, for which funds might be eliminated. After an executive session to consider program requests for handicapped children, the board heard administrative reports concerning unsuccessful efforts to sell district property once considered as a site for an elementary school and a review of the advantages or disadvantages of self-insurance. All matters required little discussion, or were tabled until the next meeting.

At subsequent meetings, board members learned that twenty-five per cent of Jamesville-DeWitt seniors had qualified for New York State Regents' scholarships, a "record that surpassed that of every high school in the county." Not only high school students excelled. Second, fourth, and seventh graders had produced test scores "well above national averages." Altogether the interest of parents, residents, and teachers had given the school district "a position of leadership recognized in the county, around the state, and across the nation," a March newsletter declared.

Discussions of educational program allowed administrators to recite accomplishments, as board members and residents shared in recent success stories. Board members felt comfortable with the ideology of educational excellence, for which they could receive at least partial credit. Only rarely did they present questions or criticisms concerning district programs. Even more seldom did administrators publicly explain the development or modification of educational programs at any level, or attempt to give board members a sense of what two writers have called the "hard choices" in the system, that is, "how much is being sacrificed in one area to meet needs or demands in another area."[9] Generally an atmosphere of civic boosterism prevailed. The board never had occasion to undertake the reevaluation of "program in the light of current needs and standards" that Coit suggested in January.

In the spring the board began its annual consideration of the budget, a process well removed from an analysis of educational program or financial constraints. During the 1960s, as enrollments had grown, so had school offerings. Like most suburban school systems, Jamesville-DeWitt did not limit its focus to the three R's but delivered an expanded curriculum that included varied classes in languages, science, mathematics, and social sciences, as well as vocational training and special education. Extensive

157

counseling and support services from psychologists, social workers, and reading specialists had come to be regarded as an integral part of the program, as were a wide array of choices in music, art, physical education, interscholastic athletics, and after-school activities. Because Jamesville-DeWitt administrators built their careers during the era of boundless expansion, they identified the good of the system with these programs as did board members who followed their lead.

In discussing school principals and closing, district officials repeatedly emphasized the importance of the system, not the individual schools. The program became sacrosanct, including even those parts developed for reasons of expediency, such as the use of field trips and sailing at a nearby lake to relieve a once-crowded gym. In the 1980s, however, some national authorities shifted their emphasis as they saw the individual school, and not the system, as needing attention. "The local school is the most critical point for analysis and improvement," said Dr. Ronald Edmonds of the Harvard Graduate School of Education. "There's a lot of genius, energy, and devotion bottled up in many local schools. They must be released."[10] This viewpoint never gained official acceptance in Jamesville-DeWitt, despite many signs to indicate its validity.

Under the mantle of bureaucratic protection, programs continued, as in the era of expansion. The school district budget developed on a year-to-year basis, and "officials often made decisions in terms of short-term political or bureaucratic concerns."[11] Instead of devising long-range plans, the superintendent concentrated on the immediate problem of securing the coming year's state aid and voter approval of the budget.

In Jamesville-DeWitt, as in most districts, officials did not collect cost information in a manner to reveal either to themselves or the public "trade-offs" among "different instructional programs or between instruction and business (or other operations)."[12] Instead, the superintendent and the business manager prepared the initial draft of the budget after receiving recommendations from other administrators. Although he consulted with staff members, Superintendent Baker maintained complete mastery of the budgetary process and school expenditures, seeing this area as critical to his power. The budget proposal presented to the board and later to voters appeared in the form of recommendations for central administration, instructional services, transportation, operation and maintenance of plant, and employee benefits, followed by an abbreviated statement of anticipated revenue. This format not only concealed significant expenditures, such as those for the district's educational communications center, but made it impossible to isolate costs at any particular school. Nor did the presentation of the budget facilitate a comparison, for example, of elementary-school reading and middle-school foreign language, or of remedial as opposed to enrichment programs. No effort was made to ask which program had greater importance, because school officials presented the assumption that each was essential.

In April board members received information calling for a budget increase of over $600,000 in 1979, or a tax increase of $3.82. Assured that a "high quality educational program for every J-D student" would continue, board members did not focus on curriculum or instruction. Carmen wondered, however, if the district could "build back the planned balance," a fund held in reserve to eliminate any interest charges in case an irregularity in the delivery of state aid or local tax revenues required the district to borrow, an eventuality that had yet to occur. In 1978 the board had voted 5-4 to cut this fund from $300,000 to $150,000, to offer the voters a reduced tax increase of under $2.00. Now Perkins, who several months earlier had expressed her "concern about the passage of the budget," mentioned restoring the planned balance as did Hopkins, another spokesman for residents who wanted to save money. Those board members most reluctant to cut the planned balance in 1978 had later opposed the motion to keep all schools open. Now, however, their statements in behalf of "building back" $150,000 of unused money were merely symbolic, a reminder of their view that the district's fiscal purity had been compromised. Given a choice, this board minority was willing to ask voters to pay more in order to save the right way.

In a characteristic preoccupation with detail rather than policy, the board gave greatest attention to a budget provision for over $200,000 in maintenance costs and "high priority" repairs. Remaining maintenance expenditures reaching almost $1,000,000 could be covered by a five-year bond issue, according to the assistant superintendent for business.[13] Turning to the housekeeping chores that she had made her forte, Perkins expressed her support for a bond issue but questioned the amount budgeted for the replacement of oil burners in two elementary schools. Carmen, too, wanted more repairs written into the budget rather than the bond issue.[14] Both Perkins and Carmen voted against what they considered a low maintenance figure in the budget, showing a willingness to offer the public a greater tax increase.

The once-controversial subject of empty chairs and surplus space now produced only occasional grumbling rather than public debate, although administrators projected a total enrollment decline of about 150. As the number of students dropped from 3505 to 3369, the proposed budget of $11.2 million showed a 5.6 per cent increase from the $10.6 million budget of 1978-1979. Furthermore, state aid provided less than half of the tantalizing figure mentioned in the governor's preliminary proposal for 1979-1980.[15] Editorials in a suburban weekly persistently chastised local school districts and demanded that budgets decrease in relation to declining enrollment.[16] But officials in Jamesville-DeWitt and other districts did not counter this shibboleth or attempt to explain what has been correctly described as "the lack of a one-to-one correspondence between changes in enrollment and the movement of school expenditures."[17]

Annual school budgets reflected the impact of inflation and increasing salary figures as well as mandated payments for social security and retirement, which require ever-mounting outlays. For the most part, school expenditures are not allocated to individual students but by subject and grade. Thus, the loss of students through the system offers no immediate return to the taxpayer. As many scholars have observed, enrollment decline at one grade level is rarely sufficient to allow personnel cuts. Moreover, even "as teacher positions are cut, tenure laws and seniority provisions usually require that the least experienced and thus least costly teachers are cut first," thus increasing expenditures per pupil.[18] And the savings of what some educators call "consolidating attendance areas," otherwise known as closing schools, are offset by continued staff costs, building maintenance, and in some districts increased transportation. Districts with declining enrollment not only have higher expenditures for instruction, they show increases that are "even more pronounced on a percentage basis, for administrative expenses." Odden and Vincent speculate that decision-makers find it easier to "reduce the number of teachers than the number of administrators in the face of declining enrollment."[19]

Although Jamesville-DeWitt administrators had twice averted a school-closing, they did not educate residents on these dilemmas of school finance. Perhaps they expected to embrace the original argument in favor of closing if public opinion shifted. In any event as "gatekeepers of information" school officials preferred to talk to board members and residents individually rather than in public meetings or hearings, which usually revealed little.[20] Quietly the administration cut positions as smaller classes moved through the school system. Starting in 1976 each year's budget provided for some attrition of staff.

In 1979 school officials also examined the rental of "extra" classroom space. In March the board established two committees to consider the appropriate use of classroom space and rental fees, a subject explored over several months. Board president Perkins carefully studied the differentiation between "rent" and "lease" in drafting a policy for classroom-rental. She next turned to non-profit status of a Montessori nursery school seeking to rent a classroom at Moses DeWitt, while Mallan wondered aloud if this nursery school's philosophy was compatible with Jamesville-DeWitt's program. Costs in utilities and maintenance were assessed.[21]

Having exhausted semantic, educational, and financial questions, the board eventually relinquished the empty rooms and completed arrangements so that the Kynda Montessori School rented a classroom at Moses DeWitt and three regional offices of the New York State Education Department rented space at Tecumseh. For the 1979-1980 school year all rooms but one were used for educational or rental purposes.[22]

Originally administrators had wanted to eliminate "surplus space" by closing a school. During the period 1977-1979 neither Superintendent Baker nor elementary principals had advocated rental of classrooms as a solution. Evidence from other districts suggests that administrators "seem to prefer schools to remain as schools only."[23] Once the district was committed to maintaining all schools, however, the rental of classrooms eliminated the delicate question of "surplus space." School officials who supported this measure considered it an expedient, a stopgap, rather than a commitment to shared space to provide community services and preserve the distinctive character of each school and area. Advocates of closing naturally resisted filling empty space, particularly in Moses DeWitt, and administrators did not want a long-term commitment to other organizations.

As the budget vote approached, so did the election of school board candidates. First appointed to the Southwood seat in 1973, DeBottis had run unopposed in 1974 and did so again in 1979. Known for his support of high school athletics and community activities in Jamesville, DeBottis first drew scathing criticism in DeWitt for voting to close Moses DeWitt in 1977 and then warm appreciation for his statement in 1979 that "schools belong to the community."[24] His service station located at one edge of the DeWittshire neighborhood behind Moses DeWitt served many patrons who took an active interest in school affairs. Having felt the intensity of support for Moses DeWitt as well as the school in his own community, DeBottis stood for the motion to keep all schools open.

Like DeBottis, Perkins had also been appointed to an unexpired term in 1973 and had run unopposed the following year. In 1979, however, she faced a contest in her reelection bid. Like Carmen, she did not withdraw when her policy preference met with apparent failure. Instead board members now sought to justify their positions by reelection. Although school board members had not usually engaged in electoral politics, board members Carmen and Perkins did not shirk this necessity or choose to retire because they had already performed their civic duty.

Perkins, like Carmen the previous year, wanted confirmation of her support in the community. Challenged by John Galletta, a resident who lived near Moses DeWitt and taught in another school system in the county, the board president had many advantages. Zeigler and Jennings found that in forty-three per cent of districts no incumbents had been forced out of office in recent years.[25] Perkins ran not only as an incumbent but as president of the board of education. She gave lip-service to the board's policy of keeping all schools open, while making her true feelings abundantly clear. "I have confined my board action to policy-making, planning and appraisal. The responsibility for board-instituted policy rests with the administration," read her campaign statement. "My goal has been to represent the ENTIRE school community without fear or favor."

Again Perkins introduced the consideration of the "fear" that she had withstood.

Perkins' campaign statement neither mentioned nor endorsed the budget proposal. In board discussions she had asked if the 1979 budget offered a minimum of "just what we can get by on," and Superintendent Baker assured her that the spending plan provided no cuts in program. Depicting herself as the representative of those seeking economies, Perkins voted both in 1978 and 1979 for budget provisions that required higher tax increases, an approach that she later followed in considering the bond issue. Whether by higher allocations for building maintenance, a restoration of the planned balance, or a reluctance to fill an "empty" classroom at Moses Dewitt, Perkins advocated the increased expenditures that might make the budget more unacceptable to the voters, thereby necessitating the closing policy she had advocated. Invoking standard school-board ideology, she officially described her policy as "one of concern for students, quality programs, fiscal responsibility, and con-science....with balanced consideration for all parties involved."

Galletta emerged as a self-starting candidate rather than a deliberate choice of Moses DeWitt parents. Because he entered the race early, parents abandoned efforts to recruit a candidate and supported Galletta at a distance. Having learned from their ill-fated support of Sugarman the previous year, Moses DeWitt parents hoped to dissociate themselves from the new candidate and allow him to establish himself as a candidate who had "a balanced consideration for all parties involved." Campaigning door-to-door in many neighborhoods and at Little League playing fields, Galletta spoke in behalf of the budget and the decision to keep all schools open.

On election day, board president Perkins won easily, defeating her opponent by more than three hundred votes. Galletta's low-key candidacy had met with no greater success than Sugarman's first-class letters, appeal for campaign contributions, and dubious support by a district-wide Moses DeWitt newsletter. But now parents realized that any candidate who supported a policy to keep Moses DeWitt would be immediately branded as not representing the entire community. The budget, on the other hand, drew a 68 per cent vote, passing by 1184 to 565 votes, or the widest margin in five years.

"We've never had a budget go down," said Perkins on

election night.[27] A newsletter before the election had declared that over a four-year period Jamesville-DeWitt "budget increases have been at less than one-half of the national inflation rate," while the school district had "maintained all schools and all programs."[28] Moses DeWitt parents used telephone calls by neighborhoods as well as their newsletter to persuade voters to go to the polls. In contrast to the private acknowledgments given to Moses DeWitt in 1978, business manager Robert Wall told the press that Moses DeWitt School had an impact on the vote. "I don't know how much of an effect that (Moses DeWitt staying open) had, but I'm sure it had some effect."[29]

Residents of the Moses DeWitt area accounted for 45 per cent of the total voting turn-out, a percentage virtually identical with their showing in 1978. Total voting turn-out declined in 1979, as the crisis atmosphere of the previous eighteen months began to fade. A more populous residential community than other elementary-school areas, Moses DeWitt consistently had a disproportionate share of the district's voters, but in 1978 and 1979 this percentage was higher than usual. The at-large electoral system prevents an analysis of "yes" and "no" votes by area, but the high turn-out from streets immediately around Moses DeWitt showed public sentiment in support of the board's decisions. In 1978, for example, 316 voters from the neighborhood immediately surrounding Moses DeWitt voted, a turn-out that fell off slightly in 1979. These voters played a critical part in supporting board policy.

As in 1978, however, the electoral results were mixed. Although the budget passed, a leading proponent of school-closing had been decisively reelected. But seeing the budget again approved by a wide margin, administrators concluded that the community accepted the policy of maintaining all schools. Even board members who had advocated closing in order "to avoid a budget defeat" now kept their peace. "We're going to do our best for another good year," Perkins had said on election night.[30] According to DeBottis, passage of the budget in 1978 "gave us an inkling that they (residents) were willing to support all schools," an indication confirmed by the 1979 vote. Curriculum Coordinator Osborn thought that the "budget vote indicates that there is a positive feeling in the district. It shows very strong support for the board and the decision they made."[31] Elected to the board presidency shortly after the budget vote, Carmen also expressed the now-official viewpoint. "I think our community is very supportive," she said. "I really am looking forward to a very good year."[32]

Having secured the all-important budget, administrators hoped to achieve greater unity in the board and the community during the coming year. As board president, Carmen would work closely with the administration for the best possible education of the children, as determined by the superintendent and his staff. Carmen's desire to see a school closed might be slaked by the satisfactions of the presidency, residents speculated. Perkins, too, might mellow following an electoral victory that confirmed her January claim that "I am not insensitive to the community."

The major business for fall was preparation of a bond issue providing for renovations in each school building. The previous spring the necessity of a bond issue had been accepted with little comment, so representatives of King and King, the school district's architectural firm, began a series of presentations at board meetings. Board members considered subjects ranging from replacement of boiler room pumps, installation of insulated metal panels in place of windows, addition of weatherstripping, repairs to the sump pump and swimming pool drain, and the relative merits of incandescent and flourescent lighting.

The bond issue had first received consideration as a way of making essential repairs. The school district's newsletter in June, for example, had pointed to the age of buildings now twenty years old. "Major roof and burner replacements are essential if buildings are to be kept in good condition. The pressures for more efficient energy use are also a factor in these considerations."[33] Gradually but perceptibly, discussion shifted from these requirements to improvements, such as air-conditioning for the guidance offices in the high school, renovation of high school locker rooms, and replacement of what district consultants called "vintage" but nevertheless functional intercoms in each building with modern internal communications systems.

Perkins now saw the bond issue as an opportunity to complete a long-needed refurbishing of school buildings. Maintenance and improvement needs "put off" from one year to the next because of budgetary limits could at last be accomplished, now apparently without regard to cost or tax implications. Even the King and King representatives expressed surprise at a board request to indicate costs for installing a new school district telephone system, saying that they could offer only a "ballpark guess" in six figures. Despite the rough estimate only Coit and Mallan opposed including this major allocation in the bond issue.

Instead of a $900,000 bond issue for a five-year period as mentioned in the spring, the board voted to present a $2.39 million bond issue over a fifteen-year period. Of this total over $700,000 was allocated to the high school. Of the $140,000 listed for the middle school, repairs for the swimming pool and its filtering system represented the greatest expenditure. For each elementary school roof replacements and other renovations amounted to $200,000-$300,000. According to the district's own newsletter, energy conservation measures accounted for only 62 per cent of the bond issue.[34]

The average tax rate for the fifteen years of the bond issue was estimated at $2.32 per $1,000 of assessed valuation. Although the bond issue would have no effect on the forthcoming 1980-1981 budget, the tax rate increase would become effective in the summer of 1981. Superintendent Baker knew that $2.32 per thousand was an appreciable amount when added to the usual tax increases to be expected in a period of high inflation. When asked at bond hearings about the possibility of a school being closed, he answered that a closing was not planned and, furthermore, buildings would have to be maintained in any case. The superintendent emphasized the district's good financial position and the prospect of substantial state-reimbursement on bond issue expenditures. Although segments of the community continued to worry about school-closing, declining enrollment, and cost-controls, Jamesville-DeWitt was to maintain the same high level of spending and excellence known during the era of expansion. The superintendent of schools in Skokie, Illinois, observed the irony in his district's policy.

> With the left hand we were doing major life-saving improvements and long-range planning to keep the schools in top shape. At the same time, we were doing enrollment projections that showed....- (severe decline) in the early 1980s.[35]

The vote on what a suburban paper called "Face Lift for JD Schools" had long been scheduled for December, not a period of peak interest in school affairs.[36] Political scientist Roscoe Martin has written that the use of separate elections for school boards emphasizes "the independence of schools, setting them apart from any and every other public activity." Moreover, separate elections render the whole electoral process "more subject to control by the schoolmen than it would be if the drama of school politics were played on a larger stage."[37] In Jamesville-DeWitt affairs the June budget and board election **was** the larger stage, and a December vote just before the holidays was a very small stage indeed, thereby underscoring Martin's conclusion that "one result of the system appears in the lack of public interest and small voter turn out."[38] On December 12, 1979, 256 voters turned out to support the bond issue, while only 126 opposed it.

As recently as June, 1977, 1,546 voters had nearly defeated the annual budget. When the tides of district politics shifted in 1978 and the budget passed easily, 968 residents nevertheless voted "no," as had 563 voters in June of 1979.[39] Now the earlier resistance to school-district spending seemed to have faded, as a fifteen-year financial commitment of significant proportions was undertaken by a handful of residents, largely parents and district employees.

Following passage of the bond issue, the board of education continued its usual business meetings, now supplemented by "communications" sessions held at individual schools. At these informal meetings the principal and staff at each building made a presentation, conducted a tour, or at one school showed a videotape of children's daily activities. Although a district newsletter asserted that "open lines of communications have been achieved," the informal meetings were not well attended.[40] One board member described them as "show and tell" evenings rather than the exchange with the public that he envisioned in advocating such sessions. When residents occasionally raised the question of school-closing, board members and administrators firmly insisted that the policy was to keep everything open.

# NOTES

1. Jamesville-DeWitt District Report, Feb. 1979.
2. **Post-Standard**(Syracuse), Dec. 13, 1977.
3. **Post-Standard**, Jan. 18, 1979.
4. J.K. McGivney and W. Moynihan as quoted by William L. Boyd, "School Board-Administrative Staff Relationships," in Peter J. Cistone, ed., **Understanding School Boards**(Lexington, 1975), 118.
5. Carolyn Coit, Statement to the Jamesville-DeWitt Board of Education, Jan. 29, 1979.
6. L. Harmon Zeigler and M. Kent Jennings, **Governing American Schools**(North Scituate, Mass. 1974), 163-164.
7. Marilyn Gittell, **Participants and Participation: A Study of School Policy in New York City**(New York, 1968), 46, 48.; see also James D. Koerner, **Who Controls American Education?**(Boston, 1968).
8. William L. Boyd, "School Board-Administrative Staff Relationships," 118; this description also fits the superintendent described by Arthur J. Vidich and Joseph Bensman, **Small Town in Mass Society**(Princeton, 1968), 196.
9. Paul Berman and Milbrey McLaughlin, "The Management of Decline: Problems, Opportunities, and Research Questions," in Susan Abramowitz and Stuart Rosenfeld, eds., **Declining Enrollment: The Challenge of the Coming Decade**(Washington, D.C., 1978), p. 322; Jamesville-DeWitt accomplishments are recited in District Report, Mar. 1980.
10. **New York Times**, Feb. 3, 1981.
11. Berman and McLaughlin, "The Management of Decline," 317.
12. **Ibid.**, 322.
13. **Suburban Life**(DeWitt and East Syracuse), Apr. 11, 1979.
14. **Ibid.**
15. **Post-Standard**, Apr. 12, 1979.
16. **Suburban Life**, June 13, 1979; June 18, 1980; Feb. 11, 1981.
17. William H. Wilken and John J. Callahan, "Declining Enrollment: The Cloud and Its Silver Lining," in Susan Abramowitz and Stuart Rosenfeld, eds., **Declining Enrollment: The Challenge of the Coming Decade**, 259.
18. Allan Odden and Phillip E. Vincent, "The Fiscal Impacts of Declining Enrollments in Four States," in Susan Abramowitz and Stuart Rosenfeld, eds., **Declining Enrollment: The Challenge of the Coming Decade**, 227.
19. **Ibid.**, 229.
20. The concept "gatekeepers of information" is discussed by Zeigler and Jennings, **Governing American Schools**, 189.
21. **Suburban Life**, May 17, 1979.
22. **Post-Standard**, Sept. 6, 1979.
23. Jean L. Jessner, "Closing Schools, Bay Style," in Betsy Wachtel and Brian Powers, eds., **Rising Above Decline**(Boston, 1979), 105.
24. **Post-Standard**, Feb. 1, 1979.

25. Zeigler and Jennings, **Governing American Schools**, 56.
26. Phyllis Perkins, campaign statement, May, 1979.
27. **Post–Standard**, June 7, 1979.
28. Jamesville-DeWitt District Report, June 1, 1979.
29. **Post–Standard**, June 7, 1979.
30. **Ibid.**
31. Lee Steinfeldt, "The School that Almost Closed (but Didn't),"
**Post–Standard**, Sept. 13, 1979.
32. **Ibid.**
33. Jamesville-DeWitt District Report, June 1, 1979.
34. Jamesville-DeWitt District Report, Special Edition, Nov.
1979.
35. Civia Tamarkin, "Skokie Tries to Close a School," in Betsy
Wachtel and Brian Powers, ed., **Rising Above Decline**, 85.
36. **Suburban Life**, Oct. 24, 1979.
37. Roscoe C. Martin, **Government and the Suburban School**(Syracuse,
1962), 46.
38. **Ibid.**
39. All voting statistics are from the Jamesville-DeWitt District
Office.
40. Jamesville-DeWitt District Report, Feb. 1980.

# XI. The Budget Goes Down

During the spring, board members and residents learned that a sharp tax increase was forthcoming in June 1980. A projected budget increase from $11.2 million to $12.3 million could boost the tax rate by as much as eight per cent, Superintendent Baker said in April. "Everything that a family faces in a home, we're facing here," he explained, noting significant increases in gas, oil, and electricity bills.[1] Nevertheless, the school district had attempted to control costs by consolidating bus routes, cutting the allotment for teachers' aides by fifty per cent, reducing the budget for supplies by twenty-seven per cent, and providing for no new equipment. In response to declining enrollment, eleven positions were to be cut, half of them elementary-school classroom teachers. Offsetting these reductions, however, were the addition of two special teachers at the elementary level and the appointment of one remedial teacher at the middle school, as required by a recent state law.[2]

Board members accepted the proposed budget increase of $1.1 million. They murmured disapproval, however, at sharply reducing the allocation for teachers' aides, a miniscule portion of the budget. Although other local school boards were also asking their voters for large increases, Superintendent Baker realized that what was now estimated to be a tax increase of $10.00 per thousand was high. "It's embarrassing to go forward with this, but if we made more cuts we'd affect things we're known as the leader on," he explained a month before the budget vote. Annual increases in state aid declined each year, as local taxpayers assumed a larger share of school financing. The percentage of the budget provided by state aid had declined from over 50 per cent in the late 1960s to only 35 per cent in the proposed 1980-1981 budget. "It's critical that we understand," explained the superintendent, "that revenues are down and costs are up." Board president Carmen reiterated the conviction that "we don't want to cut programs."[3]

The 1980-1981 budget mailed to voters called for a tax increase of $11.95 per thousand. Because of staff cuts, reductions in supplies, a $45,000-savings from the teacher-aide budget, and other economies, board members considered the proposal a "bare bones" budget.[4] By breaking the budget into three parts--basic budget, bus replacement, and interest payment on bond anticipation

171

notes--administrators described the "basic" proposal as a 6.9 per cent increase from 1979-1980. The total budget as proposed to the voters represented a 10.1 per cent increase over the 1979-1980 budget, however. The proposed tax rate showed a 9 per cent rise. The tax rate now offered greatly exceeded any previous proposal, particularly the moderate increases of the previous years, which had fallen between $2.00 and $4.00.

Nevertheless, residents seemed quiescent. The two public hearings on the budget drew a small attendance, the usual scattering of parents, teachers, and a few older residents. This handful of citizens posed several questions, largely concerning reductions in the number of teacher aides and minimal payment to substitute teachers. No person or organization challenged the budget proposal or the size of the tax increase. The bond issue provoked one or two inquiries. Board members dismissed one resident's question about the possibility of closing a school sometime in the future.

Perhaps because of the decisive approval given the last two budgets as well as the bond issue, school officials attempted no new strategy to gain acceptance of the $11.95 increase. Administrators spoke to PTA groups and again called upon their trusted circle of school-supporters in the community. "The PTA furnishes the troops of every school election," according to two authors.[5] School officials also "routinely solicit support from elite associates and 'explain' the 'need' for the tax levy or the bond project to the rotary clubs."[6] In 1980 Jamesville-DeWitt administrators followed this approach, as they had in the past. Detecting no visible critics and perhaps not wanting to produce any, the administration did not send out a pre-election newsletter again explaining the budget, as it had in 1979. Nor did Moses DeWitt parents use a newsletter as they had the previous year, when they felt acutely responsible for the budget's passage. Lulled by recent election results, school activists expected the 1980 budget to pass despite the high tax increase and instead turned their attention to the election of a new board member.

In April Carolyn Coit had revealed that she would not seek reelection. As a board member representing the Tecumseh area, she had played a critical part both in the decision to defer the closing of Moses DeWitt in 1978 and in the policy to keep all schools open in 1979, when she had recommended that a school automatically be closed

172

when elementary enrollment declined below 1,000. Both years Coit had urged the board to take time in devising careful policies and in gaining public acceptance of them.

Although some Tecumseh residents had expressed dissatisfaction with Coit's handling of the closing issue, neither of the candidates who now sought her position challenged the policy of maintaining all schools. Both candidates publicly sidestepped the closing issue by resorting to standard school rhetoric. To renege on the commitment to "a well-rounded high quality education" would be a "disservice to the students and to the community," said Benjamin D. Levine, a lawyer. Benjamin G. Berry, Jr., owner of a coin-laundry business, showed equal dedication to high ideals. "I want all children upon leaving Jamesville-DeWitt to have received the best total program for their specific needs." Campaigning door-to-door in neighborhoods near Moses DeWitt, Berry told residents that he wanted to keep all schools open. In his formal statement, however, he said, "To me, the bottom line for every board member is commitment to the children of our community."[7]

On election day Moses DeWitt parents stopped short of the special efforts undertaken in the last two years. In contrast to 1978 and 1979, they did not actively campaign for a candidate. Moses DeWitt residents acknowledged that this board seat belonged to the Tecumseh area, according to a geographical allocation of positions dating to the inception of the school district. Of the two Tecumseh candidates, many Moses DeWitt parents favored Berry, who appealed for their support while his opponent did not. The approaching election produced few signs of activity, however. Children at district schools carried home routine reminders of the budget vote. Only a few Moses DeWitt parent-group officers and school "room-mothers" made telephone checks on election day in contrast to the systematic canvassing of the previous year.

On June 4, 1980, Jamesville-DeWitt voters defeated the budget for the first time in the district's thirty-year history. As the budget fell by a margin of only thirty-five votes, candidate Berry won easily over his opponent. When asked to account for the budget's defeat, Superintendent Baker could give no specific reason. "I don't know. I can't understand it," he said. "A lot of people who normally vote didn't this time."[8]

The superintendent had correctly assessed the situation. The voting turn-out of 1715 residents was only slightly below that in 1979, but the distribution by areas and streets had changed. Whereas Moses DeWitt residents had constituted 45 per cent of those voting in 1979, they were now 38 per cent. Still the largest bloc of voters, the Moses DeWitt numbers had dwindled from a high of 1136 in 1978 to 645 in 1980. In 1980 residents from other school areas all voted in greater numbers than they had the previous year. The streets immediately around Moses DeWitt, which had produced close to 320 voters at the height of the closing controversy, now accounted for only 180. On major streets near Moses DeWitt voting turn-out fell by as much as fifty per cent in a two-year period. Critical declines also occurred between 1979 and 1980. For example, a street behind Moses DeWitt that produced 59 voters in 1979 had a total of only 22 in 1980. Turn-out fell drastically in other neighborhoods as well.

As the pressure to "save" the school relaxed, complacency returned. The policy of maintaining all schools rested on the stipulation that the community "was willing to pay for this," as Superintendent Baker had stated in January 1979. Activist parents remained committed to passing the budget as a necessary condition of keeping Moses DeWitt, and assumed that others felt likewise. But when district politics became peaceful, if not torpid, parents again turned to the usual activities in the school and community. As their vigiliance flagged, they failed to continue to educate and inspire supporters, some of whom resented an open-ended commitment to the budget. Only after the budget's defeat was the real threat of an $11.95 tax increase recognized.

School administrators apparently shared the assumption that Moses DeWitt residents would again provide the margin of support for the budget. Whereas Moses DeWitt parents had originally warned of budget defeats if their school were closed, the tables had turned. If a budget were defeated, a school would close --namely, Moses DeWitt. Although $11.95 was a sizeable increase, both administrators and parents expected well-to-do DeWitt residents to consider the proposal understandable in a period of mounting costs. Neither school officials nor parents saw the $11.95 proposal as so high that it would inevitably doom the political compromise whereby all schools remained open.

At the school board's first meeting after the budget defeat, Superintendent Baker justified the tax increase. Comparing budget increases and inflation, he described the school district as "at least 20 percentage points behind the cost of living."[9] Some board members wondered if the budget failed simply because of the indifference of voters who had expected it to pass. Board member Hopkins disagreed. "No" voters told him that the budget defeat was the "only time we've gotten you to listen to us." And a Tecumseh parent warned, "The people in the district are not going to vote 'yes' automatically year after year." But most of the thirty residents attending the meeting were Moses DeWitt parents, who assured the board that the problem was inflation, not the budget. These residents urged school officials to explain, not cut, the budget. Moses DeWitt parents took the lead in advising the board to do what it had already decided to do, resubmit the same budget to the voters. After thirty minutes of comment from the public and very little discussion among themselves, board members voted unanimously to return to the public with the budget proposal rejected on June 4.[10]

On the second try, administrators planned a more strenuous campaign in behalf of the budget. The 875-840 defeat on June 4 had been disturbing, but possibly this outcome was an electoral oddity. A deficiency of only thirty-five votes was hardly enough to require a revision of the budget proposal. To have modified the budget might suggest that the original budget had not been a good one, as one board member observed.[11] Better to protect the school board's credibility than to offer a new proposal that might make the original look "padded." Furthermore, both administrators and board members still had confidence in a community that before June had never rejected a budget or bond issue. "You have no idea--I have had excellent support from this community," Board president Carmen insisted after the June 4 defeat.[12] For the second budget vote, school officials would return to this public "once more with feeling," according to a local newspaper headline.[13]

"Tax and bond issues compel schoolmen to be politicians," conclude two scholars. A professional educator supposedly insulated from "politics," a superintendent nevertheless finds politicking an "inescapable component" of his job.[15] And no issue is more important to him than passage of the budget. To achieve success on June 20, Superintendent Baker

175

returned to a known source of support, the PTAs and the parents. PTA officers from all six schools assembled to hear the superintendent again defend his budget and call for their maximum effort, including meetings, telephone calls, and newsletters. Parent-group officers were urged to submit newsletters to the district office, where they could be reviewed as well as printed. Thus parent-supporters were to be marshaled for the cause. But with the exception of Moses DeWitt, parent-groups had never systematically studied or attempted to influence voting behavior in the school district. In the words of Robert A. Dahl, "the focus of the individual PTA is narrow."[16]

Administrators then turned to a second line of defense, those business and professional leaders active in civic and charitable causes. After many years' experience in Jamesville-DeWitt, the superintendent had a sense of what some political scientists describe as the community's "power structure." He saw a "network of influentials," a network in which he himself had long received acceptance.[17] Because of the school district's predominantly middle-to-upper income character, Baker had a high regard for an elite of business executives and their "invisible web of influence."[18] As in the past, he could call upon these men and explain the "needs" of the schools. Although sympathetic to the school district's interests, these "leaders" had never demonstrated their influence in an electoral contest.

School officials also took their case to the press and to the people. The school budget had increased 36.9 per cent in a five-year period, in the face of 49.5 per cent inflation, Superintendent Baker told a local reporter.[19] Furthermore, no schools had closed. When "community members asked" that Moses DeWitt not be closed, the administration "complied," said one article. A district newsletter to all residents explained unavoidable costs as well as economies already achieved. After presenting a grab bag of reasons to vote "yes," the report set forth what could be expected if the budget went down to a second defeat.[21] "A prominent strategy of repeat tax elections," write Hamilton and Cohen, "is a hint or a firm announcement that defeat of a levy will necessitate reductions in school programs," an approach that serves to rally parents at the risk of alienating critics who see it as intimidation.[22] In the event of defeat, the Jamesville-DeWitt newsletter foretold several possibilities, including a "contingency budget," whereby summer recreation programs would be cancelled, a revised budget reducing programs and services, or an "austerity budget," which by law prohibits purchases for library books, athletic programs, and interscholastic sports, in addition to restricting bus transportation.

Of those enlisted to support the June 20 budget, Moses DeWitt parents took their responsibility most seriously. Seeing their efforts of the last two and one half years in jeopardy, they exhorted residents to "work together for your schools and your future." In Jamesville-DeWitt elected and appointed officials had reached "a mutual understanding with the community," a Moses DeWitt newsletter reminded voters. "Continue JD's Historic Excellence: Vote Yes on the Budget," read a half-page advertisement placed in the suburban weekly.[23] Parents now organized a campaign to cover all neighborhoods and canvass by telephone--the very effort that had been missing two weeks earlier.

But as Moses DeWitt and other school-supporters made their phone calls they detected a quiet but concerted campaign against the budget. Budget-opponents did not emerge with visible leaders, organization, or literature. Indeed, because of the "symbolic appeal of education and children, and the success of schoolmen in co-opting community elites," anti-tax campaigns are frequently covert.[24] Relying on the spoken rather than the written word, these campaigns can mobilize those who dislike the property tax and oppose increases. An unprecedented $11.95 tax increase drew greater attention than the usual proposal. In addition to anti-tax sentiment, every district includes people who have specific grievances and dissatisfactions concerning the schools. Even in 1978 and 1979, years when the budget passed easily, a substantial number of residents voted "no," as Superintendent Baker had observed to be the board after the June 4 budget defeat. This consistent "no" vote, which between 1975-1980 had never dropped below 500, offered a ready-made basis for a counter-campaign.

Furthermore, resubmitting the identical budget ran the risk of intensifying the opposition instead of simply recruiting stay-at-home supporters. Two days before the election the suburban weekly commented, "JD officials are in effect punishing voters who sincerely voted 'no' by making them reiterate their stand, at the same time saying to the 'yes' faction--'We'll give you a second chance.'"[25] According to **Suburban Life**, the first budget vote showed the public's verdict on the spending plan, "yet no action has been taken to comply with that

177

directive."

On June 20, 3606 voters came to the polls, a record turn-out in Jamesville-DeWitt and more than twice that recorded for the first budget vote. Although the election drew the largest number of "yes" voters in the district's history, the budget received only a 47 per cent affirmative vote. Over 1900 residents voted against the budget proposal in what was now a decisive outcome.

The distribution of votes according to elementary-school area remained virtually identical to that seen in the first defeat. Despite vigorous efforts by Moses Dewitt parents, residents in that area did not increase their percentage of the total turn-out. Voters in all areas came to the polls in record numbers. Efforts to recruit complacent school-supporters succeeded, as the number of "yes" voters doubled. But the influence of "supportive" PTA mothers and business leaders, whose names had served many good causes, faded before an onslaught of unknown opponents. The "no" voters had broken Jamesville-DeWitt's longstanding consensus in favor of generous, even lavish, support of the schools.

Although at first surprising to residents, in retrospect the result seemed inevitable. The school district's perfect voting record had already been destroyed in the first defeat on June 4, when one elementary-school principal commented that now Jamesville-DeWitt looked like "all the other districts," where budget defeats were not only possible but commonplace. No longer did school-supporters seem invincible. Moses DeWitt parents in particular had displayed a fatal weakness, which they could not remedy by frantic pre-election telephone calls. Residents dissatisfied with the tax increase, the school-closing policy, or any aspect of the school district saw an opportunity to register their complaints.

School officials had recognized, although perhaps underestimated, difficulties in the situation. One administrator had correctly predicted that at least twice as many "no" voters would come to the polls on June 20. By stimulating a greater interest in the budget, school administrators would inevitably increase the turn-out of "no" voters. Moreover, they ran the risk of increased hostility from those residents who had voted "no" the first time and felt "punished" by resubmission of an identical budget. But the "quiet" strategy designed to avoid arousing opposition also failed in many districts. This approach sometimes brought only the determined anti-tax voters to the polls, as indicated in election results from various communities.[26]

Numerous studies of voting behavior generally show, however, that the larger the turn-out, the smaller the percentage of favorable votes cast in a school financial election.[27] Among the normal participants in school elections are parents, civic leaders, and those citizens committed to the schools as part of what Edward Banfield and James Q. Wilson describe as a "public-regarding" ethos, a viewpoint that emphasizes the good of the "community as a whole," as opposed to strictly private interests.[28] When the electorate increases, it then includes residents who rarely participate. According to one review of evidence, "this expanded voting pool frequently contains a larger proportion of no voters."[29]

Who were these "no" voters and what did they want? At their first meeting following the public's repudiation of the budget, board members attempted to determine what had happened and what to do about it. They unanimously adopted a contingency budget as of July 1, as required by law; summer recreation and driver education programs were thus cancelled. What should the board's next step be? Board member Hopkins stated that for several years residents had tried to tell the board that they wanted a school closed, only to have their wishes ignored. DeBottis disagreed, finding school board members "responsive" to the community. "Let's get this budget down to a figure where we can pass it," he concluded Recalling her vote to close Moses DeWitt three years earlier, Perkins insisted that the board "not dilute programs." Mallan reiterated the commitment to program and proposed that the board increase public understanding by authorizing a high school elective course on the American school.[30]

DeBottis returned to the problem at hand, urging his colleagues "to decide how much you want to cut." Board president Carmen then interjected, "We are not a punitive board--This is not our purpose. Our purpose is to serve our youngsters." To protect programs, perhaps the board should first cut the planned balance of $150,000, several members suggested. Perkins opposed eliminating the planned balance, however, for "then we would have no protection."[31]

Board member Luchsinger objected altogether to

submitting a reduced budget, because this would not only raise questions about the June proposal but possibly set a precedent for defeating the budget each year "in order to get the board to cut it more." Instead of relying on the administration's direction, the board should now assume responsibility by placing the district on an austerity budget for one year. Since austerity budgets prohibited spending on interscholastic athletics, library books, and equipment, and restricted busing within two or three-mile limits, residents "will see what the community stands to lose."[32]

Finally, DeBottis proposed that the board reduce the tax increase by 50 per cent, and the administration was directed to cut more than $250,000 from the budget. Dispirited after the June 20 defeat, Suprintendent Baker agreed to produce "any figure you want," but warned that "any cut is going to hurt program--don't kid yourselves." Questioned about the savings of school-closing, he answered that they would be small.

At the next week's meeting Baker returned with a list of proposals to cut $5.80 from the $11.95 tax increase. Reducing his original spending plan by $314,000, the superintendent had turned first to the planned balance. Eliminating this once-sacrosanct fund produced a savings of $3.00 per thousand. To achieve other reductions, Superintendent Baker proposed a further consolidation of bus routes and elimination of field trips, assemblies, driver education, and late-afternoon bus service, as well as an end to school board conferences, a little-noticed perquisite of office.

Board members then wrestled with the proposed changes. Perkins found it "short-sighted" to cut the planned balance instead of "saving it for a rainy day." If the board maintained the planned balance, however, it would be difficult to find another way to cut an additional $150,000 from the budget. "You can't go in slashing this and that," said the superintendent. Having hoped to pass the original budget, he regarded the cuts gloomily. "There's not that much left, baby," Baker concluded.

Luchsinger agreed, arguing that the proposed cuts went to the "heart of too many programs." He further objected to "drastic changes" made in a short period of time and again proposed an austerity budget, allowing the public to vote on separate propositions. Administrators listened but quietly favored a reduced budget, as they spoke of dangers to children walking on busy thoroughfare and the possibility that even a transportation proposition might fail.[33]

Administrators had no desire to relinquish internal control of decision-making to the public in unpredictable plebiscites. Even in adversity, they preferred, in Wallace Sayre's expression, to "maximize their own autonomous role," but they did so weakly.[34] Rebuffed by the June budget defeats, school officials apparently awaited a new alignment of public opinion. The high turn-out on June 20 indicated the kind of community conflict from which administrators withdrew. Underlying dissension had drawn new and unknown voters to the polls, as James S. Coleman found in his classic study **Community Conflict**.[35] In this volatile situation, school administrators adopted a cautious attitude and waited to see the outlines of an acceptable policy.

Before the June 20 vote, for example, Superintendent Baker had told the press that operating Moses DeWitt cost the district about $30,000 a year.[36] Even after the second defeat, he first minimized the cost-savings of closing, only to be rebuked by critics on the board and in the community. In successive weeks the superintendent made no attempt to deflect public and board comments on school-closing. Nor did he direct or intervene in board discussions. Left to take the initiative, board members floundered from meeting to meeting.

At their third session to consider a revised budget, Mallan proposed a "new approach," closing schools.[37] "In January of 1979 we voted that all six schools would remain open until the curriculum of J-D schools became jeopardized. Now it appears that the program is in jeopardy," asserted Mallan. He urged the board to commit itself to closing not one but two elementary schools. "I think we have to come to grips with this," Mallan said, as he urged immediate consideration of his proposal. Other advocates of closing did not hesitate at the clear determination to close more than one school. Hopkins declared, "I don't believe the community will buy the budget without a commitment that there will be reorganization and realignment in the JD school system."[38] And board president Carmen added her opinion that "the budget is interfaced with a commitment to close schools."

Mallan, Hopkins, and Carmen, joined by former board

181

Photograph 6. **Anthony DeBottis** insisted that passing the budget, not closing the schools, was the first priority in the summer of 1980.

president Perkins, represented the four-member minority that had opposed the board's 1979 decision to maintain all schools. Three of these board members, Mallan, Hopkins, and Perkins, had also opposed the 1978 decision to defer the closing of Moses Dewitt. From January 1979 to July 1980, however, this minority had not publicly challenged the policy of maintaining all schools. Nor did these board members urge the district to plan for future closings. Seeing the budget repudiated, however, the four members of the board minority now eagerly grasped the rationale that program was "jeopardized." As they clamored for school-closings, they neglected even to concentrate on Moses DeWitt as their primary target.

Once more DeBottis and Luchsinger resisted the board minority, protesting that passage of the budget alone deserved "first priority." Luchsinger warned, too, that a hasty decision to reorganize the school district could also produce a "no" vote on a revised budget. The board had yet to vote on a revised budget.[39]

To the administration's satisfaction, DeBottis took the lead in bringing the board's prolonged discussions to a conclusion at the next meeting. When Hopkins, Mallan, and Perkins repeatedly insisted that the board commit itself to school-closings, DeBottis argued that the public first be given an opportunity to vote on a reduced budget. Cutting the tax increase by $6.00 was the way to answer the "no" voters, he told colleagues who showed a mounting zeal to close schools. The budget reductions are "cuts that we can live with" and "won't harm our programs." Perkins, Mallan, and Hopkins disagreed, for in their judgment programs were "jeopardized" and this required school-closing. "The two issues go hand in hand," said Perkins. "Don't confuse passing the budget and closing a school," DeBottis answered this persistent advocate of school-closing. Finally, the board voted 7-2 to reject Luchsinger's austerity proposal. Then followed a 7-2 decision to offer the voters the administration's reduced budget, as Mallan and Perkins dissented.[40]

Because of strenuous efforts by DeBottis, the new reduced budget was not directly linked to a commitment to close schools. Instead, board members assured each other that they would examine reorganization and school-closings in September.[41] Perkins sought and received agreement that the reorganization question would not be put aside. "We have been treading water so long," she

183

said wearily. "We must make a commitment to resolve this question." Luchsinger and DeBottis agreed that the board should deal with the subject but not until after the budget vote. Mallan told his colleagues that they had "hit" the subject before but in the manner of "playing pattycake." The next time it would be "for real" with a decision expected in December or January, to which board president Carmen readily agreed as she directed the administration to prepare information on reorganization for September meetings.[42]

Relying heavily on DeBottis, the administration had drawn from the board a policy to present to the public. The reduced budget represented a tax increase of $6.15 instead of $11.95. The revised proposal also avoided the restrictions of an austerity budget, particularly such disagreeable prospects as an end to interscholastic athletics or the necessity of children's walking on busy roads. A district newsletter emphasized the board's concern for the "SAFETY of students." After a two-page listing of cuts made for the June budget and the additional reductions for the revised budget, the newsletter offered the prospect of school-closing for those still not satisfied. "At their July 22nd meeting, the board immediately began consideration of district reorganization and possible school closings. They will make a final decision on these matters early enough for any changes to be put into effect for the 1981-1982 school year."[43]

After many weeks of discussion and disarray, the administration at last had a policy ideally suited to its current purpose. The tax increase appeared low enough to gain public approval, thus erasing the stigma of austerity and returning control to local school officials, no longer restricted by the legal prohibitions imposed by an austerity budget. The commitment to study district reorganization and make a "final decision" for the 1981-1982 school year offered an enticing prospect for those eager to "resolve" the closing issue. On the other hand, the board had yet to act on the subject, thus not alienating Moses Dewitt supporters.

Moses DeWitt parents felt little choice but to support the budget, although this time they knew that passage would not defer the closing question. Some considered and cast "no" votes to protest budget reductions as well as the board's implicit agreement to close schools. But most interested parents were

184

faithful school-supporters who wanted a publicly-approved budget for the district and bus transportation for their children.

Having previously allied himself with Moses DeWitt supporters to pass the budget, Superintendent Baker now gave rein to closing advocates. He hoped that a new coalition would emerge to approve the budget--his foremost goal--and also indicate the district's future direction. Once the budget passed, initiative and control would again shift to the administration, which could possibly improvise tactics to avoid the obvious minefields of school-closing. On August 7, residents approved the budget by a margin of 1,474 to 1,001. But the issue of reorganization was now on "the front burner," as promised by board president Carmen at the last meeting before the vote.

## NOTES

1. **Post–Standard**(Syracuse), Apr. 10, 1980.
2. **Ibid.**
3. All quotes from **Post–Standard**, May 1, 1980.
4. **Suburban Life**(DeWitt and East Syracuse), May 28, 1980.
5. Howard D. Hamilton and Sylvan H. Cohen, **Policy Making by Plebiscite: School Referenda**(Lexington, 1974), 73.
6. **Ibid.**
7. Campaign statements in flyers distributed by Benjamin D. Levine and Benjamin G. Berry, Jr., May 1980; also **Suburban Life**, May 28, 1980.
8. **Post–Standard**, June 7, 1980.
9. **Post–Standard**, June 12, 1980.
10. **Ibid.**
11. **Post–Standard**, July 24, 1980.
12. **Post–Standard**, June 12, 1980.
13. **Post–Standard**, June 19, 1980.
14. Hamilton and Cohen, **Policy Making by Plebiscite**, 87.
15. **Ibid.**
16. Robert A. Dahl, **Who Governs?**(New Haven, 1961), 158.
17. Hamilton and Cohen, **Policy Making by Plebiscite**, 88.
18. Michael Nunnery and Ralph Kimbrough, **Politics, Power, Polls, and School Elections** (Berkeley, 1971), iii.
19. **Post–Standard**, June 19, 1980.
20. **Ibid.**
21. Jamesville-DeWitt District Report, June 16, 1980.
22. Hamilton and Cohen, **Policy Making by Plebiscite**, 110.
23. **Suburban Life**, June 18, 1980.
24. Hamilton and Cohen, **Policy Making by Plebiscite**, 111.

25. **Suburban Life**, June 18, 1980.

26. Laurence Iannaccone and Frank W. Lutz, **Politics, Power, and Policy: The Governing of Local School Districts**(Columbus, 1980), 208; also Hamilton and Cohen, **Policy Making by Plebiscite**, 110.

27. Philip K. Kiele and John S. Hall, **Budgets, Bonds, and Ballots**(Lexington, 1973), 69.

28. Edward C. Banfield and James Q. Wilson, **City Politics** (Cambridge, 1963), 38-44.

29. Piele and Hall, **Budgets, Bonds, and Ballots**, 72.

30. Jamesville-DeWitt Board of Education meeting, June 24, 1980, author's notes.

31. **Ibid.**

32. **Post-Standard**, June 26, 1980.

33. Jamesville-DeWitt Board of Education meeting, July 1, 1980, author's notes.

34. Wallace S. Sayre, as quoted by David B. Tyack, **The One Best System**(Cambridge, 1974), 147.

35. James S. Coleman, **Community Conflict**(New York, 1957); also Piele and Hall, **Budgets, Bonds, and Ballots**, 62.

36. **Post-Standard**, June 19, 1980.

37. **Post-Standard**, July 10, 1980.

38. **Suburban Life**, July 16, 1980.

39. **Post-Standard**, July 17, 1980.

40. Jamesville-DeWitt Board of Education meeting, July 22, 1980, author's notes.

41. **Post-Standard**, July 24, 1980.

42. **Ibid.**

43. Jamesville-DeWitt District Report, July 1980.

44. Voting statistics are from the Jamesville-DeWitt District Office.

# XII.   School-Closing as a Political Catalyst

Shortly before the August 7 budget vote a young couple new to the district proposed a different approach to what had become known as "the school problem."   What did people think, and what did they want the school district to do?   An opinion-survey had often been mentioned, but no information had been gathered following the Task Force questionnaire administered in early 1977.   In the winter of 1978, after the decision to defer the closing of Moses DeWitt, the school board discussed conducting an opinion-survey to accompany the new door-to-door census done that spring.   At that time the board considered asking voters a series of questions.   For example, did residents want to maintain the four elementary schools but offset the cost by modifying the middle-school program?   Or did they prefer to close an elementary school to reduce costs and maintain existing programs?[1]   Drafting the questions proved difficult, and Moses DeWitt parents quickly questioned the motivation and possible bias of the proposed questionnaire.   After considering the emotionally-charged atmosphere of the time, the board abandoned the opinion-survey and later chose to emphasize informal "communications meetings" with the public.

In the fall of 1978, the demographic committee discussed an opinion-survey, which was included in that committee's list of possible undertakings.   Again, the problem of drafting neutral but useful questions seemed insuperable.   Most committee members argued that residents would not understand terms such as "program" and "curriculum," and thus their choices would be unclear or meaningless.   A majority of committee members, particularly administrators, doubted that an opinion-survey would produce worthwhile information.   When the board reached its decision to maintain all schools in January 1979, it did so without a systematic reading of public opinion.

Following the two budget defeats of June 1980, however, some board members immediately saw a mandate for school-closings.   Public opinion was assessed on the basis of what board members heard in conversations with residents.   Instead of speculation concerning the two defeats or conclusions drawn from a few people, why not ask residents for their opinions?   This proposal was urged by Sharon and David H. Northrup, Jr., whose house faced the Moses DeWitt playground.   Like many new residents, they had purchased their house after Moses DeWitt was first named for closing. Despite the school's uncertain future, the surrounding neighborhood continued to draw young families. The average age of residents buying houses in 1978 was twenty years younger than that of previous owners.[2] These new residents now offered their ideas at a time when the closing of Moses DeWitt seemed inevitable to the original resisters.

The opinion-survey required skillful handling. Perhaps the community did in fact demand a closing. Moses DeWitt residents who gathered to plan the project rejected an early questionnaire draft that directly asked people if they wanted to close one or more elementary schools. To avoid the potentially dangerous backfire of such a query, residents would be asked to indicate areas in which the board of education should "focus its attention," generally specified as educational program, facilities, staffing, and others. Residents would have to show initiative to emphasize closing as a concern. Other subjects were to be covered as well, including feelings about the June and August budgets and an assessment of the school system's quality at all levels.

The questionnaire was designed to have a neutral appearance. It would not look professional; nor would it appear partisan. The introduction stated only that "this questionnaire is designed to help concerned citizens compile data about how the voters of the Jamesville-DeWitt School District feel about the budget and the school program." The opening questions concerning past voting and the ages of children enrolled in school were vague and unthreatening. Then followed questions about the June budget and tax proposal. ("Do you feel a tax increase of $11.95 is too high?") The question focusing on school quality at the elementary, middle, and high-school levels was designed to reveal different concerns from those discussed in the closing dispute. A question about the August 7 budget proposal preceded the critical but intentionally vague question asking where the board of education should focus its attention. The questionnaire did not build to an inevitable conclusion; if anything, it was written to avoid such a conclusion.

Moses DeWitt residents planned to distribute the questionnaire to voters leaving the polls after the August 7 budget vote. The questionnaire was to be discreetly administered by parents not conspicuously

188

identified with Moses DeWitt. Neither board members nor administrators were to receive prior consultation about the impending opinion-survey. Moses DeWitt residents, including both newcomers and longtime activists, did not expect either board members or administrators to look favorably on a project that they had not initiated. School officials were preoccupied with passing the budget. Furthermore, those board members eager to close schools would surely see the questionnaire as a last-gasp effort by their opponents. If consulted, the board of education could publicly disavow the questionnaire or urge residents to withdraw it for the "good of the district."

Administrators had purposely avoided any use of questionnaires in recent years. In a divided community a survey had a degree of unpredictability. It might produce information that would further complicate decision-making or raise issues best not discussed. An opinion-survey conducted by parents would compound these problems by being outside the administration's control.

Within two days of the budget vote, Moses DeWitt residents informed the district office of the opinion-survey. In the absence of other administrators, the assistant superintendent for finance received the call. He expressed no immediate reservations about the plans. After word reached board members, however, one appealed to residents to drop the project. Others expressed indignation and disapproval. On August 7 board president Carmen had signs posted saying that the opinion-survey was not authorized by the board of education. The district suddenly, and for the first and only time to date, enforced a 1979 amendment to the Education Law requiring distance markers at 100 feet from the polls and prohibiting "electioneering" within this area. A prohibition against "loitering" was also posted. Parents administering the questionnaire were said to be "electioneering," although Jamesville-DeWitt school board candidates had often lingered at the polls and in June one candidate had prominently displayed his name near the voting machines. Located beyond the 100-foot markers, residents found that many voters showed an interest in the opinion-survey.

Of the 2475 residents voting on August 7, fifty-six per cent filled in the questionnaire. These 1390 respondents told more about public feeling concerning the budget and the school district than did any previous analysis. Responses to questions about the budget

189

showed a good sampling of the electorate. Of those answering the questionnaire, 56 per cent favored the third budget, as opposed to 60 per cent of that day's electorate. The four elementary-school areas were represented in percentages close to those seen in elections.

The questionnaire produced solid information about those supporting and opposing district budgets. A clear-cut group had supported both the June and August budgets. The budget-supporter was typically a parent with children in the school system, as administrators had long assumed but never established. Of these solid "yes" voters, moreover, almost forty per cent were parents of elementary-school children. Parents of children in the middle and high schools also gave support, as did a smaller group of residents whose children had graduated from Jamesville-DeWitt. Not surprisingly, the questionnaire showed budget-supporters to be pleased with all levels of the school system, especially the elementary schools.

Parents in the district did not consistently support the budget, however. Only 56 per cent of parents answering the questionnaire indicated support for the June budget. Parents offered support ranging from 29 per cent positive in Jamesville, an area including lower-income neighborhoods, to 40 per cent positive in the middle-to-upper income Tecumseh section. Parents both in Jamesville and Tecumseh objected strongly to the $11.95 tax increase proposed in June. In the Genesee Hills area parents were divided in their opinions about the tax increase, but 65 per cent of these respondents nonetheless supported the June budget. In the Moses DeWitt area almost 67 per cent of parents found the size of the tax increase acceptable, while 73 per cent of these respondents indicated support for the budget. The opinion-survey confirmed a bloc of Moses DeWitt parents clearly committed to the budget. Moses DeWitt activists had worked to develop this commitment and often emphasized its importance, which administrators tacitly acknowledged. The opinion-survey offered the first concrete evidence of the variation in voting behavior from area to area.

Whereas parents differed in their views of the June budget, residents who had no children in school decisively rejected it. Responses to the questionnaire showed a defined bloc of non-users who opposed both the June and August budgets. Even after the board cut the tax increase in half, most non-users remained budget-opponents. This group also showed less enthusiasm for the quality of the schools.

On August 7, 60 per cent of those voting approved the budget. Significant voting shifts occurred not among non-users but among parents. Parents in the Moses DeWitt area again gave strong support. Sixty-five per cent of these respondents indicated a "yes" vote, as did 59 per cent of the parents in the Genesee Hills area. Cool to the June budget, Tecumseh parents now supported the reduced tax proposal. Fifty-nine per cent of these residents now voted "yes" in contrast to only 40 per cent in June. Jamesville parents shifted from only 29 per cent favorable to 45 per cent.

What is the explanation of this voting pattern? Tecumseh and Jamesville parents had strongly objected to the $11.95 tax proposal, so the reduced budget partly accounts for the change. Furthermore, most parents knew that a third "no" vote meant austerity and children's walking to school in September. Underlying the obvious concerns about money and safety, however, were deeper political and social divisions, many of them explicitly recorded in comments written on the questionnaires.

Some 350 residents, or 25 per cent of those answering the questionnaire, added their own statements of opinion. Many wrote extensive suggestions and criticisms. These comments highlighted the very issues that the questionnaire was designed to mute. School-closing remained a focus of discontent, a symbol of resentment and dissatisfaction in Jamesville-DeWitt. Of the written comments close to 200 called for school-closing and many named Moses DeWitt. Opposed to this viewpoint, however, was a substantial group of budget-supporters, willing to pay the price to keep all schools. The community's conflicting interests were temporarily contained during the eighteen-month period between January 1979, and June 1980, when two budget defeats revealed the fault lines in the school district.

About thirteen per cent of all respondents wrote comments calling for school-closing.3  Of this group the vast majority were school-users, or parents. By contrast, only one per cent of non-users specifically mentioned this subject. A significant number of parents saw the closing issue as a long-unresolved question that threatened not only their child's school but his education. These residents trusted the board's initial commitment in 1977 to close a school. That the district had somehow continued to maintain all schools seemed proof in itself that quality had been reduced. One resident wrote:

> I feel that no group has been as unconcerned about the educational program in the J-D district as those who use the "neighborhood" school excuse to divert funds from the educational programs to the physical maintenance of unused classroom space and facilties. Moses DeWitt should have been closed when first proposed to prevent the cuts in programs now forced upon the students at J-D.[4]

Board members had long referred to programs and facilities as if the two questions were inextricably connected. Public discussion also accepted the supposed contradiction between schools and programs. The costs of operating any elementary school fell well below one per cent of the district's budget, while salaries and employee benefits accounted for over seventy-five per cent. Nevertheless, the savings of school-closing loomed large in the public mind. "When a business has a shrinking market it adjusts," wrote one resident.[5] Another concluded, "There is no need to keep Moses DeWitt School open. Heat, electricity, etc. there are a major factor in expenses," stating a widespread but fallacious opinion.[6]

Because the board of education had not taken a critical economy measure when it could, the school district had reached its present plight--rising taxes and budget-defeat.[7] Some residents referred to the impact of double-digit inflation on school budgets, but others were single-minded in their interpretation. Neither economic trends nor any school policy other than the failure to close a building seemed important to this group. One parent wrote of the school board, "I feel they should have sooner followed up upon closing Moses DeWitt so we could have taken advantage of the savings before a problem with passing the budget occurred."[8]

Furthermore, the reduction in the August budget, half of which consisted of simply eliminating the planned balance, provided apparent evidence that programs had been cut.

By not closing a school we have bought the

192

worst of two worlds. Programs have been
cut. The savings from a closed school
could have been used to upgrade programs.
Now a school will be closed and programs
are already cut.[9]

Although the August budget provided for such modest
changes as the elimination of field trips and assemblies
and a consolidation of bus routes, a segment of the public
seized upon these reductions as significant, as had a
determined bloc of board members. Any change whatever
altered the quality of program and underscored the need
to close a school. "It was agreed two years ago to close
a facility when our programs were jeopardized! That
time has come!"[10]

Often residents who insisted that a school be closed
urged the board to keep all programs and develop new ones
as well.[11] "Close an elementary school! Where is your
pre-K program? Where is your talented and gifted
program?"[12] During one period Superintendent Baker had
stated that the savings of closing a school were minimal,
but this action--and failure to take it--had assumed
political proportions that far overshadowed its
financial impact. Closing a school could simultaneously
solve the district's budgetary problems and bolster its
academic reputation, secure fiscal retrenchment and open
the way to new and better educational vistas.

In the absence of specific discussion or
information from the board or administration,
contradictory viewpoints flourished. Neither administrators nor board members had consistently or clearly
explained school-closing as a measure that would simply
reduce the increase in the tax rate. School officials
had not demonstrated that the savings from a closing
would be used to enhance programs. Nor had they
dispelled that belief. Because of a paucity of
established facts, the closing issue was debated in
highly rhetorical, even emotional, terms both by board
members and by the community.[13]

True to the characteristic style of school
politics, citizens justified their position as best for
the children. "Close Moses DeWitt!" wrote one parent
who asked, "Why are you hurting our children?"[14] "It is
sad the children need to make sacrifices," concluded a
resident who urged school-closing.[15] The board should
instead "try to meet the needs of all children
educationally!" said a parent who echoed the goal so

193

often stated by school district leaders.[16]

These residents did not describe the harm inflicted on children by the policy of maintaining all schools or by the budget reductions made in August. They assumed rather than explained the benefits of school-closing "for the children." Emotional statements such as "Don't make the kids the scapegoats!" were sometimes juxtaposed with expressions of continuing faith in the system.[17] The school board still enjoyed what Zeigler and Jennings have described as a reservoir of public support.[18] Citizens declared their belief in the excellence of the Jamesville-DeWitt school system and its officials. "It's the best--and should remain so," wrote one spokesman for the long-established school ideology.[19] Said another, "This is the greatest school district--Too bad a few malcontents are causing problems."[20]

The failure to close Moses DeWitt, however, appeared as a moral weakness that undermined public confidence in the system and served to focus resentments. Local school officials had vacillated instead of taking the prescribed medicine. "Be brave! Close a school! We'll handle it."[21] A resident who described the delay in closing Moses DeWitt remarked that "other districts can make up their minds much sooner than J-D. Why the long wait?"[22]

Furthermore, the school district's failure of will specifically concerned Moses DeWitt. Financial and educational problems remained insuperable, because the district had failed to confront the closing question. "I think the Moses DeWitt problem is the crux of your entire problem," a resident concluded at the end of a long analysis.[23] "Close Moses DeWitt! **Please, please** cut at least one elementary school" expressed a deeply-felt view.[24] Almost ninety per cent of the prents who called for school-closing, however, were **not** residents of the Moses DeWitt area. A substantial majority lived in the Tecumseh and Jamesville areas.

Tecumseh residents who commented on closing saw the continued existence of Moses DeWitt as a direct threat to their own school. These parents emphasized the saleability of Moses DeWitt or the prospects of renting the building because of its proximity to a commercial location. Tecumseh parents most often commented on harm to educational programs or to children in the board's policy--or lack of policy. They resented concessions made to "selfish interests," but tried to maintain faith in the system. "I believe they (the board) are working things out," concluded one parent.[25]

Jamesville residents more often emphasized the board's unwillingness to make necessary economies and cut frills. "I advocate bare bones education and the closing of a school on Jamesville Road (Moses DeWitt)," said a parent.[26] Another resident offered only the terse conclusion, "Close a school. Stop catering to the rich," illustrating the continuing schism between Jamesville and DeWitt. Social divisions are also evident in comments describing the school district as "too high society" and "too self-satisfied."[27] Jamesville parents questioned teachers' salaries and cited school administrators, who live in Jamesville, for condemnation. A number objected to privileges and "lulus" for administrators, particularly the misuse of two district cars and credit cards for gasoline.[28]

The Genesee Hills parents who wrote comments make a less distinct group. In contrast to Tecumseh residents, Genesee Hills parents did not see Moses DeWitt as a clear and present danger to their own school. Although these parents often remarked that the school board "should have closed Moses DeWitt when they had the chance" and lamented the sacrifice of program for facilities,[29] their comments did not assume a future choice between Moses DeWitt and Genesee Hills. Parents in Genesee Hills had given greater support to the June budgets and seemed less zealous to resolve the closing problem. Again, social distinctions appear, however, as in comments that the board kept Moses DeWitt for "the rich"[30] or because of "the rich people who don't want to send their kids to Genesee Hills where there are blacks."[31]

Among the parents who discussed school issues, some specifically stated that they voted for the August budget because the board appeared willing to close a school. For example, one wrote, "Close at least one elementary school. Positive vote today based on comments that this problem would be addressed promptly."[32] This sentiment probably contributed to the shift of votes between June and August, particularly the upswing of support from Tecumseh and Jamesville parents. The August budget received approval of almost two-thirds of school-users or parents, a significant increase from that seen in June.

Yet a number of solid budget-supporters who had

voted for both the June and August proposals indicated their preference for the $11.95 tax increase. Parents holding this viewpoint registered dismay at any reductions in the district's services, whether after-school bus runs, teacher-aides, or middle-school interscholastic athletics. These respondents reflected the tradition of generous support that had prevailed over the years. Commenting on the August budget, some voters indicated support but noted preference for the first budget.33 Other residents wrote that they did vote "no" to show their displeasure with the cuts and the board's direction.34 Support from parents in Genesee Hills did in fact decline from 65 per cent approval in June to 59 per cent in August, while support from Moses DeWitt parents dropped from 73 per cent to 65 per cent.

School closing did not receive first attention from the group of parents most willing to spend and support the school system. Fifty-one per cent of these consistent "yes" voters urged the board to focus on educational program, while 32 per cent selected examination of facilities. Written comments also reflect this emphasis. Study and improvement of educatonal program is "where I feel the dollars should be going. I also like the small classes the elementary schools now have," said a Tecumseh parent who did not advocate closing.35 "Please examine educational programs and improve where possible! No school closures!" a Moses DeWitt resident advised, expressing an opinion commonly, but not unanimously, held by parents of that area.36 Suggested changes included a more "structured" or "demanding" middle school, improved counseling at the middle and high-school levels, and a strengthened English program in the high school. Financial constraints did not appear to disturb these respondents. Some thought it time to close a school, but they did not emphasize an immediate choice between program and facilities. They were willing to pay for both.

In the summer of 1980, Jamesville-DeWitt voters were badly divided, and the school district's consensus had unraveled. Residents without children steadfastly opposed tax proposals and wanted to cut "fat" and "frills" from the system. A critical segment of parents had also withdrawn approval, making support contingent upon the board's "talking seriously of action to close a school." Politicized by the budget-defeats, these residents now saw the opportunity to close a school at last. That Carmen, Perkins, Mallan, and Hopkins now determined the board's, and apparently the administration's, direction offered added encouragement. Now-hopeful residents expressed faith in the "integrity of the school board"[37] and appreciation for "the work of a dedicated board," but this endorsement required the board to act.[38] The era of "group pressures all working toward their own selfish goals" had ended.[39] Instead, the board must consider the entire community and thereby reestablish both its own authority and public confidence in the system. This position assumed the closing of Moses DeWitt but its heightened fervor left open the possiblity of other closings as well.

Arrayed against these parents were the once-dominant Moses DeWitt residents as well as others who did not see school-closing as a panacea. Included in this group were the district's strongest budget-supporters, still willing to finance and improve both program and facilities. Liberal in their view of what Jamesville-DeWitt could and should afford, these voters also had definite expectations. Those from Moses DeWitt wanted to preserve their own school, preferably not at the expense of others. Despite concessions wrung from the board of education, these parents refused to admire its dedication or integrity, and least of all did they have "faith in the board's ability to work things out." "The board should act less arrogantly and deal honestly with its constituency," wrote one Moses DeWitt parent.[40] A Genesee Hills resident thought "the school board seems to look down on those who pay the bills."[41] Willing to support the district budgets, these voters nevertheless voiced deep suspicion of the board's future actions.

Just as the 1977 decision to close Moses DeWitt had motivated residents to influence the school board, the $11.95 tax increase and budget-defeats inspired other interests to demand satisfaction. First discussed in 1976, school-closing had lingered as an issue, serving as a catalyst that activated different--and often competing--groups. In comments on their questionnaires residents wondered why the question had become divisive. "Why can't highly educated nice people--parents, staff, and board--work together? We all want the same thing."[42] Yet in the years in which closing was alternately considered and not considered, the community had become polarized. In 1980 the possibility of a simple solution was as remote as it had been in 1977.

Looking at the mass of data accumulated in the 1390 questionnaires, Moses DeWitt residents decided to code and enter responses in a computer. The vehemence of

197

written comments surprised even Moses DeWitt activists accustomed to opposition. Closing Moses Dewitt had become the focus of political interest within the school district, a goal widely expressed by people in every section and also advanced by a committed minority within the Moses DeWitt area. Furthermore, closing Moses DeWitt had assumed major symbolic importance. This act promised to solve practical problems related to rising taxes and budgets and, more important, to purify the system. The closing appeared as a practical necessity and a moral imperative. Once this action was taken, all would be well with what was otherwise a "beautiful" school district. Except for the Moses DeWitt problem, Jamesville-DeWitt had always been "the best and should remain so."[43]

After studying these comments, Moses Dewitt residents decided to prepare a report emphasizing voting behavior rather than attitudes and opinions, which were less susceptible to statistical treatment in addition to being contrary to the group's purposes. The opinion-survey did confirm the importance of Moses DeWitt parents as a voting bloc. Although Genesee Hills parents also supported the budget, the voting turn-out from that area was only about half of that of the Moses DeWitt area. As often repeated by activist parents, the school district could ill afford to ignore the wishes of its interested, well-organized Moses DeWitt constituents.

The opinion-survey also showed a suburban community's commitment to its schools. Educated, well-to-do parents wanted excellent schools for their children. Although Jamesville-DeWitt residents rated their school system very highly, they also wanted changes, especially in a middle-school program regarded as less effective than that offered in the elementary and high school levels. Board members often promised to "preserve program," while the interested public desired more than this. Forty-eight per cent of all respondents indicated that they wanted the school board to examine educational programs. Yet board members rarely discussed the public's concern with, for example, the strength of basic programs in English and mathematics, middle-school grading and discipline, or high-school guidance--all matters considered to be the administration's province.

As the school board's meeting on September 23, 1980, David H. Northrup, Jr. and John E. Hayes, Jr., both DeWitt businessmen and residents of the DeWittshire neighborhood adjacent to Moses DeWitt, presented a summary of questionnaire results. Although this was an informal communications meeting, board president Carmen proceeded through an extensive agenda, including a lengthy consideration of a forthcoming meeting of the New York State school boards' association which no Jamesville-DeWitt member wished to attend. Two hours after the meeting started, the board president acknowledged Northrup and Hayes, representing an "unidentified group" and allotted twenty minutes to speak. In their report the two residents described the voting shifts between June and August, offering profiles of budget-supporters and budget-opponents and what each group recommended to the board. They then described how voters rated the quality of the schools and briefly listed the concerns mentioned in comments. Given the community's conflicting interests, the board faced a difficult task in "reaching decisions acceptable to the community," concluded Northrup and Hayes.

After only a few questions to the speakers, the board went on to other subjects, and the opinion-survey was never again publicly mentioned. Privately, a sympathetic board member told a Moses DeWitt parent that "nothing you've ever done has made the board so mad." The residents had declined to honor the board's prerogatives, and the board declined to inquire into or use the data gathered by parents.

Nevertheless, Northrup and Hayes felt determined to achieve public discussion of the opinion-survey, so they turned to **Suburban Life.** Again the weekly highlighted the closing issue and publicized parents' efforts. The opinion-survey received a bold front-page headline and a full interior page including large-type, underscored quotations from Northrup and Hayes and a copy of a concluding sheet in the report.[44] The favorable publicity drew comment chiefly from those who had worked on administering the questionnaire or studying the results.

As in the census findings of 1978 and the four committee reports of 1979, Moses DeWitt parents regarded their opinion-survey as a substantive contribution to the school district. Thinking of new ways to consider school-closing, citizens learned about birthrates, budgets, and public opinion. Fact-finding and strategy went hand in hand to sustain the group's efforts over several years. But contrary to parents' hopes, school officials did not want their information and consistently refused to acknowledge it.

## NOTES

1. **Suburban Life**(DeWitt and East Syracuse), Mar. 8, 1978.
2. Demographic Committee, Report to the Jamesville-DeWitt Board of Education, Jan. 1979, Section 6.
3. All questionnaires including those with comments are in the author's possession; questionnaires are numbered and quotations are identified by number.
4. #1383.
5. #204.
6. #1171.
7. #373.
8. #939.
9. #778.
10. #157.
11. #1068.
12. #1041.
13. See Howard D. Hamilton and Sylvan H. Cohen, **Policy Making by Plebiscite: School Referenda**(Lexington, 1974), 110-113, on rhetoric and emotion in school issues.
14. #960.
15. #743.
16. #1365.
17. #93.
18. L. Harmon Zeigler and M. Kent Jennings, **Governing American Schools**(North Scituate, Mass., 1974), 1. 13.
19. #1038.
20. #112.
21. #108.
22. #1343.
23. #200.
24. #1114.
25. #17.
26. #936.
27. #1065.
28. #401; #316.
29. #337.
30. #1340.
31. #1088.
32. #1146.
33. #1098.
34. #502.
35. #1098.
36. #1028.

37. #17.
38. #65.
39. #200.
40. #893.
41. #1198.
42. #781.
43. #1038.
44. **Suburban Life**, Oct. 1, 1980.

# XIII. The Long Prologue

Early in September Superintendent Baker had given board members notebooks of information to use in studying the district's forthcoming reorganization. Material presented to the board included 1980 enrollment figures for each school, contrasted with peak enrollments, a breakdown of staffing for each building, a description of community use of the schools during daytime and evening hours, and a floor-plan of each school. The information, containing nothing new, was withheld from the public, drawing a protest from board member Mallan. In 1977 the board's private deliberations had left "scars." To avoid past mistakes, the community now required full discussion, "a wide-open fling-out." Vowing to attend no future executive sessions, Mallan advised his colleagues that "our information should be open to the public with rare exceptions."[1] Board members Luchsinger and Perkins agreed that executive sessions should be used sparingly.[2]

At its second meeting in September, the board devoted only a few minutes to the sparse material first included in the notebooks. Instead, board members asked the administration to evaluate a variety of reorganization "options."[3] Neither listed in the notebooks nor discussed in previous board meetings, options were first set forth in a July 24 memorandum from the superintendent, followed by a more detailed list dated September 23, 1980.[4]

In his July memorandum to board members and staff, Superintendent Baker had noted a variety of possible changes, such as creating a magnet school in one house of the middle school or moving all elementary schools to the middle school. Another proposal called for closing two elementary schools and reorganizing the remaining two, one school for grades K-2 and the other for grades 3-5, meaning "more flexibility" and the "district comes together at an early age." Attempting to balance contraction and innovation, Baker also suggested an all-day kindergarten or day-care center. Concluding suggestions called for consideration of program changes, such as flexible kindergarten entrance, gifted and talented programs, and early identification of problem students. Significantly, the July memorandum proposed that "the total focus of any change in organization center around program--what's best for students in grades K-12, short range and long range."[5]

The superintendent's September memo dispensed with any comment on the approach to reorganization or changes in the educational program and instead listed a number of plans long discussed. These options included closing two elementary schools and reorganizing as a K-4, 5-8, 9-12 system; closing the middle school and reorganizing with grades K-7 in elementary school and grades 8-12 at the high school; closing one elementary school and retaining a K-5, 6-8, 9-12 organization; and, last, closing two elementary schools, making two K-3 elementary schools, a 4-8 middle school, and a 9-12 high school.[6]

At the board's September 23 meeting, Baker explained the efforts of the administrative staff in assembling information on grade organization, drawing "input" from principals, teachers, and parents, and listing options. "We are trying to find out what kind of organization we feel is best for Jamesville-DeWitt," the superintendent stated. Once the "priority order of organizations" is established, "the rest is up to the board." At that point the school board "will determine which buildings to affect, which to close or not," and the administration will determine how to implement the board's decision.[7]

For the public's benefit Baker rapidly read off the options described in his September memo, explaining the variants of each one. Each plan had a number of permutations, and the superintendent's hurried recital left the impression of a multiplicity of choices. At least one and possibly three administrative meetings would be necessary to rank the organizational plans. Nevertheless, Baker forecast a "narrowing down of options" and recommended that the board first consider the K-4, 5-8, 9-12 plan. Board members decided to await the administration's report on the options and then reach decisions based first on educational program and, second, on finances. The board appeared in agreement until the meeting's end, when DeBottis and Scibilia asked if the decision to close a school had already been reached and, if so, when.[8]

A week later, on September 30, the board of education met again in special session. President Carmen opened the meeting by saying that the voters had spoken in two budget defeats, directing the board to close a school, and "we are here tonight to make that decision." Luchsinger immediately challenged the board

204

president for calling a meeting without explaining its purpose to board members, none of whom knew of the evening's agenda. He observed that Carmen had declined to describe the purpose of the meeting to her colleagues, yet she herself had read from a prepared statement. "You can't make a decision and then give everybody the shuffle," he said. "I don't know who's doing this, whether it's you or Lance (Baker), but it's got to stop. If we're going to be discussing closing schools, you'd better make sure everybody knows we're meeting."[9] Other board members also voiced irritation at the evening's proceedings.

As the mood darkened Superintendent Baker intervened to say that the administrative staff had met, and he was pepared to give the board the report promised the previous week. But "the decision to close a school has to come before the discussion of options," he now maintained in a direct reversal of the position he had stated a week earlier.[10] "We can discuss options of organization any year. First you decide to close a school, then consider options." Baker further explained that administrators were willing to keep all schools open if that was what the board wanted.[11] Taken aback, several board members asked why the decision on closing now took precedence over consideration of reorganization plans and program goals. "I expected a weeding out of options. What happened to that?" said a puzzled Ben Berry, now in his third month of office. Luchsinger, Cargian, and Mallan, who had often differed on other questions, asserted that program and organization should receive first consideration as originally planned. Perkins, however, declared herself ready to discuss closings. In her judgment, "We're treading water. We keep putting things further and further into the future."[12] In obvious disarray, the board voted to adjourn and place the subject of school-closing first on the agenda of its October 14 meeting.

Board president Carmen later told the press that she and Superintendent Baker had decided to call the special meeting to see if board members truly wished to close a school.[13] Before the August budget vote, Baker had exploited the board's tacit agreement to close one or two schools. The district's newsletter of July 29, 1980, had described the board's consideration of district reorganization and school closings, saying that a final decision would be reached in time "to be put into effect for the 1981-1982 school year." But when two board members asked when or why the decision to close a school had been made, the superintendent decided to shift the question back to the board. The administration was "not going to recommend closing a school." Instead, Baker now offered "to take the pressure off" the reorganization process and await the board's judgment.[14]

When differences within the board and the community again seemed inescapable, administrators withdrew. Once again the board of education advanced, or was pushed, to the fore as the spokesman for education, as Roscoe Martin has written of the characteristic pattern of crisis politics in school districts.[15] Having executed a precipitous retreat from his statements of preceding months, the superintendent avoided public criticism, even for the September 30 meeting. Instead, attention focused on the school board, variously described by the residents as "unpredictable," "unresponsive," and "uncommunicative the minute a crisis comes up."[16] Michael Marge, a professor of education and onetime dean at Syracuse University, accused the board of trying to "railroad" a school-closing on September 30, a viewpoint shared by Moses DeWitt parents who hurried to the meeting after an alert was sounded. Lynda Rill, president of the Moses DeWitt Parents' Group, complained of an important session held without "great notification." The superintendent blandly explained that the meeting's purpose did no concern "any one school in particular."[18]

An experienced politician, Baker did not intend to be impaled on an issue he had learned to know, if not master. As superintendent, he constantly assessed the interests and influence of different segments of the community and parlayed the desires of board members and residents, generally securing approval for his proposals. Skilled in the private negotiations of day-to-day school politics, Baker and other adminstrators did not direct the board's discussion, or comprehension, of public issues. Martin has written, "The superintendent and his aides, though skillful and experienced at the infighting which characterizes 'school board politics,' step out of character when they essay roles of leadership in the public forum."[19]

Furthermore, administrative theory stipulated that the superintendent implement the will of the "employer." The school superintendency had developed early in the twentieth century as a "learned profession," for which specialized university training and qualifications were required.[20] Administrators commanded reputed technical

206

Photograph 7. Board president **Joyce Carmen** and Superintendent **Lansing Baker** contemplate school-closings, 1980.

knowledge, community respect, and public positions, not to be squandered in political conflict. The board had to "clarify the stand on school closings," so that the administration could safely implement the decision.[21] To satisfy their professional ethic and guarantee their own survival, administrators now deferred to the board for leadership. In a rapid sequence of events, this direction was established.

On September 30, Perkins submitted her resignation effective immediately following the board's special meeting. In a statement to the local press, the former board president expressed feelings of "futility" and "frustration" that made her position on the board "untenable."[22] Despite the board's apparent agreement in July, the necessity of school-closings and reorganization remained in question. Long thwarted in her desire to close a school, Perkins had seen the issue again postponed at her last meeting.

In her farewell address the embattled Perkins expressed disappointment with board members, residents, and administrators. "The Jamesville-DeWitt school board members, for whatever reasons, are unwilling to take a stand and appear afraid to make a decision." Also at fault were those citizens who speak only in the voting booth, expecting "elected persons to operate without public support." Denied the much-needed public presence and voice of her own supporters, Perkins had also suffered when she "was personally attacked for taking an unpopular stand" in voting to close Moses DeWitt. Administrators, too, had contributed to her displeasure. "Over the years I have expressed many concerns, but have been given to understand that one must not ask controversial or embarrassing questions," wrote the departing board member. "Time and again issues are brought up only to be abruptly dropped or glazed over. Answers are evasive and information requested is not always received. I am frustrated at every attempt to get forthright action on issues." Convinced that board members and school administrators had again retreated from their commitment to consider school-closing, Perkins resigned.[23]

The school board's October 14 meeting convened before an audience of 150 residents, some of them standing in the aisles and halls. Board member Hopkins opened by honoring Phyllis Perkins, a representative who thought only of "the interest of the children" and "the entire J-D district." Reading from a prepared address,

208

Hopkins recalled his term as board president in 1976-1977 when Perkins headed the Task Force. "We knew then that we would face surplus classrooms," recounted the Jamesville board member. Having studied the Task Force data, the board voted to close a facility, only to reverse the decision in response to the "affected part of the community." Finally, in the summer of 1980 the board had "to cut the heart out of the J-D program." In August the budget passed after assurances that something would be done.24 "Now," Hopkins concluded, "we are in a position to consolidate and reorganize." He then moved that the board of education close two schools at the end of 1980-1981.25

Mallan seconded the motion, but added that the board should still consider the kind of program "the facilities should facilitate." DeBottis found Hopkins's motion premature and asked that it be withdrawn until other board members had a chance to offer their opinions on options for reorganizaion. Berry still wanted to know what the administration recommended, while Cargian described a discussion of options as the first step. "Why isn't the motion a first step?" asked Hopkins. Finally, Luchsinger called for the administration's recommendations.26

Superintendent Baker reported that administrators had met "to discuss the best educational program for kids." Anticipating the necessary board commitment on school-closing, the superintendent now felt prepared to discuss options for reorganization. He returned, albeit unconvincingly, to the subject of the ideal grade-organization and program for Jamesville-DeWitt. Baker ruled out placing grades 6,7, or 8 in the high school; likewise, administrators did not find it appropriate to return grades 6, 7, or 8 to elementary school. Nor did they want too many levels in the school system, as in dividing the elementary years between a K-2 and a 3-5 school. Placing the fifth-graders in the middle school did seem feasible, however, because these children could either be isolated in one part of the building or grouped with sixth-graders. Again, the emphasis was directed to a K-4, 5-8, 9-12 grade-organization, as in the previous month's presentation. Baker did advise the board that "politically it might be easier to close the middle school," because "our four quarters are rather unique."27

Board member Luchsinger saw the desirability of changing elementary-school boundaries, now recognized as obsolete. He recommended closing two elementary schools and reorganizing the other two as K-2 and 3-5 schools. Instead of the regional loyalties endemic to Jamesville-DeWitt, the youngest children would come "together at the outset," and "parents can build together rather than tear down together."[28]

"We could also individualize teaching programs as well as pupil program," agreed Mallan as he supported Luchsinger's proposal. Furthermore, "new experiences are good for children and they would be moving with their peer group." Mallan anticipated sufficient savings to establish a pre-kindergarten program and "do other things."[29]

Superintendent Baker interjected that the degree of savings from school-closings remained unknown. The administration had not addressed savings, only program. Incredulous, Scibilia exclaimed, "You didn't address finances?" Demanding the cost savings of school-closings, Scibilia declared, "We're not going to have any schools or anything else if we close a school every time we defeat a budget!"[30] After describing elementary schools as the place were "kids get the basics," he prophesied that "the savings will amount to little compared with the effect of closings on this district."[31]

Other board members continued to consider "what is best for the children," the discussion of the new grade-organization overshadowing the proposal to close two schools. President Carmen attempted to set the board on course by explaining that the grade-organization had "nothing to do with the motion," and Superintendent Baker assured board members that "you can close two schools." Hopkins agreed, "We've got the objective of closing two schools on the basis of the Task Force," he said. "We'll consolidate in two buildings and the administration can figure out how to work things in."[32]

As members of the overflow audience called out to be heard, DeBottis proposed that the board take twenty minutes for public comment, and Luchsinger offered a motion to enable residents to speak. Her objective now within reach, president Carmen felt confident of her authority. Having earlier warned residents that the board would recess if comments from the audience continued, she now cast the decisive "no" vote that blocked Luchsinger's motion. "A tie vote means the motion is defeated!" the president announced after joining Cargian, Mallan, and Hopkins in preventing

Photograph 8. Board member **Frank Scibilia** demanded figures on the cost savings of school-closings. He predicted that the savings "will amount to little compared with the effect of closings on this district." Scibilia alone opposed the motion to close two schools.

public comment. "Where's democracy?" shouted a man from the back of the room. A wave of indignation swept through the room, as voices rose and order was barely maintained. When the vote was taken, all board members except Scibilia supported Hopkins's motion, which passed 7-1.[33]

The only resident to speak to the issue was Lynda Rill, representing the Moses DeWitt Parents' Group. Having learned in 1977 that the school board could act quickly, allowing no opportunity for public comment, Moses DeWitt parents had taken the precaution of formally requesting a place on the agenda. Even so, the decision had already been taken when Rill stood before the board. "I am extremely angry that a decision to close not one but two schools could be allowed to happen with no input from residents," she told board members. "To close elementary schools is to cut at the very heart of the Jamesville-DeWitt school district."[34]

After voting 8-0 to leave Perkins's position open until the May election, the board methodically continued with the rest of its agenda. The decision to close two schools had been reached without figures as to cost-savings, determination of grade-organization, or consideration of which schools to select for closing. Only Scibilia had voiced the misgivings others had shared about the impact of school-closing.

By October board members either favored closings or accepted this policy as inevitable. Early in the board's consideration of reorganization, Luchsinger had told Mallan that he would not support a motion to close only one school--unquestionably Moses DeWitt. Mallan also regarded two closings as a genuine reorganization and an opportunity to discuss educational program. By contrast, closing only one school was certain to create a "knee-jerk reaction from the Moses DeWitt people," and thus damage the prospects for change. Having taken opposite positions in the decisions made in 1977, 1978, and 1979, Mallan and Luchsinger were now willing to consider educational innovations and theories within the context of two closings.

Cargian and DeBottis did not share an enthusiasm for educational experimentation or reorganization as such, but they wanted to end the years of conflict. "Try to roll with the punches," DeBottis told a Moses DeWitt parent after the October decision, although he had predicted only months earlier that Jamesville-DeWitt

212

would never close a school. First taking a cautious position, Berry declared himself not ready to vote until he had information on cost savings, the numbers of children that could be accommodated in two buildings, and the impact of closing on art and music rooms. Nevertheless, when the vote was taken, Berry sided with the majority.

For Carmen and Hopkins, however, the motion to close two schools satisfied a much-needed belief. At last they had stopped the administration's vacillation and aimed a presumably fateful blow at the school board's Moses DeWitt challengers. Returning to the Task Force, they could justify their own position and redeem the honor of the absent Perkins. After three long years came the opportunity to un-do the efforts of Moses DeWitt parents. The board had finally taken the action necessary to close Moses DeWitt and yet another school, as recommended in the long-neglected Plan A of the Task Force. The new policy's momentum was such that the choice of the second school seemed unimportant. Although she had only recently despaired of any action, Perkins was "not surprised" at the board's October decision. "Declining enrollment has held true," she told the press. "We knew all this three years ago. The figures were all in place. I would rather have done it three years ago," she said, disregarding the second closing just voted.[35]

The board had provided the direction that Superintendent Baker had declined to give. The administration could now prepare to explain and implement the board's decision. Despite new information gathered in recent years the Task Force Report was to provide a useful rationale, for there it was written that a second school be closed in 1980-1981. Administrators, too, wanted to erase any record of error and change in the years between 1977 and 1980. Furthermore, two school-closings might actually offer political advantages. Before the schools were selected for closing, opponents could not mobilize, and afterwards they could conceivably cancel each other out. Closing two schools further served to deflect the attention and hostility of Moses DeWitt critics. In the opinion of one administrator, the two closings would also "answer this whole problem for once and for all." Instead of first closing Moses DeWitt and then, after an interval, another school, the district could meet, solve, and leave the problem. Administrators did not seem unhappy with the October decision.

213

Shortly before the board's second October meeting, Superintendent Baker reminded a local reporter that the Task Force had recommended closing one school in 1978 and a second in 1980-1981, so the district was "on target" with that report.[36] Soon thereafter the administration forecast an estimated $331,550 in savings by two school-closings, a reduction "about the same as that predicted by a 1977 task force."[37] At the October 14 meeting, before he had addressed the subject of finances, the superintendent had cautioned the board that he "would not like to get people's hopes up that we are going to save a pile of money." The administration now projected a reduction of two classroom teachers by the two closings. But consolidating "specials" in two buildings--that is, eliminating positions for art, music, physical education, reading, and remedial instruction--would offer significant savings. So-called "excessing" of staff also extended to nurses, secretaries, and custodians.[38]

The single sheet of figures submitted to the school board on October 28 showed a reduction of two principals, one per "ECB," or each closed building. In fact, both principals would continue to hold administrative positions, and no administrator in the system was to be cut, as later acknowledged. In the face of declining enrollment school districts frequently reduce the number of teachers rather than the number of administrators.[39] Although it had a small administrative staff, Jamesville-DeWitt also followed this pattern, and school-closing was not to bring the cuts in administrative personnel or costs that some citizens had called for in questionnaire comments.

The reported savings drew little public interest, for the decision to close two schools had already been reached. Over the years many different numbers had been used in discussing the cost savings of school-closings. The new figure of a $331,550 savings was not "about the same" as that predicted by the Task Force. According to the Task Force Report, two closings were expected to yield a savings of $483,000 without attrition of staff.[40] As recently as June 1980, moreover, Superintendent Baker had used the figure of $30,000 to describe the cost of operating Moses DeWitt.[41] In 1978-1979, administrators had said that one closing would produce a savings of $70,000.[42]

At its October 28 meeting the board of education did

214

not linger over the financial statement, although budget-defeat and cost-control provided the ostensible reasons for school closings. Flanked by the school-district attorney and the superintendent, president Carmen outlined a meticulous timetable for the board's future deliberations and actions, leading to a public hearing and then a final decision on December 9.

The board first discarded the proposal for a K-2, 3-5, 6-8, 9-12 plan. Seated at the table with the board members, school principals reported that the staff did not favor the plan supported by Luchsinger and Mallan. The principals, performing as the superintendent's housecarls, entertained questions and explained that teachers wanted the "current configuration" or a K-4 plan.[44] As attention shifted predictably to a K-4, 5-8 plan, board members weighed problems of psychological adjustment, social maturity, and the advent of puberty. Now allowed to comment, parents also expressed concern about placing children in the middle school at an early age. Looking at enrollment, Superintendent Baker remarked that the 5-8 plan had the advantage of "filling up the middle school."[45]

School principals now turned to the PTAs to secure endorsement for the inevitable K-4, 5-8 organization. "Often laced with and frequently dominated by key administrators," the parent-teacher groups played the role of "kept organizations," as described by several authors.[46] Adroit administrators attempted and usually succeeded in capturing these organizations to reduce conflict and build support, as now occurred. Responding to the issue, the Tecumseh Parent-Teachers' Organization advised the board of education that "we endorse and urge a program consisting of grades K-4 to be housed in two of the existing elementary schools," offering the added reassurance that the Tecumseh PTG is "supportive of the J-D school board."[47] The Genesee Hills Parent-Teachers' Organization wrote "expressing gratitude" to the board for "listening to the public" concerning the K-2, 3-5 grade organization. Jamesville and Moses DeWitt parents expressed concerns but continued to emphasize community feeling in Jamesville or what was now reduced to "the spirit of the neighborhood concept," as described in the Moses DeWitt letter to the board.[48] Moses DeWitt parents specifically rejected a request by their energetic new principal Patrick Tamburro that they endorse the K-4 plan. No organization opposed placing the fifth grade in the middle school despite widespread reservations and public concern that even sixth-graders did not belong in the middle school.

On November 11, the board of education voted unanimously to move fifth-graders to the middle school. An anticipatd 1981-1982 enrollment of 1060 children in grades K-5 could not be accommodated in two elementary schools. Many hours of discussion notwithstanding, the school board had effectively ended the K-5 elementary organization the night it voted to close two schools. With only two K-5 elementary schools, "every classroom would be needed for instruction, leaving no space for art, music, reading, or resource teachers."[49]

To reduce "disruption for the kids," Superintendent Baker next asked the board to consider "pairing schools," a proposal quietly initiated by board president Carmen. According to "pairing," children from a closed school would move together to another school. Located at opposite ends of the district, Genesee Hills and Jamesville were too far apart to make a feasible pair. Nevertheless, all other combinations would work, including Moses DeWitt and Genesee Hills, Tecumseh and Jamesville, Tecumseh and Genesee Hills, and Tecumseh and Moses DeWitt--the last being a spurious combination in that the remaining two schools, Genesee Hills and Jamesville, could not be paired. The different pairs produced enrollments that varied between Tecumseh and Jamesville, at 386, and Moses DeWitt and Genesee Hills, at 473. All combinations could fit in the buildings and work equally well, no matter what the selection, said the Suprintendent.[50]

At its second November meeting the board attempted to study the various mutations possible from the district's once-familiar schools. Again, the apparent multiplicity of possibilities enumerated by Super-intendent Baker concealed a more defined choice. Administrators reiterated that each building could accommodate the enrollment and provide the program as well as any other, a viewpoint consistently supported by building principals in the weeks and months ahead. Even travel time between the schools varied by only two minutes. Everything being equal, how was the school board to make its final selection? Working from a list prepared by the administration, board members and residents contributed miscellaneous points to be taken into account, including playground space, number of walkers, safety, sidewalks, provisions for the handicapped, recreational and athletic uses, sale or leasing possibilities, and potential population growth--

216

all considerations to be treated equally.51

Pairing first drew support from board members and residents who approved of keeping neighborhoods and children together. Neither parents nor board members had challenged the administration's litany of equality, despite a known and abiding conviction that all four schools were distinctive. The Tecumseh Parent-Teachers' Organization had written that "all four buildings are adequate and suitable" for quality education.52 If all buildings were equal, any combination could be plausible. The Genesee Hills and Moses DeWitt parents' organizations specifically endorsed pairing, albeit with different expectations as to which building would serve as the "receiving school." Only when board member DeBottis declared support for a particular pairing did controversy erupt. Close Tecumseh and move the children to Jamesville, and close Genesee Hills and shift those children to Moses DeWitt, said DeBottis, the sole board member to indicate his opinion. "I don't think we can close Jamesville," he explained. "It's a community by itself."53

Board members and parents who took alarm at this direction now began to insist on further discussion of redistricting as opposed to pairing. Administrators had not prepared detailed redistricting plans for the November 18 meeting, because they assumed that the board favored pairing. After repeated questions, Baker offered to "work up" any redistricting plans requested, an undertaking eventually completed in February.

At the public hearing on November 25, board president Carmen called for a special meeting "to consider the possibility of redistricting," as urged by Tecumseh residents who sensed danger. The largest and newest of the elementary schools as well as the only one equipped for handicapped children, Tecumseh had once seemed likely, if not certain, to remain open. Because of its twenty-six classrooms, in contrast to the twenty-one or twenty-two available at other schools, Tecumseh could easily accommodate children from any closed building, provide special program rooms, and still allow space for future changes in enrollment. But linked with Jamesville, a school whose interests were represented by three board members, Tecumseh's prospects paled, perhaps to the astonishment of the board leader who first proposed pairing. Mallan supported Carmen's new-found interest in redistricting, a subject he had raised several times.54 Even after four board members

217

indicated that they did not want a special session at which to discuss redistricting, Carment disregarded the deadlock and searched in vain for a meeting date.

Residents who spoke at the public hearing expressed doubt and uneasiness about the board's forthcoming decision. Many parents advocated keeping their own elementary school open. "Each neighborhood holds its school to be the heart and soul of the district," said a Tecumseh resident.[55] According to an officer in the Genesee Hills Parent-Teachers' Organization, the "low profile" taken by that group in district conflicts did not indicate lack of concern. A Jamesville mother felt that her community needed and deserved to have a school, while another resident reminded the board that "Moses DeWitt remains at the center of a highly populated area, particularly of elementary school students."[56] If both Genesee Hills and Moses DeWitt were closed, the school district's population center would have no elementary school.

Other speakers questioned the procedure that the board would use on December 9. "I think the board owes it to the people in this room to look at every pairing, every possible combination," said a worried Tecumseh parent.[57] Another resident observed that "much will hinge on the first person to make a motion," an observation that held true of the board's decisions from December 1977, when Mallan proposed closing Moses DeWitt, to October 1980, when Hopkins had seized the initiative to move that two schools be closed, to the distress of Moses DeWitt residents in the audience. Now board pesident Carmen assured the public that the voting procedure to be used would be carefully considered because of "great concern in the community."[58]

Even more important, by exactly what criteria would the schools be closed? Residents had repeatedly raised this question during the preceding month. Board member Luchsinger shared their concern and asked that the administration provide professional advice. Reading aloud, Luchsinger summarized a detailed statement of criteria that he had sent to his colleagues and to the administration. He hoped that board members would add to this list, and administrators could then assist the board in weighting each criterion. Otherwise, Luchsinger continued, "each board member will rate their criteria differently based on their own experience," which could make the decision an emotional one. As professionals, administrators, "work with children and buildings on a daily basis" and have the expertise to rate the criteria for school-closing.59

Superintendent Baker later said that the administration had made no attempt to rank the fourteen criteria now on the board's list of considerations.60 Privately, he told a board member that he was "not going to get involved in this mess." The superintendent continued to look ahead to the way out and so, apparently, did president Carmen, who told the press after the public hearing, "I will be happy when we have a decision. That is when the work will really begin to provide the best education possible for all of the youngsters in the district."61

Many Tecumseh residents did not feel sanguine about the forthcoming decision, however. Anticipating a decision "based on politics and emotionalism," parents now feared that Moses DeWitt--the school they had cast as their nemesis--would remain open. Resentment at the reversal of the board's 1977 decision flared again. "I feel very sorry for some of the board members who were under extreme economic pressure after the first vote to close Moses DeWitt," said a Tecumseh mother who incorrectly alleged that a board member had suffered a "40 per cent loss of business." Other parents complained of Moses DeWitt's wooden floors, open stairwells, and location "one and on-half blocks from a major commercial center."62

Turning their attention from Moses DeWitt, Tecumseh residents looked at Jamesville, where they found potential health hazards for children and teachers caused by the Alpha Portland Cement Company, located near the school. Unlike Jamesville Elementary School, Tecumseh "is far away from potential damage from emissions" of the factory, soon to close. A Tecumseh parent informed the press of a "possibility that sometime in the future the Alpha factory might be a site to incinerate toxic wastes --liquid toxic wastes similar to those at Love Canal." Although he had told the board only days earlier that his children would be served in any of the four schools in the district, this physician now urged the school board to act prudently and close the Jamesville school.63 Advancing the argument in conversations and in a mimeographed flyer, Tecumseh parents failed to find allies, and in a suicidal step angered Jamesville members who had always held decisive votes in board decisions.

Moses DeWitt parents felt equally pessimistic about the prospects. If board members were to agree on anything, that subject would be closing Moses DeWitt. Trying to anticipate the final decision, Moses DeWitt residents who had long followed the issue expected the board first to "pair" Genesee Hills and Moses DeWitt and then forever close the school that had provided the focus of public controversy. Having taken this long-desired action, perhaps the board would become stalemated over other schools and retreat to closing only one building, according to one speculation.

As the decision neared, Superintendent Baker had scrupulously avoided any comment or commitment to guide the board's selection, just as he had earlier withdrawn from the decision to close schools. By characterizing all buildings as equal and all pairs and choices as equally feasible, Baker had devised a way to accommodate to any possible decision. No group could criticize the superintendent for dictating the outcome or, in his expression, "putting pressure on the process," and after the decision he could not be held accountable for the result.

Describing the problems of school-closing as seen by a superintendent, William F. Keough, Jr. has written that this divisive issue disturbs and "frightens even the most able school people."[64] Baker had already weathered such experiences as "community backlash," anti-administration press comment, "whittling away of credibility," "pages-long petitions," actions by "special interests to keep open local schools," and "angry phone calls from constituents." Many districts fired superintendents in the course of such conflicts, inspiring the American Association of School Administrators to offer a session entitled "Superintendents Under Siege: When to Fight, When to Run."[65] In Jamesville-DeWitt Superintendent Baker still retained a remnant of community trust, and he perhaps hoped to preserve both his present support and future prospects by isolating himself from the final stages of the district's internecine strife. By periodically abdicating leadership in the years between 1977 and 1980, however, the superintendent had contributed to the conflict he hoped to avoid.

As elected representatives, board members now made policy but uncertainly. According to a typical description of school decision-making, the superintendent and his top aides "are the ones who initiate action, who make proposals for change, who recommend that this or that be done."66 By contrast, board members rarely initiate proposals themselves. Normally, the Jamesville-DeWitt school board accepted administration reports and routinely approved housekeeping measures. Now, however, as in 1977, the board found itself charged with reaching a major policy choice, for which it had minimal preparation or direction.

The board's meetings in the fall of 1980 failed to develop public confidence in the forthcoming decision. In the absence of leadership from the administration, board members offered little discussion to satisfy residents' questions. Not thinking of themselves as politicians, board members still recoiled from criticism, and only one had the temerity to explain his school-closing choices and reasoning before December 9. School-closing advocates Mallan, Hopkins and Carmen said nothing to offer direction in selecting the schools for closing. The closing ideology apparently produced no strategy or coalition by which to achieve its ends. Both residents and board members assumed that each member would protect his own school, but beyond this further decision-making remained very much in doubt.

### NOTES

1. **Post-Standard**(Syracuse), Sept. 11, 1980.
2. **Ibid.**
3. **Post-Standard**, Sept. 25, 1980.
4. Lansing G. Baker, Memorandum to Board Members and Staff, July 24, 1980; List of Options, Sept. 23, 1980.
5. Lansing G. Baker, Memorandum, July 24, 1980.
6. Lansing G. Baker, List of Options, September 23, 1980.
7. Jamesville-DeWitt Board of Education meeting, Sept. 23, 1980, author's notes.
8. **Post-Standard**, Sept. 25, 1980.
9. **Post-Standard**, Oct. 2, 1980.
10. **Ibid.**
11. **Ibid.**
12. **Ibid.**
13. **Ibid.**
14. Statements made at Jamesville-DeWitt Board of Education meeting, Sept. 30, 1980, author's notes.
15. Roscoe C. Martin, **Government and the Suburban School**(Syracuse,

1962), 100.

16. **Herald-Journal**(Syracuse), Oct. 4, 1980.

17. **Ibid.**

18. **Ibid.**

19. Martin, **Government and the Suburban School**, 100; see also Arthur J. Vidich and Joseph Bensman, **Small Town in Mass Society** (Princeton, 1968), 196.

20. David B. Tyack, **The One Best System**(Cambridge, 1974), 135.

21. **Herald-Journal**, Oct. 4, 1980.

22. **Suburban Life**(DeWitt and East Syracuse), Oct. 8, 1980.

23. **Ibid.**; also **Post-Standard**, Oct. 9, 1980.

24. **Suburban Life**, Oct. 15, 1980.

25. **Post-Standard**, Oct. 16, 1980.

26. **Suburban Life**, Oct. 15, 1980.

27. **Ibid.**

28. **Post-Standard**, Oct. 16, 1980.

29. **Suburban Life**, Oct. 15, 1980.

30. **Ibid.**

31. **Herald-Journal**, Oct. 16, 1980; **Suburban Life**, Oct. 15, 1980.

32. **Suburban Life**, Oct. 15, 1980.

33. **Post-Standard**, Oct. 16, 1980.

34. **Ibid.**

35. **Post-Standard**, Oct. 23, 1980.

36. **Ibid.**

37. **Post-Standard**, Oct. 30, 1980.

38. **Ibid.**

39. See Allen Odden and Phillip E. Vincent, "The Fiscal Impacts of Declining Enrollments: A Study of Declining Enrollment in Four States," in Susan Abramowitz and Stuart Rosenfeld, eds., **Declining Enrollments: The Challenge of the Coming Decade**(Washington, D.C., 1978), 229.

40. Jamesville-DeWitt Needs Assessment Task Force, **Report**(Mar. 1977), Introduction, Section E.

41. **Post-Standard**, June 19, 1980.

42. **Post-Standard**, Aug. 16, 1980.

43. **Post-Standard**, Oct. 30, 1980.

44. **Ibid.**

45. **Ibid.**

46. Quote from L. Harmon Zeigler and M. Kent Jennings, **Governing American Schools**(North Scituate, Mass., 1974), 99; also see James D. Koerner, **Who Controls American Education?**(Boston, 1968) and Robert A. Dahl, **Who Governs?**(New Haven, 1961), 155-156.

47. **Suburban Life**, Nov. 26, 1980.

48. **Ibid.**

49. **Post-Standard**, Nov. 13, 1980.

50. **Ibid.**; also **Post-Standard**, Nov. 20, 1980.

51. **Post-Standard**, Nov. 20, 1980; **Post-Standard**, Nov. 27, 1980.

52. **Suburban Life**, Nov. 26, 1980.

53. **Post-Standard**, Nov. 20, 1980.

54. **Post-Standard**, Nov. 27, 1980.

55. **Ibid.**
56. **Suburban Life,** Nov. 26, 1980.
57. **Post-Standard,** Nov. 27, 1980.
58. **Ibid.**
59. **Post-Standard,** Dec. 4, 1980.
60. **Ibid.**
61. **Herald-Journal,** Nov. 26, 1980.
62. **Herald-Journal,** Dec. 9, 1980.
63. **Ibid.; Post-Standard,** Nov. 27, 1980.
64. William F. Keough, Jr., "Enrollment Decline: The Dilemma from the Superintendent's Chair," in Susan Abramowitz and Stuart Rosenfeld, eds., **Declining Enrollments: The Challenge of the Coming Decade,** 334.
65. **Ibid,** p. 335.
66. Roland J. Pellegrin as quoted by Koerner, **Who Controls American Education?,** 138.

## XIV. The Infamous Decision

On December 9 board members assembled in the high school auditorium before an audience of some 400 residents. The expectant crowd gazed down at a board table wedged between the stage and the auditorium's first row. No longer did board members conduct meetings on stage, as in the tumultuous evenings of December 1977, or January 1978, when residents had demanded that the table be relocated so that board members faced the public rather than each other. Nevertheless, spotlights and television cameras focused on the eight board members, seated with the school district's attorney and Superintendent Baker.

As the critical meeting opened, board members had reached no agreement on common criteria to use in school-closing. Despite residents' questions and Luchsinger's late-November appeal, the board had declined to accept, or rank, a definitive set of criteria. Nor had board members voted on pairing as an approach to school-closing, although this subject, too, had been considered in the preceding three meetings. President Carmen had promised careful consideration of voting procedure, but board members had yet to establish a format or process whereby they would reach their conclusion.

Calling upon her colleagues in alphabetical order, Carmen solicited statements of opinion. Some board members developed and explained their own criteria, while others also addressed pairing, the merits of individual schools, and voting procedure. Some justified their own motives and actions, or deplored those of others. Only rarely, however, did board members consider questions from a common starting point, incorporate the arguments of others, or reach a shared conclusion. Each member wanted his own school to remain open, but no one offered a rationale for the closing-selection that seemed convincing to more than one or two colleagues. Few points of consensus appeared in the eight statements, ranging from standard school rhetoric to bitter political counterpoint and emotional catharsis.[1]

Berry struck a familiar note when he explained his commitment to serving all of the children. He then outlined his own criteria, including among other points accessibility, number of classrooms, and provisions for the handicapped, the last condition receiving particular

225

emphasis. Berry reminded the public that the board's decision would produce no winners and no losers, for "the children will benefit wherever they go." Elected as the representative of the Tecumseh area, he found that this school best met his criteria; Genesee Hills also met most of Berry's requirements.

Cargian reminded board members that Jamesville Elementary had the necessary space, classrooms, and parking. Furthermore, Jamesville had long ago closed its high school, leaving the elementary school as the only school at the southern end of the district, where distances and travel time were greater. Thus, "it is important that this school remain open."

Next Cargian considered alleged environmental hazards in Jamesville. "I have found out that I will have to move in order to not use a respirator," he grumbled in response to complaints about air pollution from the Alpha Portland Cement Company. Contrary to the opinion of Tecumseh critics, air pollution in Jamesville was below the average in the county, and "incidentally, the winds blow towards Tecumseh!" The boisterous audience interrupted to roar delight or disgust at this sally. Cargian then went on to explain that representatives of Alpha Portland denied any proposal to burn toxic wastes as alleged by Tecumseh parents, and in any event this could not occur without the town government's approval. Referring to his twenty years on the school board, Cargian described himself as ready to leave, now drawing applause from Tecumseh parents. Having already asserted that Jamesville should remain open, Cargian described all buildings as suitable and recommended that the board discuss pairing.

Summarizing his eight years on the board, DeBottis could think of no action he had taken to hurt the school district or any child. He reiterated his November statement that Moses DeWitt and Jamesville should remain open, a position that sparked frantic efforts by Tecumseh parents. Disregarding the complexities of criteria, Debottis simply stated, "Jamesville is a vital part of its community....Don't take it away."

DeBottis next addressed the allegation that he supported Moses DeWitt to protect his business, as charged by a Tecumseh resident in that evening's paper.[2] The suggestion that economic pressure determined his position was a "cheap shot," he said, to the sustained applause of supporters, some of whom had once discussed cutting credit cards used at his service station. Having survived scathing criticism but no organized boycott from his Moses DeWitt patrons, DeBottis recognized the commitment of these residents not only to their school but to the district in recent budget elections. His judgment and his interest reenforcing each other, DeBottis was, in his expression, "firmly planted" as he faced fierce new opposition.

Following DeBottis, Hopkins again reviewed the troubled history of recent years. Still smarting from the success of Moses DeWitt parents in undermining the board's 1977 closing decision, he insisted that "our data has proved correct." The school board could have and should have closed one school in 1979-1980 and a second at the end of the 1980-1981 school year as planned, said Hopkins, misstating even Task Force Plan A, which was now applied retroactively to decision-making in 1977. Both Hopkins and Baker returned freely to the Task Force to justify current actions; neither board members nor the superintendent hesitated to revise the historical record according to their own needs and beliefs. In 1977 the school board had actually emphasized Task Force plan C's recommendation of one closing in 1978-1979 and minimized discussion of a second closing. After the selection of Moses DeWitt, a district newsletter stated that closing the largest school "will delay by at last two years (until 1982-1983) the need to close a second school."[3] Nevertheless, Hopkins argued that the board was now doing what it had planned all along.

Author of the October motion to close two schools, Hopkins correctly observed that the board was again subjected to a barrage of public demands. Three years ago it had seemed illegitimate to Hopkins as well as to Perkins when Moses DeWitt parents resisted the closing decision, which was reversed "due to pressures brought on some members of the board." Now, however, it was obvious that this behavior was not unique to Moses DeWitt as once believed. Indeed, the board was "pressured" by residents of every area. Elected to serve the entire district, board members should remember their responsibility to all residents and thus provide a facility in each geographical area, or quadrant, including Jamesville.

Having reached this conclusion, Hopkins reverted immediately to his preoccupation with the events and concerns of 1977. Because "the original reason to close Moses DeWitt Elementary School has not changed, an all-

out campaign to keep Moses DeWitt Elementary School has
continued to confront the board members." Making no
reference to meetings held in the fall of 1980, Hopkins
described the board's decision as based on data that best
took in the "interests of students and educational
programs" as developed by administrators and board
members. Whether he referred to the 1977 decision to
close Moses DeWitt or his own motion to close two schools
is unclear. Again, Hopkins telescoped the events of
1977 and those of 1980, and attempted to offer one
interpretation to cover the decisions of both years.
Now, he continued, concerns for students and programs
"have been thrown to the winds." Instead, "deals have
been reached by some members of this board." At first
startled, some residents applauded as they detected an
effort to discredit the current decision-making. "I
have been approached by board members to get on the
bandwagon," continued Hopkins. "If I want to keep
Jamesville School, I must vote to keep a particular
school open."

Again, Hopkins had pinpointed, albeit indirectly,
Moses DeWitt School and its supporters. For Hopkins,
the preservation of Jamesville Elementary could not be
linked to Moses DeWitt. Even the possibility of an
alliance to maintain both schools place the Jamesville
postmaster in an untenable position. Although he had
offered the motion to close two schools in a display of
decisiveness, his foremost political goal was closing
Moses DeWitt. As a longtime resident of Jamesville,
however, he could not jeopardize the future of his own
school. Rather than associate himself in any way with
Moses DeWitt, Hopkins alleged that deals had been made--a
situation "in direct conflict with my ethical
principles." After deploring references to Jamesville
as "the Love Canal area" of the school district, Hopkins
offered his resignation effective December 31.

After a brief comment from Luchsinger suggesting
that the board first vote on pairing, Mallan took the
microphone. "I must admit that I am dumbfounded by this
board of education! Shame on you!" he shouted to
applause. "Shame on us!" Repeating Hopkins's allegation of a deal--"which means from people among this
body"--Professor Mallan rebuked his colleagues. "And I
am supposed to sit here and honor your commitments and
your statements?" he demanded. Then, suddenly, he
shifted to past events, recalling the resignation of
Phyllis Perkins. Again, the resentments of preceding
years flared. No one had called the former president to

Photograph 9. **William J. Hopkins** charged that "deals have been reached by some members of this board."

compliment her on a job well done. "What are you running here? A meat factory?" Some residents responded with applause, as others attempted to comprehend what had been said.

The indignant Mallan next apologized for having said in July that the school board did not make politically-motivated decisions. "My God, Mallan, you were the one who said it!" He had heard rumors of people being approached, of board members' making connections, but he had disregarded these stories. "I'm naive--I'm just a silly professor not with the feet on the ground, playing a card game, O.K.?" Referring to colleagues with whom he had worked for three or four years, he exclaimed without explanation or evidence, "These people are going to turn and play this game!" Board members and residents listened intently as the outburst continued. "And we talk about, publicly, the education of kids! We don't even have an education ourselves!" As his anger subsided, Mallan demanded to know if anyone had in fact been involved in a deal and suggested that the board recess to get an answer. His temper again rising, he concluded, "I'm not going to vote when this whole thing is rigged!"

As the next speaker, Scibilia quietly explained that all board members set their own priorities and reached their own conclusions. The sole member to vote against closing two schools, he reminded his colleagues that any decision would inevitably alienate fifty per cent of the parents. Attempting to restore calm, he also reassured the public that "this is still the Jamesville-DeWitt school district."

Having listened to all of her colleagues, president Carmen now presented her views. Resorting to the rhetoric that had served so well in the past, the board president asserted that "educational needs must be served." An advocate of educational excellence, she also believed in fiscal responsibility and a safe environment. Children should learn in the least restrictive setting, free of architectural barriers and physical hazards, for "this board has never propositioned the safety of our children." She urged colleagues to rise above enrollment decline "for the sake of all the children." Two schools, Tecumseh and Genesee Hills, best served the interests of flexibility, safety, and long-range planning.

Nevertheless, Carmen seemed uncertain that these

maxims answered the current problem. She next addressed the question of voting procedure that assured equal consideration for each facility. "In keeping with fairness to all, through the democratic process," she suggested that the names of the four schools be written on slips of paper and placed in a hat. As the clerk drew the names from the hat, discussion of each school would follow in that order, and motions to close would be offered in the same sequence. After each board member had cast two votes, the totals would be computed and those schools with the highest votes would be closed. Under this recommendation board members would not choose between Jamesville and Tecumseh, the alternatives unexpectedly created by Carmen's earlier concept of pairing. Furthermore, considered alone, Moses DeWitt could still be expected to gather the greatest number of votes. Belatedly recognizing Jamesville's strength on the board, Carmen calculated or at least hoped that board members would choose Genesee Hills as the second school to close.

After hearing the board president's elaborate proposal, Cargian commented, "I want to react to that-- your rabbit in the hat trick. I don't think it's necessary." Directing a disdainful gaze at the president, the veteran board member said that he did not need any such system, temporarily ending discussion of the point.

Luchsinger then moved that the school board recess to consider Hopkins's allegation. Seconded by Mallan, the motion called for an executive session to discuss "personnel." Although both Luchsinger and Mallan had earlier disavowed the use of executive session except for narrow technical reasons, both now wanted an opportunity to talk in private.

DeBottis, who had immediately seen himself as the object of Hopkins's accusation, declared that he preferred to talk in public. Acknowledging that he had called some board members, DeBottis named each one, starting with Hopkins. "I do not want to be accused of trying to arrange a deal!" he exclaimed as he faced Hopkins across the table. "I tried to point out the importance that I placed on a small school in a small community," he continued. "I did not ask any one of these board members to vote specifically, and I wish you would say so right here and now!" Berry among others answered that he had not been approached, and, furthermore, "there is no way in hell that I would be part

231

of a deal for your child or my child!"

After a forty-five minute executive session, Luchsinger reported that board members "all seem to be satisfied that we've all made independent decisions." Mallan confirmed this conclusion but ambiguously. "My satisfaction is, to be honest with you, that I know I am going to make those independent decisions--I never had any doubt about it. I cannot speak for others," he said, thus leaving his own position clear but the process in doubt. Other board members expressed satisfaction that the question was settled. "I, too, follow suit," said Hopkins as he endorsed this position, at least for the moment.

The board now struggled with the matter of voting procedure. Berry moved, seconded by Mallan, that the board vote on individual schools, according to the procedure suggested by president Carmen. Mallan recommended a consideration of individual schools rather than pairs, because "pairing narrows the decision by fifty per cent." He proposed his own framework by which the school board would provide a facility in each geographical area contiguous to the boundaries of adjacent school systems, a rationale very similar to what he had used in advocating the closing of Moses DeWitt in 1977, when he also wanted peripheral areas to have schools.

Luchsinger countered that his approach to decision-making required a discussion of pairs, not individual schools, in order "to take a total view of the school district." After presenting an elaborate ranking of schools according to a diverse list of criteria, including number of rooms, walkers, population centers, and provisions for the handicapped, Luchsinger concluded that Jamesville and Moses DeWitt should remain open, a recommendation that surprised no one. Like Berry, Luchsinger interpreted criteria to serve his own school and political allegiances.

"We're fooling ourselves if we think we have criteria in its intended sense. That implies standards," said Mallan. Listing the same considerations cited by Berry and Luchsinger, Mallan favored Jamesville in the southern quadrant of the school district and Genesee Hills in the northern segment. "I do push for Genesee Hills," said Mallan as he, too, cited reasons and criteria to justify his own school. Uneasy about the board's discussion, president Carmen reminded her colleagues that they had declined her request to adopt a list of criteria in November. Now any reassessment of criteria came too late to solve the board's predicament. When the motion was called only Carmen, Mallan, and Berry wanted to vote on schools individually.

After this motion failed, board members again attempted to set forth their views on pairing and school-closing. Cargian stated that he favored Mallan's recommendation of what was ineptly described as the "four corners" plan. According to this proposal, Jamesville and Genesee Hills would occupy the southern and northern corners, or quadrants, while the middle school and the high school presumably served the eastern and western corners. Like Cargian, Scibilia also wanted to pair Tecumseh and Jamesville, retaining Jamesville Elementary as the school for the village of Jamesville at the southern end of the district. But in the northern section Scibilia found that the impact of school-closing on the surrounding community "leaves only one school to remain open--and that's Moses DeWitt." As some segments of the audience groaned, he explained that homes in the Genesee Hills area are not affected as much as homes in the Moses DeWitt neighborhood. "I'm sorry--this is how I feel," he said as residents hissed. Hopkins reaffirmed his support for Jamesville as the school in the southern end of the district. Using the same logic in the northern area, he continued tentatively, "the northern most school should be the school that is left open. I would say that Genesee Hills is the school that is left open for that reason."

After repeated statements linking Tecumseh and Jamesville, Carmen interjected her concern that schools offer "full access" to all children, including the handicapped. As a larger one-story building, Tecumseh offered "ample rooms for all youngsters" now and in the future and provided for the possibility of increased enrollment, a subject she had not emphasized in the past. Mallan shared Carmen's concern for handicapped children, having just described Tecumseh and Genesee Hills as the best schools "in terms of physical facilities." Now, however, he stated that he was not concerned that the district have a "physical facility in every area." Furthermore, "handicapped children do not need to bear the onus for the decision....There's enough on them already," concluded Mallan as he definitively jettisoned Tecumseh.

After this exchange, Cargian moved that Tecumseh and Moses DeWitt be closed, seconded by Mallan. As confusion prevailed, Luchsinger asked if the board had already decided on pairing as opposed to redistricting. Had the administration or faculty offered a recommendation as to which approach would be best? Administrators, including school principals, had emphasized pairing in all preceding meetings and conversations and elicited parents' support for this approach. Now, however, Superintendent Baker shifted responsibility. "We heard pairing fom most people." Not having prepared redistricting plans for previous meetings, he nevertheless said, "We are prepared to talk about redistricting and we are prepared to talk about pairing." Again removing himself from the board's continued dilemma, Baker concluded, "We can do anything you want to do."

President Carmen protested that while the board had made no decision to pair schools, the names of two schools appeared in the same motion. "A fair consideration of each school is needed," she reiterated. Her fears at this point were groundless, because together Moses DeWitt and Tecumseh had enough advocates to defeat the motion easily. Only Cargian and Mallan supported their proposal to close Moses DeWitt and Tecumseh, and Luchsinger abstained. Luchsinger supported closing Tecumseh, and he had prepared himself to accept Genesee Hills "if this is the school the community wants" to keep.

In 1977 Luchsinger had suffered condemnation from both residents and board members for casting a minority vote and then cautiously aiding Moses DeWitt parents in their effort to reverse the closing decision. Moses DeWitt residents turned most often to him for information and advice, which he stated with qualifications and pauses that required careful deciphering. After voting to close two schools, Luchsinger had explained to critical constituents that this strategy saved Moses DeWitt from certain extinction. In recent weeks, as often in the past, Luchsinger despaired of Moses DeWitt's prospects. Eventually, he thought, residents needed to unite and stop "tearing down" the district; thus, if Jamesville and Genesee Hills offered the most acceptable choices, he would support these schools, as he did in abstaining on the motion. Before the December 9 meeting Luchsinger had urged Moses DeWitt parents to accept, and even advocate, Genesee Hills as their second line of defense for keeping a school in the northern, populous part of DeWitt.

Many interested residents expected the board to maintain Genesee Hills and Jamesville. By that compromise, the 10,000 residents of the Moses DeWitt and Genesee Hills areas would continue to have an elementary school but not the one which had become anathema to much of the public. A given in the situation because of the original Jamesville-DeWitt centralization and the board's composition, Jamesville Elementary would continue as the school for that small but separate community and the 3,000 some residents of the Tecumseh section as well.

Genesee Hills had only Mallan as a strong advocate on the school board, however, while every other school had at least two or three spokesmen. Although Berry and Carmen had expressed support for Genesee Hills, they would not vote for this school at the expense of closing Tecumseh--not when they still hoped to save their own school. Using "the same logic" that he applied to Jamesville, Hopkins had identified Genesee Hills as the school for the northern quadrant, but he failed to vote for the choice of Jamesville and Genesee Hills when the motion was offered. Mallan had not negotiated an alliance that committed the Jamesville postmaster to his position. His weakly worded statement to the contrary, Hopkins supported Tecumseh and Jamesville. Apparently dumbfounded at the possibility of conversations or agreements among board members, Mallan lacked the connections to achieve the outcome he wanted. As a solution for what Berry had called a no-win situation, Genesee Hills and Jamesville seemed more plausible to residents than they did in the context of board decision-making.

Berry next proposed, and Hopkins seconded for purposes of discussion, closing Jamesville and Moses DeWitt. "Lopping off Jamesville" would be a mistake, protested Mallan, who in previous discussions had emphasized programs and minimized the importance of localities. Buildings did not make a school system, he had often said in justifying closing to Moses DeWitt parents. Staffing, programming, and curriculum notwithstanding, Mallan, too, favored particular buildings in particular places. Alone among the four schools, Jamesville clearly had the support of a board majority, and the motion was easily defeated, 6-2. Only Carmen and Berry voted to close both Moses DeWitt and Jamesville.

As the hours wore on, board members exhausted

themselves in endless procedural roll calls as the previous question was called, followed by the subsequent roll call on the motion. Periodically, board members interrupted to ask, "What is this we're voting on now?" Following each vote were long intervals in which board members engaged in side conversations with each other and referred questions of parliamentary procedure to the school district's attorney, who studied **Robert's Rules of Order.** The longest interruption came when Mallan proposed dividing the motion to close Jamesville and Moses DeWitt, presumably in order to consider Moses DeWitt alone--a possibility that first the superintendent and then the attorney found unacceptable.

Late in the evening, the board turned to yet another possibility. Luchsinger moved, seconded by Scibilia, that Genesee Hills and Tecumseh be closed. Mallan quickly urged board members to study a few tattered maps before them, drawing protests from weary residents. "To close those two schools," he said, pointing at Genesee Hills and Tecumseh, "would be to take your borders and retrench right on in, and it just doesn't make sense in this day and age!" Board members listened to the continuing discussion of borders and corners, attempting to grasp at some rationale for what they were doing. Only a little earlier Mallan had referred to Jamesville as a border area in which a school should be maintained. The boundary concept had limited value, however, for the education professor himself had described Jamesville-DeWitt as a small school district in which "we can do anything." In 1977 Mallan had advocated closing the "hub" school, because doing so would "not collapse any other part of the district geographically." Least of all did he wish to "retrench" to Moses DeWitt in 1980. Committed to Jamesville, Mallan had sacrificed Tecumseh as well as any consistency in his desire to locate schools in buffer zones. Tecumseh was as close to the Syracuse city line as Genesee Hills, but in the end it was not his school.

The motion to close Tecumseh and Genesee Hills produced a deadlock, thus going down to defeat. Scibilia and Luchsinger, representing the Moses DeWitt constituency, supported the motion, as did DeBottis and Cargian of Jamesville. Opposed were Carmen and Berry of Tecumseh, as well as Mallan and Hopkins. Both Cargian and Luchsinger supported this motion after having earlier agreed to the proposal to close Moses DeWitt and Tecumseh.

The board had apparently exhausted the possible pairs of schools. Having only eight members, the school board faced a stalemate that now seemed a salvation to board members who saw their schools threatened. In October the board had voted unanimously to keep Perkins's position open until the May election. Those who advocated and those who opposed closing Moses DeWitt both feared an unknown person who would "come in cold" and tip the balance in one direction or the other.4 Now it appeared that an eight-member board served Moses DeWitt's interest by making it difficult for a majority to coalesce behind any proposal. Only two months earlier the board had violated the district's tradition of filling vacancies by appointment, only to find itself now lacking the ninth member who could cast a decisive vote.

After the motion to close Tecumseh and Genesee Hills went down to defeat, president Carmen proclaimed, "What is the pleasure of the board? There is a deadlock decision!" Momentarily relieved that her colleagues would now retreat from the dangerous pairing concept, she attempted to chart a new course. After hearing a voice from the audience advising the board to vote on schools individually, president Carmen repeated this possibility. Noting that she did not want to put words into his mouth, she elicited a motion by Mallan, seconded by Berry, that the board reconsider its earlier decision not to vote on schools individually.

Having exhausted further pairs, board members now readily agreed to vote on each school separately. Far more difficult, they next attempted to find a procedure whereby they could accomplish this task. Would board members consider the four schools one by one, or would they vote their closing preferences in one motion? When Cargian suggested voting alphabetically, this worried the board president. "If you do it in alphabetical order, this does not allow you necessarily to vote on each school as the motion was made," said Carmen, struggling with the conundrum that she saw. "It's certain if your first options do not close, then what you are saying is that the other ones go by default," she concluded. "And I do not believe that's what this board has in mind!" -- an exclamation that drew applause from Tecumseh residents in the audience.

Looking into nearby rows of Moses DeWitt parents in the front of the auditorium, DeBottis saw tally sheets held up by residents. Responding to parents' suggestions, he asked, "Why couldn't I just put down on this piece of paper I've got the two I prefer, give it to Mrs. Carmen, and have her read it?" Board members first ignored the suggestion of a paper ballot as they struggled over a motion by Luchsinger, seconded by Cargian, to allow each board member to vote on two schools. Luchsinger proposed that the board consider each of the four schools separately, as members voted in alphabetical order. Again, president Carmen objected. "This is not an equitable way of voting, because the first person either will pass or vote to close a particular school. The next person will of course do the same. But then as you get towards the conclusion in the alphabetical order of roll call vote, there is more weight put towards the end than there is towards the beginning," she explained. "And I maintain that this is not the democratic process!" Residents who shared her apprehensions about the outcome cheered.

DeBottis took this opportunity to return to his suggestion. "Let me place my two votes on a piece of paper with my name. You read this to the board with my name, how my two votes are." Carmen did not respond favorably to this solution. She reminded her colleagues that Luchsinger's motion was on the floor, and "any other motion is really not in order." Luchsinger countered that DeBottis had raised a procedural question related to the same motion. Furthermore, Luchsinger was happy with DeBottis's procedure. After president Carmen tried to bring Luchsinger's motion to a vote, he and Cargian withdrew it.

DeBottis then moved, seconded by Berry, that each board member write the schools he wished to close on a piece of paper, submitted to the clerk. "We must vote on the procedural motion first," advised the board president, although Luchsinger had already withdrawn his motion. Attempting to buy time, Carmen repeatedly asked her colleagues for questions and suggested that the board "wait a minute to make sure everyone is clear" on the procedure. Near midnight, the board voted unanimously to use paper ballots.

The audience broke into conversation as board members recorded their choices. Finally, after a long interval, Berry asked the clerk to read the results, only to have Carmen interject that she was not yet finished. When the clerk started to announce the results, he was interrupted by Moses DeWitt parents seated in the first row. "No! No! You have to read the papers!" objected a

238

Moses DeWitt resident. Although residents were normally forbidden to interrupt official board agendas, the clerk and board members assented to the demand that each vote be read.

Proceeding alphabetically, the clerk read out the final choices, as parents tallied the results and attempted to sort out the voting pattern. Berry had voted to close Moses DeWitt and Jamesville, consistent with his original statement. He alone took this position. Having originally subscribed to Berry's position, Carmen had shifted her vote. During the long deliberation in which she had discarded several sheets of paper, Carmen selected Moses DeWitt and Genesee Hills, not Jamesville, for closing. Like Carmen, Hopkins chose Moses DeWitt and Genesee Hills, showing an allegiance to the board president's convictions not shared by any other colleague. Only Carmen and Hopkins voted to close both elementary schools at the northern end of the district. Cargian, too, changed an earlier position. Having supported Genesee Hills only hours before, he now chose to close that school and Tecumseh. Willing to support Genesee Hills if a majority had emerged for that school, Luchsinger reverted to his first choices. True both to his criteria and longstanding commitments, he preferred to close Tecumseh and Genesee Hills, as did Scibilia and Debottis, who had clearly expressed this viewpoint. Mallan voted to close Moses DeWitt and Tecumseh, the only member to take the position that once seemed a probable board decision.

As the clerk read the totals, many residents remained silent and uncomprehending: 1 vote to close Jamesville; 5 votes to close Tecumseh; 4 votes to close Moses DeWitt; and 6 votes to close Genesee Hills. At first stunned, Moses DeWitt residents broke into applause. Having labeled the first tape cartridge for the five-hour meeting "The Infamous Decision," an officer of the Moses DeWitt Parents' Group spoke into the tape recorder, "In case you haven't heard, it's a keeper!" Least expected by parent activists, the impossible had happened. Moses DeWitt remained open.

As evident in earlier voting, Genesee Hills had no solid coalition behind it. Unlike Moses DeWitt, it had no determined enemies but it also lacked strong friends. Only Mallan and Berry voted for Genesee Hills; Cargian and Hopkins fell by the wayside as supporters. Considered a natural ally, particularly by her friends in the Genesee Hills Parent-Teachers' Organization, even

Carmen had voted to close the school. Describing her vote to the press, Carmen said that keeping Genesee Hills was her "first preference," but she shifted her vote "when it became obvious" that other board members would vote to close the school.[5] She also saw a majority for Jamesville and realized that choosing to close that school was a wasted vote.[6] Possibly Carmen hoped to create a deadlock in the voting for Genesee Hills and Tecumseh. By voting last she might conceivably have stalemated any choice among the three DeWitt schools. But the paper ballot, like the much-discussed alphabetical roll call, deprived the president of the opportunity to cast a decisive tie-vote, a prerogative she had used in the past.

Tecumseh, moreover, held a precarious political position. Although Moses DeWitt parents often described Tecumseh as the favorite of administrators and board members, effective support for the school had dwindled. Known only recently for the academic record of its students, innovative programs, and excellent building, Tecumseh had only two board advocates, Carmen and newcomer Berry, supported by their ineffectual ally, Hopkins. After the board linked Jamesville and Tecumseh in discussions of pairing, Tecumseh parents had issued maladroit warnings about their children "attending school in the shadow of a toxic waste incinerator." In addition to Jamesville opposition, Tecumseh's proponents faced their original problem, Moses DeWitt.

Certain to remain open, Jamesville drew the support of all board members except Berry. Moses DeWitt, the school slated for closing, had the advantage of a few committed adherents. In an eight-member board, a bloc of three provides a significant starting point, as some residents began to fear in November when DeBottis publicly aligned himself with Moses DeWitt. In the midnight vote Cargian also joined Luchsinger, Scibilia, and DeBottis in supporting Moses DeWitt. After other possibilities failed, Cargian decided to cast his vote for the school that seemed more likely to gain the board's support. Moses DeWitt parents had long recognized the critical part played by the board's senior member. In 1978 Cargian had voted to defer closing Moses DeWitt, and in 1979 he had offered the motion to keep all schools open, describing school-closing as the district's worst problem in his two decades on the board. Cargian recognized that a decision must finally be made. Having voted to close two schools, he could live with Jamesville and Moses DeWitt.

In the face of their colleagues' confusion and disarray both Cargian and Luchsinger had remained steady. Whether in checking the proposal to vote by lot, restoring apparent agreement after Hopkins's and Mallan's outburst, or thwarting the president's effort to sidetrack the paper ballot, both men narrowed the board's choices. As Cargian and Luchsinger alternately blocked her efforts at parliamentary maneuver, Carmen had little chance to set the board's direction. Both men saw their opponents' disunity and thus calmly entertained each motion as the hours passed. When the pairing motion to close Moses DeWitt and Tecumseh failed, the possibility of keeping Moses DeWitt became obvious. Luchsinger and Cargian could be certain of the position of DeBottis and Scibilia, unlike other board members who shifted according to different calculations.

In accounting for their votes, board members resorted to various public explanations. "I was assured by the administration that education would not suffer no matter which two schools were closed," said Debottis, who defended going back to "our original districts" in DeWitt and Jamesville.7 Luchsinger and Berry referred to their criteria. Showing a changing interpretation of geography, Hopkins said that he wanted Jamesville to serve the district's southern section and Tecumseh for the northern area as well as for handicapped children.8

Hopkins, Mallan, and Carmen left the December 9 meeting, doubly defeated. They had waited three years to shut Moses Dewitt forever, only to see two other schools closed. Somehow, the phoenix had risen from the ashes. Originally confident of closing Moses DeWitt, these three board members were responsible for the board's October decision to close two schools. During the long December meeting, members of this troika feared an outcome contrary to their premeditated calculations. Thus each one cast doubt on the final stage of the two-closing process that they had set in motion and advanced ever since July. Hopkins recoiled from deals that said "keep my school open and I'll keep yours open." He refused to join the bandwagon, not being "ready to be pressured into dealing."9 "Shame on you! Shame on us!" said Mallan, who now thought the board needed to do a lot of homework before reaching any decision. Carmen gave her attention to the absence of adopted criteria and the public's "great concern for the decision-making process." Both residents and board members should look back at a decision-making procedure that appeared "fair

241

and just" as well as "consistent with the democratic process."10

The architects of the two-closings policy had failed to reach agreement about which schools to close. Now facing the probability of being out-voted, they saw collusion, giving no consideration to the common purpose they themselves had pursued since the June budget defeats. Confronted by unanticipated opposition, those who spearheaded school-closing looked again to the democratic process. Now important, "fair and just" decision-making, adopted standards and criteria had not mattered two months earlier, when Hopkins, Mallan, and Carmen had secured the 7-1 majority in favor of two closings. What was not "political" in July when the board discussed closing two schools became a "game" or a "deal" when the selection of schools began to be evident.

Believing their own rhetoric, Carmen, Hopkins, and Mallan thought they wanted to close two schools. By trying to appear fair and pretending to have a policy, they created a situation in which they failed to concentrate on their primary objective of closing Moses DeWitt. Only belatedly did Carmen and Mallan recognize the real problem of saving their own schools. When it became clear that certainly Tecumseh and possibly Genesee Hills would close, no board member offered a motion to consider only one school. Emotionally committed to school-closing, members of the troika lacked the political flexibility to retreat to a motion to close one school. A last-minute strategic withdrawal would require these board members to renounce their own ideology and draw predictable opposition. Seeing an almost-certain defeat, members who had briefly dominated the board did not seek another bulwark from which to define a new position and defend common interests. Instead, Mallan, Carmen, and Hopkins relied on melodrama and parliamentary tactics, hoping at least to divert or deadlock the school board. Thus, it happened that Jamesville-DeWitt closed two schools, as planned by neither the administration nor the board of education.

## NOTES

1. All quotes from the Dec. 9 meeting come from a tape-recording made by Moses DeWitt residents and now in the author's possession;

the Jamesville-DeWitt Central Office also taped the meeting.

2. **Herald—Journal**(Syracuse), Dec. 9, 1980.
3. Jamesville-DeWitt District Report, Special Edition, Dec. 22, 1977.
4. **Post—Standard,** Oct. 16, 1980.
5. **Suburban Life**(DeWitt and East Syracuse), Dec. 17, 1980.
6. **Herald—Journal,** Dec. 17, 1980.
7. **Suburban Life,** Dec. 17, 1980.
8. **Ibid.**
9. **Post—Standard**(Syracuse), Dec. 11, 1980.
10. **Suburban Life,** Dec. 17, 1980.

# XV.  Rattling the Wrong Cage

"They've definitely rattled the wrong cage," said a spokesman for an organization formed immediately after the December 9 decision. The new Jamesville-DeWitt Concerned Citizens' Committee was "organizing for a fight," ran a local newspaper headline.1 Two nights after the decision about 300 residents had assembled to protest the board's action and plan a strategy of resistance.2 Parents from Genesee Hills and Tecumseh quickly seized upon possible improprieties in the decision-making as a justification for their opposition. Protesting parents expressed concern that the district have an "honorable board."3 Furthermore, the board had not closed Moses DeWitt. "They voted to close Moses DeWitt three years ago and then reversed that decision. The school certainly hasn't improved since that time," said the president of the Genesee Hills Parent-Teachers' Organization, now co-chairman of what became known as the JDCCC.

As local news stories focused on deals and improprieties, board members were again asked to comment on their decision. Luchsinger, Scibilia, Cargian, Berry, and DeBottis dismissed the new organization's discussion of improprieties. Mallan did not comment, and Hopkins preferred not to discuss a situation he found "difficult." He did say, however, that "the process used in the decision making was proper."4 Board president Carmen explained, ambiguously, "If there were improprieties, I would hope that the situation would be addressed in a professional, unbiased, objective manner." Describing herself as "horrified," she did not wish to discuss the situation further.5 Further protecting ties to the new protest organization, Carmen issued a public statement accounting for her vote to close Genesee Hills. For three years she had consistently voted to close Moses DeWitt, and only when it became "obvious there was no hope of closing Jamesville" did she realize that "it was a new ballgame." With only three schools under consideration, she faced the unenviable task of voting to close one of the newer buildings.6 Never emphasized or even discussed before December 9, the age of the schools now appeared as a significant consideration.

Within a week of the December 9 decision, the JDCCC held a second meeting to introduce officers and explain plans. The organization's steering committee consisted of officers from parents' groups at Tecumseh and Genesee Hills and interested residents from both areas. In addition to a few longtime board-watchers, three lawyers, three physicians, an engineer, and a Syracuse University professor came to the fore as protest leaders. The group's composition, including PTA mothers and newly-activated professionals, was similar to that of the Moses DeWitt Special Committee which had organized spontaneously three years earlier. Although JDCCC leaders attempted to involve residents from all areas, they achieved only token success in this effort.

Demonstrating the seriousness of their commitment, JDCCC officers announced that they had hired a local lawyer to file a complaint against the school board with the New York State Commissioner of Education. Attorney John A. DeFrancisco, who served as president of the Syracuse school board, advised his clients that they faced an "uphill battle" to prove that the December 9 decision was "arbitrary and capricious."[7] He called upon residents to offer cooperation and written evidence to help persuade the commissioner that the local school board should take a new vote. "The best solution to the problem would be to talk to the school board and have them voluntarily decide to take a new vote on which schools to close."[8]

Despite the lawyer's cautionary note, JDCCC speakers established a goal of raising $15,000 for legal expenses. The organization had already raised "about $7,000," of which approximately $3,000 came from the playground fund of the Genesee Hills Parent-Teachers' Organization. "People have really opened up their purses," continued steering committee member Benjamin Levine, an attorney defeated as a school board candidate the previous June.[9]

After he outlined the legal strategy, Levine further noted that the new protest would be sound and reasonable, in contrast to the emotional campaign three years earlier. Although the JDCCC planned to contest the board's authority, it would do so in a sensible fashion. Steering committee members accepted the board's decision to close two schools but questioned the procedure used in making the decision. "We're not telling the board to keep four buildings open," said Levine.[10] Instead, the JDCCC wanted "clearly stated criteria for the school selection" and evidence that the final decision is "rational and non-political regardless of which two buildings are eventually closed."[11]

The evening's highlight came when former board president Perkins addressed the audience. Perkins told parents that her heart ached for the school district's "turmoil," which dated to the board's decision to close Moses DeWitt. She reminded the audience that she had voted to close Moses DeWitt in order to preclude closing a second school, the official justification developed shortly after the 1977 vote. Keeping the emphasis on 1977, she did not say whether she now wanted to close two schools or mention any school other than Moses DeWitt. Instead, she deplored the absence of long-range planning by the administration and the board and explained that her "personal ethics made it impossible to continue in an untenable situation."[12] Perkins declined to join parents in fighting the school-closings as such. Which schools were closed did not concern her, she said, a statement at odds with her preceding sentences emphasizing Moses DeWitt. Instead, the former board member saw the main question as "the issue of ethics--of legal and moral considerations."[13]

When local reporters questioned her public support for the JDCCC, Perkins merely repeated that she is a "firm believer that a school be closed." Again making no reference to the policy of closing not one but two schools, she repeated that the decision to close is necessary "in order not to penalize the taxpayer." Despite her eagerness that the board stop "treading water" and take action, Perkins shared the JDCCC's unhappiness with the decision-making process. She found the present situation "absolutely different" from that in 1977-1978, when she had not considered public criticism justified.[14]

JDCCC members asserted that they did not necessarily want the school board to "flip-flop" its December 9 decision, but they repeatedly referred to Moses DeWitt and Jamesville as the district's "older schools."[15] Newspaper articles referred almost nightly to the older and newer buildings, never citing construction dates for any school. With the exception of a four-room wing of Moses DeWitt, elementary-school construction in Jamesville-DeWitt had all taken place within the decade of rapidly-expanding enrollment between 1952-1962. Rarely replying to public criticism, Superintendent Baker informed the morning paper, "All our buildings are in good shape and relatively new."[16]

Not only the age of buildings but the presence of

247

Photograph 10. Former board president **Phyllis Perkins** addressing the JDCCC said that her heart ached for the district's "turmoil" dating to 1977.

staircases at Moses DeWitt and Jamesville provided an issue. Access to handicapped children offered the most effective rallying point in what JDCCC leaders had earlier defined as a "non-emotional" protest. A pediatrician who specialized in the treatment of cerebral palsy resigned from the Jamesville-DeWitt Committee on the Handicapped, charging the school board with taking a "step backward in education, not only in providing quality education for handicapped students but for all students in the district." The physician cited a possible violation of the federal statute guaranteeing handicapped children the right to be educated in the least restrictive environment. Dr. Phillip T. Swender also saw a "potential tragedy involving not only handicapped children but all children," given increased enrollment and ever-growing commercial traffic in the vicinity of Moses DeWitt.[17]

On January 8, one hundred residents assembled to review the JDCCC's efforts "to bring about a review and reversal of the decision that selected Genesee Hills and Tecumseh Elementary as the two buildings to be closed," as the organization's purpose was described in its first newsletter.[18] Addressing a diminished audience, attorney DeFrancisco again warned parents that they would have to overcome "long odds" in winning an appeal to the commissioner of education. Nevertheless, the main legal avenue was to be this appeal. In attempting to show that the December 9 decision was arbitrary and capricious, DeFrancisco offered a grab bag of arguments. For example, the school board had voted in 1979 not to close schools until the quality of educational program was "jeopardized," but the board had never established that quality was threatened. When members of the JDCCC steering committee expected other schools to close, they felt certain that program was jeopardized and publicly insisted that the board take action.[19] As circumstances changed, so did arguments. DeFrancisco planned to argue that the board had failed to fill the Perkins vacancy and never fully documented savings from closing two schools, also points raised by Moses DeWitt parents but ignored by others when they felt their schools were safe. The board, moveover, had lacked objective criteria for a closing process in which alleged improprieties occurred.[20]

Earlier in the week DeFrancisco had achieved a momentary success when he obtained a "show cause" order from a State Supreme Court justice. This order required the school board to explain why the December 9 decision

249

should not be voided as a result of violation of the Open Meetings Act (Public Officers Law) and prohibited actions to implement the closings.[21] Notice of the appeal to the commissioner was officially delivered to board president Carmen, along with a JDCCC request to address the board on January 13.[22]

The school board also took actions, however. After an appeal by the district's attorney, Leslie Deming, the "show cause" order was quickly rescinded, requiring the JDCCC attorney to "re-serve" the motion. In a court hearing scheduled for late January, DeFrancisco planned to challenge the use of an executive session on December 9 to discuss Hopkins's allegations, as well as "any other executive meetings involving school-closing discussions." The young lawyer cautioned parents against placing their hopes in this approach, however. Answering questions at the JDCCC's meeting, DeFrancisco explained to Phyllis Perkins's husband that a closed meeting or even a deal as discussed by Hopkins offered no basis for a criminal proceeding. Indeed, the Open Meetings Law permitted board members to talk in private, get together for discussions, and even reach deals. At the evening's end, JDCCC officers announced that they had signed over $5,000 to DeFrancisco.[23]

On January 13, spokesmen for the JDCCC appealed to the board to adopt a resolution deferring the October 14 and December 9 decisions until the 1981-1982 school year, pending a complete review of costs, educational program, and criteria for the closing of schools, to be implemented in the 1982-1983 school year.[24] Speakers cited various problems, complaining tht the administration had not made information readily available to them. William Johnson, a Syracuse University economist, described the district's information on cost-savings as inadequate, but stated that he had not established an answer. Dr. Swender could not see the logic of closing newer, more accessible schools. Jamesville-DeWitt had never before settled for minimal standards, he said, as he read a letter from parents of a wheel-chair child scheduled to enter kindergarten in the fall. Robert Herman, a professional engineer with a Ph.D. in electrical engineering, next considered the condition of school facilities. "We are letting ourselves in for a catastrophic failure....With rusting pipes, you are asking for a problem," he said of Moses DeWitt. At Jamesville Elementary, the engineer forecast that it "was only a matter of time before the

250

septic tank fills up."25

JDCCC leader Levine then made the organization's major argument to the board.26 He expressed concern that the December 9 closing decision represented "an unprecedented step backwards, a retreat from the best." Levine contrasted the JDCCC and previous protesters. The new organization appeared before the board "in a positive fashion, without harassment, intimidation, or public outcries for personal reprisals," he said, "but with respect for which your office is entitled."

Never alluding to the JDCCC's legal action against the school board, Levine returned to the issue that had long held the community's attention. In 1977 the board had determined to close Moses DeWitt, based on "established factors and agreed-upon criteria." The 1980 closing decision, by contrast, reflected "regionalism and neighborhood politics." According to a "criteria-based decision," Moses DeWitt should have been closed. Indeed, the reasons for closing Moses Dewitt "remain unchanged to this day." To illustrate his argument, Levine showed on an overhead screen a copy of a district newsletter of December 1977, listing a number of **ex post facto** reasons for closing Moses Dewitt, a document that had never been mailed. The more modest rationalization about delaying a second closing, as described in the published newsletter, had galvanized Moses DeWitt activists who knew that this reasoning had never been presented before the closing decision. Now "established factors and agreed-upon criteria" were projected back to 1977, when board members met in all-day private sessions, seldom expressed opinions in public, and scarcely realized the complications of school-closing. But for those who wanted Moses DeWitt closed the history of 1977 was indelibly rewritten by opinion and desire.

Finally leaving Moses DeWitt, Levine turned to Jamesville Elementary. Because of the board's composition that school "was placed on a pedestal." The use of uniform criteria requred that Jamesville be considered on a par with other schools. "We come with facts and unanswered questions," concluded Levine, who described the JDCCC's attitude as neither arrogant nor hat-in-hand. "We confront a decision not seasoned with reason but spiced with regionalism....That a precedent exists for a review and a reversal is beyond dispute."27

The audience of 250 residents waited attentively

251

to hear the board's reaction to the JDCCC ninety-minute appeal. After an interval of silence, Berry addressed the question. "As far as I am personally concerned, I would like to go to court and get this resolved," he said. "To rescind and go back is not in the interest of our total community, because it delays the process," Berry maintained, to the dismay of Tecumseh constituents. "I, too, don't want to reverse the decision at this time," said Mallan, making it clear that the JDCCC had sympathy but no real support on the board. A lawyer, Luchsinger found it inappropriate for the school board to take any action while a lawsuit and an administrative appeal were pending, because this could "jeopardize our position legally."

During the evening Carmen had jotted down her own thinking about the school board. "In my opinion responsiveness, respectability, and responsibility are the key elements in effective decision-making," the president declared. "Historically, the board of education at Jamesville-DeWitt has prided itself on being responsive to the desires of the community." Carmen, however, had not sided with the board majority in 1979 when five members concluded that the community wanted to maintain all schools. At that time she discounted residents' interest in passing the budget and the strong support for local schools seen by her colleagues.[28]

Now the board president recalled that "just three years ago the board was asked and was willing to review its position in response to the concerns of one segment of the community," she said identifying Moses DeWitt. "I would hope that the board of education would not now choose to violate a commitment to the responsiveness and responsibility to the larger community!" The terms "one segment" and "larger community," like "responsiveness," served as ideological code words, stimulating sustained applause from JDCCC supporters.

Cargian then observed that no board member had actually offered a resolution, and he did not wish to discuss the subject. DeBottis argued that board members knew from the outset that they would face questions, possibly litigation. Even if the board voted to close the other two schools, "we'd be right back here" facing legal action. Berry, too, preferred to be "sued now" rather than later; the court action should be settled now, not for the school board but for "the little kid going into second or third grade."

Berry's comments caused the board president to explode. "Are we saying on this board of education that as the Jamesville-DeWitt school community we are not looking to mediate?" Having long countered Moses DeWitt residents by restricting or preventing public comment, Carmen had achieved only tactical success. Confronting failure, she committed herself to "mediation." But mediation, answered Berry, is not the problem. "We are going to court." Returning desperately to the events of 1977-1978, the president recalled that the board faced a threat of litigation at that time.

DeBottis now challenged the board president. The board had not failed to talk to anybody in the community, he stated. "Who do you suggest we talk to first? Who do you want to mediate with first?" The board had voted to close two schools. Mediation first with Tecumseh and Genesee Hills, then with Moses DeWitt and Jamesville, would not solve the problem. "Am I to believe tht you do not support this suit? Yes or No?" To this Carmen replied, "If need be I will answer that in a court of law!" for which she received a standing ovation.

Berry then moved, seconded by Luchsinger, that the board of education defend its interest in the lawsuit and the administrative action, as directed by attorney Deming, who had spent hours at school board meetings with the expectation of such a result. Board president Carmen cast the sole dissenting vote on the motion. When asked to account for her position against the board's legal defense, Carmen told the press that she would have to hear the motion read back to her word by word in order to explain her vote. "Now that the board has made its decision, it is purely academic," she concluded.[29]

Following their presentation, JDCCC leaders had sharply criticized Deming for not revealing that DeFrancisco had proposed an out-of-court settlement if the board adopted the resolution to defer the closing decision.[30] Deming had presented this choice to board members in an executive session immediately preceding the January 13 meeting. When board members rejected the offer, president Carmen had left the executive session.[31]

Except for Carmen, the board stood united in defense of its closing decision. Mallan had testified for the JDCCC's appeal to the commissioner of education that he "did not have all of the data requested from the

superintendent's office to make a rational decision" on
school-closings. He further stated that he was not
satisfied in his own mind that a deal had not been made.
Nevertheless, the education professor did not want to
rescind the board's closing decision. Elected as the
school board's Tecumseh representative, Berry also
declined to support the JDCCC. Despite criticism from
residents in his area, Berry remained true to his
statement at the close of the December 9 meeting, when he
told the audience that "it's all over" and time to begin
again.

Administrators also presented a solid phalanx; no
principal defended a particular school, as opposed to the
program and the district. The era of Moses DeWitt's Ted
Calver had passed. Principal at Tecumseh for fourteen
years before his transfer to Jamesville in 1978, Fred
Weir said, "The teachers and educational program at
Tecumseh are excellent. We have an equally outstanding
staff and program here."[32] Using almost the same words,
the current principal at Tecumseh, Robert Dewey, agreed,
"All four elementary schools have outstanding staffs and
programs that have earned the district an excellent
reputation."[33] Dr. Robert T. Catney, who was principal
of Jamesville for nine years before moving to Genesee
Hills in the 1978 rotation of principals, said, "The
educational program won't be damaged in any way because
of closing two elementary schools. We'll have the same
teachers, students, and programs."[34] Midway through his
first year as principal, Patrick Tamburro told the press,
"None of my kids would have lost anything by going to any
of our other elementary schools, and no one is going to be
losing anything by joining us here at Moses DeWitt."[35]
Superintendent Baker said repeatedly, "Buildings do not
make a program. Staff does."[36]

Having emerged with their school open, Moses
DeWitt parents took the anomalous position of defending
the board and the administration. Adopting the rhetoric
of their opponents, they too considered what was best for
all of the children. Moses DeWitt Parents' Group
president Lynda Rill thought it important that all parts
of the community "get moving along so the children can
make a smooth transition." Considering the criticism
from the JDCCC, Rill continued, "I understand that
everyone wants to keep their school open. But the
children are not going to be jeopardized by being in Moses
DeWitt."[37] Moses Dewitt activists resented the lack of
past support by Tecumseh and Genesee Hills parents who
had urged school-closing when they felt nothing at stake.

Furthermore, JDCCC spokesmen such as Levine clearly emphasized closing Moses Dewitt above other goals. As a result Moses DeWitt parents refused to make common cause with new critics who adopted their arguments.[38] Those who wanted to retain K-5 elementary schools remained silent, knowing that if only one school closed it would be Moses DeWitt. When JDCCC leaders arranged a late-January meeting with Moses DeWitt activists, assembled parents arrived at no agreement or shared purpose.

JDCCC members were offended by the reaction of the board and administration to the January presentation. Board members had rebuffed protesting parents, and Superintendent Baker had said nothing, using pending litigation as his justification in private conversations. "The official position taken was to ignore our findings. This is the crux of our complaint," said a full-page JDCCC advertisement.[39] Having failed to persuade the board, JDCCC leaders hoped that the legal strategy would bring results.

A State Supreme Court justice ruled that the board of education must answer JDCCC charges that it had violated the Open Meeting Law by the executive session on December 9, thus giving some hope to dissatisfied parents.[40] In a second court session on February 10, DeFrancisco also argued that Jamesville-DeWitt board members had participated in private meetings before the December 9 meeting. "Board members deny that deals were made," he continued, but all admit that "prior conversations" occurred concerning school-closings.[41] The JDCCC lawyer further argued that Hopkins had not retracted his statement that deals were made. Deming readily refuted these contentions. The Open Meetings Law applies only to meetings with a quorum, he explained. "At no time did any board member attend any meeting that was closed to the public or any meeting when a quorum was present. They attended nothing but public meetings." Each board member, Hopkins included, had sworn in affidavits that he did not make a deal. Furthermore, continued Deming, discipline or removal of an individual goes to the heart of personnel, a legitimate reason for executive session.[42] Several weeks later a State Supreme Court justice ruled that the December 9 executive session did not violate the Open Meetings Law. The judge further dismissed charges that illegal meetings occurred before the December 9 meeting.[43]

Meanwhile, parents continued to assail the board. President Carmen allowed unrestricted comment by a largely JDCCC audience at a communications meeting in late January. In addition to raising questions about class size, program rooms, and provisions for the handicapped, residents expressed interest in redistricting. Carmen had offered "just for discussion" a modification of pairing, whereby 56 children from one wealthy Moses Dewitt neighborhood would be shifted to Jamesville Elementary.[44] By redistricting it might still be possible to inflict punishment on Moses DeWitt adversaries. "We've heard over and over again that the children will adjust. Well, the children will adjust to redistricting, too," said JDCCC leader Levine.[45]

On February 10, Superintendent Baker made his first forceful presentation in many months. Explicitly and without qualification the administration recommended pairing, because it caused the least disruption for students. When Luchsinger urged the board to settle the issue and move on to other topics, Carmen protested that she was "not sure that programming questions had been asnwered" concerning redistricting. Having decided in January to leave Hopkins's position vacant, the seven-member board voted 6-1 to send all children from Genesee Hills to Moses DeWitt and all from Tecumseh to Jamesville Elementary. Carmen again cast the sole dissenting vote.[46]

Defeated in their lawsuit and in the symbolic effort to redistrict Moses DeWitt, JDCCC adherents turned to their pending appeal before the commissioner. Before an audience of only fifty residents, DeFrancisco described legal actions as of mid-March. Although disappointed by the outcome of their lawsuit, parents felt satisfied that they had done what was right. DeFrancisco explained that he had hoped for a hearing in order to obtain full information from board members. "We would have won if the judge had ordered the board members to testify about their secret agreements under oath," said one parent. DeFrancisco next summarized arguments to be made before the commissioner on March 24. He planned to use Luchsinger's November appeal for criteria to support the JDCCC's position. Other arguments were to focus on provisions for handicapped children and the board's reversal of the 1977 decision to close Moses DeWitt. At the meeting's end, JDCCC officials reported that the organization had spent $7,500 in legal fees and anticipated a total cost of $10,000.[47]

As the meeting ended conversation turned to the

forthcoming May election, in which four board positions would be open. In late February Mallan had announced that he would not seek reelection, and Cargian had earlier said that he was ready to leave.[48] With two board members retiring and two having resigned, new candidates could seek election without having to challenge an incumbent. As early as their December meeting, JDCCC members had considered changing the board's composition.[49] From the outset DeFrancisco had urged his clients to use the political and electoral process. In February a JDCCC spokesman declared the organization's intention "to elect four people to the board in May."[50] Moses DeWitt parents had first considered possible board candidates in mid-January. Before the filing deadline in early April, both groups attempted to determine the plans of the other and field strong candidates in an election that could tip the balance of the board.

A newspaper summary of legal papers presented to the commissioner showed that DeFrancisco had used the JDCCC's familiar arguments. Acknowledging that the commissioner has found no board arbitrary and capricious in the area of school-closings, the JDCCC appeal nevertheless asserted that "there is no case with reported facts that even approaches the arbitrariness of the (Jamesville-DeWitt) decision," an extraordinary statement considering the several hundred schools closed in New York State in the previous decade.[51]

JDCCC parents hoped to set a precedent in educational law by their appeal to the commissioner. Placing their hopes in the commissioner, parents expected the educational bureaucracy to pass judgment on itself. Bureaucracy, according to Roscoe Martin, is a natural corollary of professionalism in education. Over many years professionals created what Martin has termed education's "peaceable kingdom," an organization designed to guarantee the autonomy of educational decision-makers. As described by Martin, "the leaders of education have erected for their enterprise a fortress which seems all but impregnable."[52] At the pinnacle of the state's educational bureaucracy sat the commissioner. To expect him to allow one parents' group to assault the fortress was unreasonable.

Deming held secure ground when he argued that school-closing was "a reasonable and rational exercise of its (the school board's) discretionary powers." Not only the incumbent commissioner but no commissioner in

257

ten years had upheld a challenge to a closing decision. The JDCCC's legal case "must be based upon more solid legal ground than mere disappointment," argued Deming. Furthermore, the JDCCC petitioners had over three months' notice and five opportunities to present their material before the decision was made. Instead, parents collected information after the fact.[53]

The commissioner's decision was expected in four to six weeks. In the meantime, the school board continued with other matters. Board members unanimously approved a $12.6 million budget for the school year 1981-1982.[54] The budget proposal restored cuts made the previous year, including field trips, assemblies, parent-teacher conferences, and driver education, as demanded by parents. The new budget proposal raised the tax rate by only 2.8 per cent or $3.48 per $1,000 of assessed valuation. The district planned to cut six elementary-school teachers, two as a result of the closings and four by staff attrition in response to declining enrollment.[55] The budget proposal was a reasonable figure, in contrast to the previous year's $11.95 tax increase.

In April ten candidates filed for the school board positions. Immediately after the filing deadline, board president Carmen startled residents by submitting her resignation. "We have all been through stressful times," she wrote. "Unfortunately, this board's reaction to these stresses has been internal divisiveness as well as an obvious blatant contempt for the community we serve."[56] Carmen resigned, because she could no longer answer for and justify the board's actions. The board president declined to cite particular incidents or individuals in her condemnation. "It's not a person I'm talking about. It's a way of operating."[57] Superintendent Baker expressed ritual shock and dismay, describing the departing board member as "a very classy woman who always has been a strong supporter of the programs for the children."[58] Carmen's resignation came at an odd time, just as four JDCCC candidates hoped to gain election to the Board. Carmen held the fifth vote necessary for the JDCCC's success.

The four JDCCC candidates had all been intimately involved in the protest organization. Two served on its steering committee, as did the husband of a third candidate. The fourth candidate's wife was a JDCCC petitioner to the commissiner. Of the four candidates, Benjamin Levine was the organization's most prominent spokesman as well as a petitioner to the commissioner.

After much consideration Moses DeWitt parents fielded two candidates for the DeWitt board positions. For the Moses DeWitt seat, parents backed John E. Hayes, Jr., who had served as the Moses DeWitt representative on the facilities and program committee in 1978-1979 and later had an instrumental part in the opinion-survey conducted in August 1980. For the Genesee Hills position, activists supported their own political organizer and past president of the Moses DeWitt Parents' Group, Mary Jane Fennessey. Having experienced only failure in school board elections, Moses DeWitt parents attempted to build alliances by supporting two Jamesville candidates, achieving in one case a close working relationship. Moses DeWitt parents now clearly supported the **status quo**, an advantage they realized. For the first time, they escaped the stigma of disrupting the district.

The board candidates used standard school rhetoric, relying on only a few key phrases and the work of supporters to identify their positions. Candidates all agreed on the need for unity and improved communication. "Faith must be restored and positive spirit must be returned to our district," said a JDCCC candidate. "Open communication between a responsible board and a concerned, informed community is the only solution," agreed a Moses DeWitt contender.[59] Candidates saw a need for a responsive school board that would work with adminstrators to achieve innovative programs for the children and serve the district's total welfare. Businessmen seeking election discussed fiscal management and long-range planning. Most candidates emphasized passing the budget and maintaining quality education.

Questioned about a reversal of the school-closing decision, all candidates but one sidestepped the issue by cautiously answering that any decision would be subject to review by a new board. When asked about their decision to sue the school district, JDCCC candidates described the action as part of the democratic system. Reporters and residents turned the question to Moses DeWitt candidates who had condoned the expenditure of parent-group funds in resisting the board three years earlier.[60] Neither side could claim a consistently supportive role.

Working throughout the district, parents'

organizations adopted a more forthright approach than that seen in the public positions of candidates. JDCCC adherents circulated a sheet listing their candidates and appealing for support "if you want honesty, fairness, and a possible reconsideration of which schools should be closed." Immediately before the May 6 election members of the Moses DeWitt Parents' Group distributed several thousand newsletters in their area. After condemning the JDCCC's legal and political strategy, the newsletter identified the four board positions. Those candidates supported by Moses DeWitt parents were conspicuously described, in contrast to a stark identification of their JDCCC opponents. Informed rather than consulted about the newsletter, Moses DeWitt principal Tamburro later expressed concern about the document's partisan character and hoped that such actions would not occur in the future.

On election night Moses DeWitt candidate Hayes achieved a narrow victory, as Fennessey lost in an equally close race against a past president of the Genesee Hills Parent-Teachers' Organization. The Jamesville candidate who had worked closely with Moses DeWitt parents led all candidates, achieving an easy victory. Facing two candidates who divided his opposition, Levine was also elected by a substantial margin. Thus, the JDCCC gained two of the four positions. In contrast to the previous year, the budget passed easily. As voting turn-out subsided to 2535, 54 per cent voted "yes." Residents who had turned out in record numbers to vote "no" on June 20, 1980, stayed home, as parents committed to board candidates supported the budget. Passage of the budget appeared to give the community's seal of approval to the closings policy.[61]

Two days after the election the commissioner upheld the board's closing decision. "The responsibility for managing the affairs of a school district rests with the board of education," he wrote. The commissioner devoted only one line to alleged improprieties discussed by the JDCCC. As in twenty-five other school-closing appeals in the previous year, the ruling supported the local school board.[62] Levine criticized the commissioner for failing to address the JDCCC's issues, but hoped that board members may have learned that it is "more expedient to listen than to defend a lawsuit."[63] The JDCCC had raised $10,000 to cover fees for its futile legal strategy, while the district's costs for the lawsuit and the administrative action amounted to $17,000.[64]

260

In a special election in June to fill Carmen's position a JDCCC candidate gained election in a three-way race.65 After months of effort and a major financial commitment, the JDCCC had gained three of nine board positions. The protest organization had pursued legal action destined to fail, for all precedents supported the school board. The group's political strategy was equally flawed. From the outset the JDCCC supported the board's decision to close two schools, thereby limiting the possible choices. Retreating to a policy of one closing could have focused attention on Moses DeWitt, as desired by JDCCC protesters. Because of their public support for two closings during the fall, JDCCC leaders did not attempt the necessary volte-face.

If two schools closed, Jamesville was certain to remain open, a political reality usually acknowledged by JDCCC parents. Even if Moses DeWitt were selected for closing, either Genesee Hills or Tecumseh would be the second school closed. Because their organization represented parents from two schools, JDCCC leaders never clearly determined which school they wanted to save, although Tecumseh received greater emphasis as a building fully accessible to the handicapped. At best JDCCC parents could keep only one of their schools. Instead of concentrating on that goal, however, they emphasized past grievances by insisting on the closing of Moses DeWitt, a measure that did not solve the problem. Again, a policy of keeping three schools offered the only recourse. If JDCCC parents had considered a radical approach, they might have attempted to save Tecumseh at the moral cost of keeping Moses DeWitt. By allying themselves with Moses DeWitt parents, JDCCC members might have created a political interest strong enough to reverse the board's direction. If their own school was secure, many Moses DeWitt parents preferred to maintain at least three elementary scools. But because of past history an unholy alliance between Tecumseh and Moses DeWitt never received serious consideration.

After the election, the board's majority dispelled JDCCC charges that Moses DeWitt presented fire hazards and then agreed to lease Genesee Hills to the Jewish Community Center.66 Tenants at Tecumseh included the New York State Education Department, a nursery school, and a dance program, among others. In July trucks appeared at the closed schools and the move began.

After only two weeks of calm, local newspapers

261

carried the announcement that Superintendent Baker was resigning to become executive vice president of Utica College, a branch of Syracuse University.[67] Baker denied that the resignation, effective September 15, was related to the controversy concerning school-closing. That conflict was "just part of the job," said Baker. "It's part of the workload superintendents today face." If he had stayed in the public schools, he would have remained at Jamesville-DeWitt but the superintendent wanted another challenge.[68]

Case studies have pinpointed board turnover as a prelude to a change in a local district's superintendent.[69] Baker had not seen the defeat of incumbents that often signals a superintendent's dismissal, but board members had resigned or retired, showing a decreased commitment to the system. While Jamesville-DeWitt incumbents traditionally sought reelection to serve the district or in recent years to prove that they were right, they now retired from the scene. As superintendent, Baker retained the support of a majority but the board was significantly altered by its five new members. Justified by the passage of the budget, legal decisions, and a board majority that supported the closing decision, Superintendent Baker found an opportune moment to leave.

## NOTES

1. **Suburban Life**(DeWitt and East Syracuse), Dec. 17, 1980.
2. **Herald—Journal**(Syracuse), Dec. 11, 1980.
3. **Suburban Life**, Dec. 17, 1980.
4. **Ibid.**
5. **Ibid.**
6. **Herald—Journal**, Dec. 17, 1980.
7. **Post—Standard**(Syracuse), Dec. 18, 1980.
8. **Herald—Journal**, Dec. 17, 1980.
9. **Post—Standard**, Dec. 18, 1980.
10. **Ibid.**
11. **Herald—Journal**, Dec. 17, 1980.
12. **Post—Standard**, Dec. 18, 1980.
13. **Herald—Journal**, Dec. 17, 1980.
14. **Post—Standard**, Jan. 1, 1981.
15. **Herald—Journal**, Dec. 17, 1980.
16. **Post—Standard**, Jan. 1, 1981.
17. **Herald—Journal**, Dec. 16, 1980.
18. Jamesville-DeWitt Concerned Citizens' Committee, Newsletter

#1, Jan. 1981.
19. See **Post—Standard**, Oct. 16, 1980.
20. **Herald—Journal**, Jan. 9, 1981.
21. **Ibid.**
22. **Herald—Journal**, Jan. 7, 1981.
23. **Herald—Journal**, Jan. 7, 1981; author's notes of JDCCC meeting, Jan. 8, 1981.
24. **Herald—Journal**, Jan. 14, 1981.
25. **Post—Standard**, Jan. 15, 1981.
26. Unless otherwise indicated, all quotes are from a tape-recording of the meeting made by the author.
27. **Post—Standard**, Jan. 15, 1981.
28. See **Post—Standard**, Feb. 1, 1979.
29. **Suburban Life**, Jan. 21, 1981.
30. **Post—Standard**, Jan. 15, 1981.
31. **Herald—Journal**, Jan. 14, 1981.
32. **Herald—American**, Jan. 18, 1981.
33. **Herald—American**, Jan. 25, 1981.
34. **Herald—American**, Feb. 1, 1981.
35. **Herald—American**, Jan. 11, 1981.
36. **Post—Standard**, Jan. 1, 1981; **Herald—American**, Jan. 11, 1981.
37. **Post—Standard**, Jan. 1, 1981.
38. **Post—Standard**, Jan. 22, 1981.
39. **The Scotchman**(DeWitt, Jamesville), Feb.4, 1981.
40. **Herald—Journal**, Jan. 27, 1981.
42. **Ibid.**
43. **Post—Standard**, Mar. 12, 1981.
44. **Herald—Journal**, Jan. 28, 1981.
45. **Suburban Life**, Jan. 28, 1981.
46. **Post—Standard**, Feb. 12, 1981.
47. **Herald—Journal**, Mar. 12, 1981.
48. **Suburban Life**, Feb. 25, 1981.
49. **Herald—Journal**, Dec. 15, 1981.
50. **Herald—Journal**, Feb. 25, 1981.
51. **Post—Standard**, Mar. 19, 1981; figures on school-closings are from the Bureau of Educational Statistics, New York State Department of Education.
52. Roscoe C. Martin, **Government and the Suburban School** (Syracuse, 1962), 90, also 95-101.
53. **Post—Standard**, Mar. 19, 1981.
54. **Post—Standard**, Apr. 2, 1981.
55. **Post—Standard**, Mar. 5, 1981.
56. **Herald—Journal**, Apr. 8, 1981.
57. **Post—Standard**, Apr. 9, 1981.
58. **Herald—Journal**, Apr. 8, 1981.
59. **Post—Standard**, Apr. 30, 1981.
60. **Ibid.**
61. Voting statistics are from the Jamesville-DeWitt District Office.
62. **Post—Standard**, May 14, 1981.

63. **Ibid.**
64. **Suburban Life,** Apr. 15, 1981; **Post–Standard,** May 14, 1981.
65. **Suburban Life,** June 10, 1981.
66. **Post–Standard,** July 2, 1981.
67. **Herald–Journal,** July 21, 1981.
68. **Post–Standard,** July 24, 1981; in Aug. 1982, Baker was named president of Utica College.
69. Laurence Iannaccone and Frank W. Lutz, **Politics, Power, and Policy:  The Governing of Local School Districts**(Columbus, 1970), 232, also chapters 6 and 7.

# XVI. What to Do

As the 1981-1982 school year opened, the principal architects of the district's closing policy had resigned or retired from office. Only DeBottis and Luchsinger, now the board's president and vice-president, and Scibilia had served on the board that first considered school-closing in 1976-1977. Perkins, Hopkins, Mallan, and Carmen, who had forced the school-closing issue the previous year, had all left the board, and Superintendent Baker now held what the school district described as a "position in Higher Education Administration."[1]

Although the board had decided in 1979 not to "jam" elementary schools, it did so in 1981. Jamesville Elementary's extra classrooms for a historical museum and a senior citizens' group were eliminated. At Moses DeWitt teachers again worked with small groups in the hallways, and class-size in several sections rose above the promised 22-24. Despite the previous year's reassurances to the contrary, the building lacked the flexibility to accommodate an additional classroom section and teacher. The district's reorganization also filled the middle school. In September 1981, almost 1,000 children enrolled in grades 5-8, a student population virtually identical to the middle school's enrollment in 1971. By adding fifth-graders, Jamesville-DeWitt leaders offset a 21 per cent decline in middle school enrollment over the 1970s but at the cost of truncating elementary education and sacrificing neighborhood, or even community, schools.

For years Jamesville-DeWitt officials had struggled to keep pace with the growing influx of children. As in other districts the 1950s and 1960s were spent in construction programs to provide for the enrollment boom. But growth was politically easy. New schools presented visible symbols of progress and civic pride, and each year brought new programs to satisfy every interest. The period of school expansion was an "era of promise and fulfillment in the goodness of the American way of life."[2]

Rapidly growing enrollments and a multiplication of programs strengthened the autonomy of professional educators. Early in the century administrators had established their importance in running the schools, and a burgeoning clientele accelerated the trend.[3] Americans considered education a unique public function.

The educational process must be non-political and a professionally trained superintendent entrusted to make choices based on educational merit rather than political considerations. A facade of school board-control continued as a token to the American belief in representative government.4 But in the postwar years, as Roscoe Martin astutely observed, the superintendent's professional reputation and community position combined to give him an "almost irresistible voice in school affairs."5 Adequate in an era that valued consensus, this pattern of decision-making was first challenged in urban districts by demands for desegregation or community control. In less heterogeneous districts the closed system ruptured only under the impact of declining enrollment. In the late 1970s it became apparent that no crisis embroils suburban areas more than "attempts by school boards and administrators to close schools."6

In dealing with declining enrollment Jamesville-DeWitt's elected trustees gave wide latitude to the superintendent, just as they had throughout the district's history. During what became a four-year controversy over school-closing, Superintendent Baker adopted changing positions but played a consistent role. When an organization of senior citizens and disgruntled taxpayers threatened the passage of the budget in 1977, the superintendent first set in motion plans to close a school. The board could follow recommendations set forth in the Task Force Report, a study instigated after the near-defeat of the budget in 1976. Strongly influenced by administrators, the Task Force outlined three plans, all involving elementary school-closing. To Baker and his staff closing a building seemed painful but nevertheless preferable to altering their programs. Not surprisingly, a superintendent who linked his own reputation with programs opposed their modification. The administrator's reputation and the district's became one and the same. In the event of budgetary constraints, the conventional remedy was to close an elementary school.

Superintendent Baker recognized perils in closing but failed to prepare for them. Likening school-closing to a death in the family, he said, "It's probably the hardest decision a board has to make."7 But he neither directed nor prevented the decision to close Moses DeWitt, carefully leaving that choice to the board. Following intense public criticism, Baker helped the school board retreat from the closing decision. The superintendent's foremost concern at this time was not the margin of error in the district census or whether Moses DeWitt was the right school to close. Moses DeWitt residents now presented a larger problem--an organized interest that threatened the budget--and passage of the budget held the key to Baker's professional success.

After the budget passed as promised, the superintendent agreed to the policy of maintaining all schools. During the brief period in which Moses DeWitt parents seemed able to fulfill their commitment to the budget, school-closing became officially unmentionable just as it had earlier been unavoidable. Committed to the dogma of keeping all schools open, the administration neither considered nor advanced plans for an eventual school-closing.

When voters rejected an unprecedented tax increase, however, the school-closing issue predictably appeared. Superintendent Baker did not propose scrutiny of his spending policies but defended the district's programs as having earned Jamesville-DeWitt's reputation. After Moses DeWitt parents failed to provide the necessary help in the June budget vote, Baker abruptly jettisoned this alliance and its arguments. He now accommodated himself to school-closing advocates and returned to the Task Force for justification. As superintendent he relied on two choices: pass the budget or implement the Task Force Report.

To protect his own interest Baker recoiled from the board's decision-making process in the fall of 1980. By telling board members and residents that all schools were equal and all choices equally feasible, the administration again threw the critical decision back to the board. When later asked to compare the JDCCC protest in 1980-1981 and that of Moses DeWitt parents three years earlier, the superintendent told the press that the decision to reopen Moses DeWitt reflected the "support of the community toward the budget." Thus "the one big difference is the budget defeat."8

Passage of the budget held paramount importance. Only by the annual consent of the voters did administrators secure discretion in spending and freedom to shift funds to chosen programs and interests. As former principal of the middle school, Baker effectively protected and eventually enlarged this school. Proposals to alter the middle school never received serious discussion in board and administration counsels. Confronted by repeated questions concerning the middle school's grading system and discipline, Baker parried comments and publicly ignored evidence of dissatisfaction. When residents challenged the expenditure of $100,000 for middle-school counseling, the superintendent insisted that the program was important for the children. In this and other instances board members accepted administrators' explanations, because they were professionals trained to deal with a sacred object--the child.9

The board of education failed to fill the leadership vacuum left by the superintendent's public role. Not wanting to repudiate the administration, board members accepted policies despite reservations. Occasionally board members attempted to modify the administration's direction but were thwarted by incomplete information or apparently technical material concerning school finance or state requirements.

During several years' controversy the most significant effort at board leadership came in 1979 when Coit and Luchsinger proposed an automatic school-closing when elementary enrollment dropped below 1,000 students, a workable plan that drew approval from at last one board colleague, a principal, and parents, including those from Moses DeWitt. Superintendent Baker rejected this proposal, however, in favor of an open-ended motion designed to give the administration more latitude, and a board majority acquiesced. Ultimately, both the decision to close two schools and the selection of the schools appeared impulsive and personal rather than planned. Non-political in ideology, board members had lacked the equivalent of a mayor to counter the administration's strategies or organize coalitions. When frustrated in efforts to influence the superintendent, board members did not criticize him directly or present issues in public forum. Instead, they resigned.10

Just as board members felt uncertain in challenging the administration, they regarded the public warily. Elected representatives supposedly devoted to the principle of local control, these officials did not fully embrace the democratic ethos. In the district's thirty-year history board members had never established a tradition "for expressing dissent honestly and loyally without threatening the entire educational enterprise."11 When Moses DeWitt parents tried to establish themselves as a loyal opposition, resisting decisions they considered wrong but supporting the good of the district, board members responded with distaste to what Perkins described as intimidation and coercion. Gradually the board came to expect an interested constituency at its meetings. When prerogatives were involved, however, board members did not care to hear from an opposition party. Affronted by the Moses DeWitt opinion-survey or demands for comment before the decision to close two schools, the board chose to exclude the public.

Neither the superintendent nor the school board offered the sense of direction badly needed. Unwilling or unable to provide leadership, school officials failed to clarify issues or even to moderate public discussion. Despite accumulated information on enrollment trends and each school's classroom space and operating costs, administrators and board members did not restate the choices before the community. Instead, the district's dominant style continued to follow the small town's "etiquette of gossip" whereby private complaints and rumors circulated in lieu of a public confrontation of issues based on the same facts.[12] The district's direction shifted spasmodically as the superintendent gauged community opinion, periodically leaving critical decisions to a board unaccustomed to cooperative action. Policies developed by year-to-year improvisation deepened divisions among board members and residents.

In successive battles the Moses DeWitt and JDCCC parent-groups displayed a new determination to influence how the school district used its resources. Both groups showed that administrators had underestimated the attachment to local schools. In the protracted controversies over school-closing residents challenged not only the result but the process of decision-making. Although protesting parents failed to unite among themselves, they left a warning against educational decisions made in isolation from community values and objectives.[13]

Jamesville-DeWitt's experiences in 1977-1981 were not unique. During the period 1970-1980, total public school enrollment in the United States dropped from 45.9 million to 40.9 million--a decline of 11 per cent.[14] Districts across the country responded by closing thousands of schools, mainly at the elementary level. Between 1970 and 1980 New York State's total number of elementary schools fell by over 400, a trend expected to continue and even accelerate during the 1980s.[15] The 1980s' epidemic of school-closings will be especially severe in the North Central states and the Northeast, where some states are expected to close as many as several hundred schools in one year.[16] Only areas of population growth will escape a problem that affects both suburban and urban districts.[17]

Enrollment trends merely reflect underlying demographic changes. The population is shifting to the southern and western states, which accounted for over 90 per cent of the nation's increase between the 1980 census and July 1981.[18] Onondaga County and nearby upstate counties showed a population decrease during the 1970s, as did other parts of the region. Furthermore, between 1970 and 1980 non-metropolitan areas grew almost twice as fast as metropolitan areas. During the 1960s era of suburban expansion metropolitan growth rates had been triple those of non-metropolitan areas.[19]

By 1980 the once-booming suburbs were aging and losing population. Between 1970 and 1980 Jamesville-DeWitt's total population declined by more than 2,000, or 11 per cent, and the character of the community changed significantly. The percentage of residents 65 and over went from 6 to 13 per cent, while there were now only half as many children ages 5 and under. The average number of persons per household plummeted from 3.5 to only 2.6.[20] Writing in 1953, William H. Whyte, Jr. found 40 per cent of the population in Levittown, Pennsylvania under age 10.[21] By 1980 Jamesville-DeWitt's percentage in this age bracket fell below 10 per cent.

Residents whose children have grown and left home often found themselves pitted against younger parents willing to pay school taxes. Facing demographic changes and budgetary pressures, school officials have forged away to close schools despite bitter controversy, whether in suburban Chicago, Philadelphia, Boston, New York, Baltimore, or Syracuse. A superintendent who presided over school-closing in a suburban district in Nassau County declared, "I can tell you there is absolutely nothing easy about this process."[22]

Nevertheless, school-closing is routinely chosen as the first solution. Why? School officials everywhere are looking for "simple answers to complex problems," Professor Robert I. Rotberg told Moses DeWitt parents in May 1978.[23] Administrators prefer not to examine educational programs, and board members accede to their recommendations. A closed building, moreover, offers a visible economy measure, a symbol of change indicating that a community has successfully weathered its "mid-life crisis."[24] Each elementary school, however, accounts for only a fraction of one per cent of a typical district budget. Seventy-five to eighty-five per cent of a budget goes to personnel costs, which are not significantly altered by school-closings. After a building is closed administrators and most teachers are shifted to remaining buildings; school-closings consolidate very few teachers in special areas and cut only one or two classroom positions not already eliminated by normal attrition of staff. The utility, custodial, and secretarial costs of any one building are modest, and even rental revenue from a closed school is absurdly small.[25]

School districts move ahead from closings with meager or non-existent tax savings. Although Superintendent Baker used figures varying from $180,000 to $70,000 to $30,000 as the cost-savings in closing Moses DeWitt, and later $331,550, or up to a million dollars over a five-year period, from closing two schools, the actual savings have not been assessed.[26] School-closing has greater symbolic than financial importance. In the most extensive survey of school-closing available, Professor Richard Andrews found that most districts did not analyze cost-savings; of those that did two-thirds found no savings or increased costs.[27]

"Closure is a simple solution to the problem of excess space," wrote Andrews. "But at the same time, closure is most assuredly a source of other problems." The environmental and neighborhood impact of school-closure is now recognized, particularly in urban settings.[28] In suburban areas schools have provided a magnet for families, and several studies indicate that school-closing actually accentuates out-migration and enrollment decline. For the first time in Jamesville-DeWitt's experience, kindergarten enrollment in 1981 and 1982 dropped below the total births five years earlier. School-closings may well delay the rejuvenation of aging first-ring suburbs. A school administrator in Arlington, Virginia reported, "Young families have done more selective house-buying since the closures."[29] Likewise, a detailed analysis of Seattle showed families moving from an area after a school-closing.[30] Because of public education's traditional autonomy, school officials reach decisions **in vacuo,** ignoring important economic and social influences affecting the future of their districts.[31]

In most districts little public review is given even to educational questions, including the criteria by which to determine school-size. In the judgment of school-board consultant Stanton Leggett, "We have a notion in this country that the larger the school the better the school." Leggett sees the specialized services of larger schools as less important than good teachers and close relationships between teachers and parents.[32]  A task force in Eugene, Oregon, for example, reported "no clear evidence that a school of less than 150 is inferior to a larger one," and a study of Lexington, Massachusetts described small schools as educationally effective, even outstanding.[33]

A comprehensive eight-year examination of public schools supports the same conclusions. Study director John I. Goodlad found American schools at all levels too big. "None of the schools rated the most satisfactory by students, parents, and teachers was large, and none of the least satisfying was small." Goodlad recommends that "school districts think twice about closing schools," or reorganize larger elementary schools into houses of only 100 pupils. In a small setting children can remain with the same group of teachers for several years and receive the individual attention lacking in schools organized for economies of scale.[34]  Mounting evidence indicates that small schools are "intrinsically good" by virtue of their small classes, intimate, cohesive atmosphere, and parental support.[35]

In Jamesville-DeWitt the subject of ideal school-size received attention only according to political necessity. When closing seemed imperative to save the budget, the large enrollments of the 1960s received emphasis to highlight excess space. Only the demographic committee attempted to develop a standard of school-size to provide for small classes, special program rooms, and flexibility in building-use, but this committee's report had no lasting impact. When Superintendent Baker supported maintaining all schools, the use of itinerant special teachers, the number of sections per grade, and school-size did not seem critical as long as the budget passed. The administration never considered a reorganization of program--for example, multi-age classes--specifically to maintain small schools. Neither did it make careful preparations to gain public acceptance of an eventual closing by gradually altering attendance areas or pinpointing a date for an anticipated closing, as done in nearby districts.

Although elementary schools were negotiable, Superintendent Baker was committed to the program that had made Jamesville-DeWitt a leader, as he repeatedly explained.[36] The administration did not cut services such as videotaping and duplicating or an allocation of almost $300,000 for guidance and counseling in the 1981-1982 budget. The district emphasized the very services discounted by consultant Leggett. In addition to the nine professionals of the counseling staff, Jamesville-DeWitt employed a complement of remedial and resource teachers, special area teachers, and over 60 coaches and assistants. Despite declining enrollment throughout the system, school officials did not compromise offerings at the middle and high-school levels. The preservation of programs ranging from volunteer fire-fighting to photography and driver education took precedence, and parents who wanted to keep local elementary schools never extracted cost savings in other areas.

As professionals the superintendent and his staff protected the programs and grade-organization that seemed important to them. Administrators emphasized career values in influencing the community's decisions. Handicapped by incomplete information and limited time, amateur board members never held an equal voice with administrators but simply hoped that their decisions served "all the children." Protest leaders found sustained political activity difficult, for parents' concern with public education naturally and inevitably reverts to their own children. Thus the public school system functioned essentially as a private institution, characterized by loyalty, resistance to innovation, and brisk defensiveness in the face of criticism.[37]

Jamesville-DeWitt's prolonged imbroglio over school-closing shows the critical need to reexamine relationships among school officials, educational program, and the community.[38] First, citizens must restore what James Koerner described as a balance of powers in education.[39] Because of deference to educational experts, the school superintendent now commands too much latitude in decision-making. In regard to questions such as educational goals, curriculum, and grade-organization, school professionals do not enjoy a monopoly of knowledge. Despite countless studies little is known about how children learn or what makes a good teacher.[40] Educational prognosis remains an uncertain art at best. Laymen can assert their opinions without fearing that they will reduce educational quality or hurt the children.

Certainly, school administration is a specialized task as is teaching, and professional educators know the operation of schools better than anyone else. What this study recommends is a change of emphasis. Communication with parents should not be considered the "bane of every administrator's existence" as stated in one problem-solving guide for the profession.[41] Administrators should not only entertain suggestions but assiduously cultivate public support. Only if educators work in partnership with parents and patrons "can they secure the community of interest that public education demands."[42]

Furthermore, the commanding position and salary granted the superintendent tend to obscure the contribution and potential of other administrators, relegating them to needless subservience. During the 1981-1982 school year, for example, Jamesville-DeWitt's curriculum coordinator and business manager implemented the difficult closing policy unaided by any superintendent. The building principal, moreover, is a critical figure in making a school work well. In the classrooms, hallways, and playgrounds, he is the problem-solver who sets a school's atmosphere. As parents instinctively knew when they fought to save their schools, curriculum plans and policies from the central office matter less than what is happening in a particular classroom or building. According to the Harvard education school's Ronald Edmonds, the local school, not the district, presents the critical point for analysis and improvement and commands the loyalty of parents. "The larger organization has to be rethought in a way that is more supportive of the local school," says Edmonds.[43]

To restore a balanced viewpoint as well as a balance of powers, the role of the school board should be strengthened. If board members are to fulfill a representative function, they should speak for the community to the superintendent rather than the reverse, as is commonly the case.[44] A salutary and long-overdue dose of politics will best clarify the board's powers and responsibilities. Rhetoric to the contrary, decision-making in education is political, involving competing values and interests.[45] Openly competitive political campaigns and elections will enhance the board's autonomy as well as its accountability to the community, just as the appointment process makes an insulated inner circle dependent upon the superintendent.

274

Changed procedures are also needed to make the school board more responsive to its constituency. Citizens should not be required to wait three or four hours until adjournment to raise a question long after the board has discussed or acted upon the subject. The West Irondequoit school district near Rochester, New York offers a model. Residents there have the opportunity to offer comments following each item on the board's agenda or to address the board at the start of a meeting. As a minimum of democratic procedure documents and reports presented at board meetings should be distributed to the audience.

Board members, moreover, should seek--not shun--public participation in their study committees and important decisions, including administrative appointments.[46] As recognized by only a few Jamesville-DeWitt board members and administrators, vigorous protest activities such as those of Moses DeWitt parents or the JDCCC reveal a renewed dedication to public education. But this vitality cannot be tapped by communications sessions devoted wholly to routine housekeeping subjects, PTAs restricted to coffee-and-cookies functions, or board actions taken without public involvement. Shared decision-making rather than secrecy as again practiced in the selection of Superintendent Baker's successor will build support for public schools. As repeatedly seen in closing controversies, an open discussion of problems, choices, and criteria serves to create public trust, a quality perhaps not appreciated until it is damaged.[47] Thus, a board's executive sessions should be used sparingly, and the private meeting's catch-all justification of "personnel" narrowly construed to apply to problems concerning individual teachers.

As elected officials, board members should be more than figureheads. According to the Jamesville-DeWitt policy handbook, "the Board of Education accepts full responsibility for education in this district."[48] Board members should fulfill this responsibility by overseeing their appointed administrators and taking an active part in budgeting, planning, and monitoring school programs. Instead of playing a ceremonial role by appearances at meetings and school musicals, board members should assume a personal sense of liability for the school district's actions. In the words of Zeigler and Jennings, "school boards should govern or be abolished."[49]

275

In many communities teachers also exercise significant influence in educational decision-making, as they have used collective bargaining to set conditions in regard to class-size, schedules, and school program. In Jamesville-DeWitt, however, teachers emphasized salary and fringe benefits, taking no part in the public controversy over school-closing or grade-organization. In exchange for reaching an average salary of $25,000 in 1982, the faculty saw the ranks of classroom teachers depleted, while special teachers remained relatively stable and new positions were created in resource or remedial areas. Difficult decisions about staff attrition, salary structure and annual increases, and class-size were made with no public knowledge of teachers' views. According to one recommendation, negotiations with teachers' representatives should be conducted with board members and lay citizens present.[50] Again, a balance is needed so that the public knows what it is paying and what it is losing in contract negotiations.

Changing populations and financial limits make it imperative that the pattern of school decision-making be reformed. As the percentage of the population with children under age 18 drops to only one-third or, in some areas, one-fourth of the population, local districts will confront decisions about what they can offer. Federal and state budget reductions and the underlying commitment to curtail public services in the face of economic recession present serious constraints to local decision-makers. Despite increasing dollars the percentage of state aid declines annually, forcing school officials to ask local tax-payers to finance a greater share of the budget. And because of inflationary pressures--meaning rising costs, salaries, and benefits--school districts will inevitably pay more for fewer teachers and students.

Declining student numbers and new financial pressures make public participation and careful planning even more important than in the halcyon days of growth. Retrenchment should not repeat the crazy-quilt pattern of the boom years. During public education's years of expansion district lines were drawn without regard to population growth, natural communities, or political jurisdictions. School districts often constructed buildings without adequate forecasts of residential development, or located schools in close proximity to those of an adjacent district. Educational programs grew by yearly accretions or in response to the prevailing vogue, e.g., the early adolescent--the middle school, and later to meet demands and requirements for particular groups such as the handicapped.

During the 1970s school administrators responded to declining enrollment by staff reductions and school-closings made for symbolic rather than clearly-defined educational or financial reasons. By incremental budgeting and piecemeal adaptations school officials attempted to preserve a shrunken version of the 1960s educational status quo.51 In the decade of the 1980s, however, high school enrollment will drop drastically, showing an average decrease of about 25 per cent or often as much as 40 per cent or more in hard-hit districts.52 In Jamesville-DeWitt high school enrollment is projected to decline by almost 50 per cent between 1981-1990.

Instead of again improvising patchwork solutions, communities should at last reexamine the purpose of their schools. By addressing educational goals after decades of "doing it the way we always have," both citizens and school officials can develop guidelines as to what is essential and what is not. These guidelines will provide criteria in determining what choices to make from a suburban school system's smorgasbord of academic, social, athletic, and recreational offerings.

As an elected body, the school board should provide a forum for this new and wider debate concerning public education's purposes. The superintendent of schools should be charged with renewing the coherence of the educational program and public commitment to it. Planning will be more important than ever, as all decisions are subjected to review in place of the special haven offered to programs that serve administrative interests or have the protection of their own lobbies. Financial planning should take the form of long-term budgets to forecast anticipated spending. Population projections and a close scrutiny of the community's migration patterns will continue to be critical, because the lower grades of elementary schools will begin to gain enrollment during the mid-1980s.53

During the coming decade, residents, board members, and administrators will have to join together to consider objectives at every level of the school system and balance these interests. Political decisions about programs, quality, and staffing at every level and every building can no longer be negotiated privately but must

277

instead be confronted by the process of public discussion and planning. Although this new order of decision-making will not spare school districts controversy, it may avoid the self-destructive features of Jamesville-DeWitt's travail over closing.

**NOTES**

1. Jamesville-DeWitt Central School District, "Announcement of Vacancy in the Office of Superintendent of Schools," Sept. 1, 1981.
2. Katherine E. Eisenberger and William F. Keough, **Declining Enrollment: What to Do**(Arlington, 1974), 10.
3. David B. Tyack, **The One Best System**(Cambridge, 1974), especially 182-198.
4. Louis H. Masotti, **Education and Politics in Suburbia: The New Trier Experience**(Cleveland, 1967), 154-155.
5. Roscoe C. Martin, **Government and the Suburban School** (Syracuse, 1962), 61.
6. Robert I. Rotberg, **New York Times**, June 3, 1976.
7. Lee Steinfeldt, "School Closings Unhappy--But Inevitable," **Post-Standard**(Syracuse), Dec. 8, 1977.
8. **Post-Standard**, Jan. 1, 1981.
9. L. Harmon Zeigler and M. Kent Jennings, **Governing American Schools** (North Scituate, Mass. 1974), 251.
10. See Laurence Iannaccone and Frank W. Lutz, **Politics, Power, and Policy: The Governing of Local School Districts**(Columbus, 1970), 18-23 for a good discussion of the characteristic pattern of board-administration relations; also Zeigler and Jennings, **Governing American Schools,** 249-254.
11. Iannaccone and Lutz, **Politics, Power, and Policy,** 22.
12. Arthur J. Vidich and Joseph Bensman, **Small Town in Mass Society**(Princeton, 1968), 41-42.
13. Cf. Brian Powers, "Fitting Schools to Fewer Students," in Betsy Wachtel and Brian Powers, eds., **Rising Above Decline**(Boston, 1979), 14-15.
14. National Center for Education Statistics, **The Condition of Education, 1981 Edition**(Washington, D.C., 1981), 48; U.S. Department of Education, "Statistics of Public School Systems," Fall 1980.
15. Estimates for closings across the nation are around 10,000 with some variation in figures because of name changes and grade reorganization. New York figures are from the New York State Department of Education, Office of Education Statistics.
16. **Herald-Journal**(Syracuse), Aug. 5, 1981.
17. **New York Times**, Mar. 31, 1981, on problems of suburban districts in the Northeast.

18. **New York Times**, May 17, 1982.

19. Ellen Bussard, **School Closings and Declining Enrollment**(New York, 1981), 1-3.

20. Information is from U.S. Bureau of the Census, population count and age data, 1980, available at the Syracuse-Onondaga County Planning Agency.

21. William H. Whyte, Jr. as quoted by William Severini Kowinski, "Suburbia: End of the Golden Age," **New York Times Magazine**, Mar. 16, 1980.

22. **New York Times**, Mar. 31, 1981.

23. **Post-Standard**, May 25, 1981.

24. Eisenberger and Keough, **What to Do**, 10.

25. The Jewish Community Center offered to pay $18,000 per year plus utility costs of about $40,000 a year for use of Genesee Hills School, and received a five-year lease. **Post-Standard**, June 11, 1981.

26. Figures were presented as follows: $180,000, Jamesville-DeWitt Board of Education meeting, Dec. 5, 1977; $70,000, Jamesville-DeWitt Board of Education meeting, Aug. 14, 1978; $30,000, as stated by Superintendent Baker to the **Post-Standard**, June 19, 1980; Jamesville-DeWitt Board of Education meeting, Oct. 28, 1980, reported in **Post-Standard**, Oct. 30, 1980.

27. Richard L. Andrews, "The Environmental Impact of School Closures," (Seattle, 1974), 32.

28. Paul Berman and Milbrey McLaughlin, "The Management of Decline: Problems, Opportunities, and Research Questions," in Susan Abramowitz and Stuart Rosenfeld, eds., **Declining Enrollments: The Challenge of the Coming Decade**(Washington, D.C., 1978), 324.

29. Quoted by Andrews, "The Environmental Impact of School Closures," 27.

30. City of Seattle and Seattle Public Schools, **Schools and Neighborhood Research Study** (Seattle, 1976), 6, 18.

31. Martin, **Government and the Suburban School**, 65.

32. MacNeill/Lehrer Report, Transcript, "Shrinking Schools," WNET Channel 13, Sept. 7, 1979; also Stanton Leggett, "Sixteen Questions to Ask and Answer Before You Close a Small School," **American School Board Journal**(Apr., 1978), 38-39.

33. **Small Schools Task Force Report**, School District 4J, Eugene, Oregon(Eugene, 1976), 29; **The Lexington Elementary Schools**, Report by the Educational Program Study Committee(Lexington, 1976), 107.

34. Directed by John I. Goodlad and sponsored by the Institute for the Development of Educational Activities, "A Study of Schooling" is widely described as the most comprehensive study ever made of American schools. Goodlad summarizes his findings in **A Place Called School: Prospects for the Future**, to be published by McGraw-Hill in late 1983. Quotes are from an article on the study, **New York Times**, July 19, 1983; also interview with Goodlad, **New York Times**, July 26, 1983.

35. On the same subject, Robert I. Rotberg, **New York Times**, June 3, 1976, and **Post-Standard**, May 25, 1978. To close small schools is

"educational folly," said Rotberg.
36. **Post-Standard**, May 1, 1980.
37. Martin, **Government and the Suburban School**, 60, characterization of the "bureaucratic progeny of the public school mythology."
38. Brian Powers, "Fitting Schools to Fewer Students," 15.
39. James D. Koerner, **Who Controls American Education?**(Boston, 1968), 155.
40. Zeigler and Jennings, **Governing American Schools**, 248; Koerner, **Who Controls American Education?**, 156-162.
41. James J. Lewis, Robert M. Bookbinder, and Raymond R. Bauer, **Critical Issues in Education: A Problem-Solving Guide for School Administrators** (Englewood Cliffs, 1972), 114.
42. David B. Tyack and Elisabeth Hansot, **Managers of Virtue: Public School Leadership in America, 1820-1980**(New York, 1982), 254; on the same point, see Lawrence A. Cremin, **The Transformation of the School**(New York, 1964), 350.
43. **New York Times**, Feb. 3, 1981.
44. Zeigler and Jennings, **Governing American Schools**, 249.
45. An early and still excellent article on politics and public education is Thomas H. Eliot, "Toward an Understanding of Public School Politics," **American Political Science Review**, Vol. 53(Dec. 1959), 1032-1051.
46. See, for example, Mary Lou Meese, "Hiring School Administrators Can Be a Group Decision," **American School Board Journal**, Sept. 1981, 40-41.
47. Ellen Bussard, **School Closings and Declining Enrollment**, 5; on the value of citizen-action groups, see Tyack and Hansot, **Managers of Virtue**, 233.
48. Jamesville-DeWitt Central School District, **Board of Education Policy Handbook**, 104.
49. Zeigler and Jennings, **Governing American Schools**, 254.
50. William L. Boyd as cited by Tyack and Hansot, **Managers of Virtue**, 242.
51. Brian Powers, "Fitting Schools to Fewer Students," 15.
52. Ellen Bussard and Alan C. Green, **Planning for Declining Enrollment in Single High School Districts**(Washington, D.C., 1981), 1.
53. Russell G. Davis and Gary M. Lewis, "The Demographic Background to Changing Enrollments and School Needs," in Susan Abramowitz and Stuart Rosenfeld, eds., **Declining Enrollments: The Challenge of the Coming Decade**, 5.

## About the Author

Jean Stinchcombe holds a B.A. degree from Swarthmore College and an M.A. and Ph.D. from the University of Michigan. She is the author of **Reform and Reaction: City Politics in Toledo**(Belmont, Calif., 1968).